Marketization and Democracy

As the East Asian financial crisis continues to leave a path of destruction economically and politically in its wake, people all over the world seek to know what went wrong. Many blame the illiberal markets of the countries involved and many blame their political leadership. This book explores how strong, open, liberalized markets create a counterbalance to crony capitalism and corruption and form the basis for a foundation of political liberalization. Using both a quantitative model and qualititative country studies, this work analyzes the experiences of China, Taiwan, Indonesia, and Korea in moving toward both marketization and democracy.

Samantha F. Ravich is a Fellow in the Asian Studies Program at the Center for Strategic and International Studies in Washington, D.C. She formerly served as Program Officer in the International Security and Foreign Policy Program of the Smith Richardson Foundation based in Westport, Connecticut. Dr. Ravich previously conducted research on Asian economic, security, and political trends at RAND, where she received her doctorate from the RAND Graduate School. Prior to working there, she conducted commercial real estate assessments for overseas Chinese and Japanese institutions in the Los Angeles area. She is a member of the Council on Foreign Relations and the National Committee on American Foreign Policy.

RAND Studies in Policy Analysis

Editor: Charles Wolf, Jr., Senior Economic Advisor and Corporate Fellow in International Economics, RAND

Policy analysis is the application of scientific methods to develop and test alternative ways of addressing social, economic, legal, international, national security, and other problems. The RAND Studies in Policy Analysis series aims to include several significant, timely, and innovative works each year in this broad field. Selection is guided by an editorial board consisting of Charles Wolf, Jr. (editor), and David S. C. Chu, Paul K. Davis, and Lynn Karoly (associate editors).

Also in the series:

David C. Gompert and F. Stephen Larrabee (eds.), *America and Europe: A Partnership for a New Era*

John W. Peabody, M. Omar Rahman, Paul J. Gertler, Joyce Mann, Donna O. Farley, Jeff Luck, David Robalino, and Grace M. Carter, *Policy and Health: Implications for Development in Asia*

Marketization and Democracy
East Asian Experiences

Samantha F. Ravich
Center for Strategic and International Studies,
Washington, DC

CAMBRIDGE
UNIVERSITY PRESS

PUBLISHED BY THE PRESS SYNDICATE OF THE UNIVERSITY OF CAMBRIDGE
The Pitt Building, Trumpington Street, Cambridge, United Kingdom

CAMBRIDGE UNIVERSITY PRESS
The Edinburgh Building, Cambridge CB2 2RU, UK   http://www.cup.cam.ac.uk
40 West 20th Street, New York, NY 10011-4211, USA   http://www.cup.org
10 Stamford Road, Oakleigh, Melbourne 3166, Australia
Ruiz de Alarcón 13, 28014 Madrid, Spain

© RAND 2000

First published 2000

Printed in the United States of America

Typefaces Sabon and Futura 10/12 pt.   *System* MS Word   [TB]

A catalog record for this book is available from the British Library.

Library of Congress Cataloging in Publication Data
Ravich, Samantha Fay.
    Marketization and democracy : East Asian experiences / Samantha F.
Ravich.
       p.   cm.
    ISBN 0-521-66165-X
    1. East Asia – Economic conditions – Econometric models.   2. Free
trade – East Asia – Econometric models.   3. East Asia – Economic
policy.   4. Democracy – East Asia.   5. East Asia – Politics and
government.   I. Title.
HC460.5.R38   1999
320.45′09′045 – dc21   99-40315
                                                                  CIP

ISBN   0 521 66165 X   hardback

Contents

v

Figures

Tables

Preface

In the wake of the Asian financial crisis, old theories and new realities about the relationship between economics and politics are being debated—and debunked, validated, or discarded as obsolete. Around the world, the academic and policymaking communities are wrestling with the question of where to pin the blame for the crisis and trying to decipher the lessons that can be learned from the suffering. At the heart of these discussions lies an intense debate over the importance of economic and political liberalization in halting, reversing, and correcting the problems that beset East Asia.

This book describes the experiences of the countries of East Asia as they have moved toward economic and political liberalization since the mid 1950s. The book's thesis is that marketization vests an increasing percentage of the population in the economy and leads citizens to seek political representation to protect their newfound economic opportunities. The relationship between marketization and democracy in East Asia over the past 40 years is tested and explored with an econometric model, along with four comparative, historical country studies. The primary research for this book was supported by RAND's National Defense Research Institute (NDRI), Project AIR FORCE (PAF), the Arroyo Center, RAND's International Policy Department, and the RAND Graduate School (RGS).

The book does not examine the causes and consequences of the financial crisis, nor does it offer specific recommendations on how to rectify the calamity. But it is hoped that a better understanding of why and how marketization creates needs and incentives for citizens to press for democracy will lead to more effective and efficient policymaking. As the governments of East Asia struggle to create and implement reform packages, for both economic and political institutions, this is a particularly opportune time to study the lessons of the recent past. This work should be of particular interest to policymakers, both in the United States and abroad, who recognize that Asia's future prosperity must rest on the principles of marketization and democracy.

Acknowledgments

This work benefited from the comments and guidance of a large number of people, although I alone take responsibility for its content.

I would like to thank Dr. Charles Wolf, Jr., whose writings on the subject of markets and states gave me the original idea for this work. In this, and many other matters, he has been a true inspiration and a very valued mentor. Other thanks go to Lynn Karoly, Jonathan Pollack, David Trinkle, Cathy Krop, Mary Anne Doyle, Michael Kennedy, C. Richard Neu, Kirsten Speidel, and the support team at the RAND Graduate School. I am especially grateful to Marin Strmecki, Nadia Schadlow, and the good people at the Smith Richardson Foundation.

I wish to dedicate this work to my family: to my parents who instilled in me the love of learning and the organizational skills to complete this massive undertaking; to my precious cherub, Isabella, who helped me keep my priorities straight while I was writing the dissertation upon which this book is based and who taught me the nature of a true labor of love; to my darling angel, India, who arrived on the scene in time for the revisions and kept me smiling even in the wee hours of the night; and to the man of my dreams, my husband, Dr. Richard Anthony Brahm, without whom nothing would be worth it.

1

———————————————————————————————

Introduction

This book explores and empirically analyzes the connections between marketization (the process of moving away from a centrally controlled economy and toward an open market) and democracy in East Asia. The underlying hypothesis of this research is that certain economic conditions may be necessary to provide a foundation for a competitive system of government. If this indeed is the case, then to increase democracy in East Asia, the United States must look for those specific policy levers that will strengthen these economic conditions.

Over the last 50 years, substantial effort has been dedicated to understanding the linkages between a country's political institutions and its economic development. Three main theories of polity and economic development arose from this research: the authoritarian model, the democratic model, and modernization theory. The authoritarian model suggests that authoritarian regimes can control the market, thereby creating optimal conditions for economic growth. The democratic model predicts that a democratic system has the means to promote long-term economic growth well beyond the capabilities of an authoritarian regime by rationally determining economic choices—a position that is nearly impossible in a regime with concentrated power and the exploitation of government office. What both of these theories lack, aside from empirical validation, is a logically sound, intuitively viable, causal explanation relating regime type to economic growth.

A much stronger argument, describing the relationship between polity and development, evolved from Lipset's 1959 classic work, *Some Social Requisites of Democracy: Economic Development and Political Legitimacy.* Modernization theory posits that a country must strength-

1

en and stabilize its economy before it can institute democratic reforms.[1] With a resulting rise in general prosperity, citizens will seek certain political rights to accompany their newfound wealth.

Modernization theory may provide insight into the correlates of democratic reform, but a more comprehensive understanding of the effect of socioeconomic development on political democracy in East Asia requires an expansion of the theory in three respects. First, much of modernization theory is based on understanding the correlates of economic development with little investigation of the market mechanisms underlying such growth. The work presented in this book broadens this research by incorporating a theory of marketization into an economic-development/democracy model. The basis for this approach is that although economic development may be a precondition of democracy according to Lipset, marketization provides the foundation of democracy by introducing choice, competition, and public accountability. Economic concepts such as market competition, and the inefficiencies that arise from its absence, shed light on how a country can move toward democracy. Economic competition usually brings numerous players into the market and forces the need for consumer choice. Citizens are no longer presented with a single product. With an open market, products are tailored to particular preferences and consumers can achieve their highest utility preference given their budgetary constraint. The same theory of choice and welfare that applies in the marketplace may also hold true in the political realm. In this respect, democratic "learning" may arise from marketization.

Second, although previous empirical work has built on modernization theory in testing cross-national databases, few have paid attention to the particular histories and events of East Asia. A growing number of Asian scholars are suggesting that "Asian" democracy may not be synonymous with "Western" democracy. Developing an appropriate U.S. policy to foster and enhance democracy in East Asia requires a resolution of this issue. This book analyzes the modern histories of South Korea, Taiwan, Indonesia, and China, using a country study approach, to strengthen the predictive power of the econometric model and to deepen our understanding of "Asian" democracy.

1   Inkeles and Smith (1974) wrote that the "defining features of a modern nation . . . include mass education, urbanization, industrialization, bureaucratization, and rapid communication and transportation."

Finally, most econometric models that test modernization theory rely on simplistic measures and models of economic development. Energy consumption per capita and gross domestic product (GDP) per capita have been the preferred proxies for economic development in many previous works. In relating marketization to democracy, however, a much stronger measurement device is needed. The present model uses *mtwo* (currency plus demand and time deposits) as a percentage of GDP as a measure of "financial deepening." A key component of a market system is the ability for internal savings to be channeled into productive investment. The strength of these channels is assessed by *mtwo* as a percentage of GDP.[2] Stock market capitalization is used as an instrument to identify marketization within the system of equations.

In determining the appropriate way to empirically test the above assumptions, one must consider the research objectives, the independent and dependent variables, and the availability of data. As this work studies the relationships between marketization, prosperity, and democracy, it is of primary importance to understand the intricacies of the appropriate East Asian economic and political systems. Therefore, concurrent with the construction of an econometric model, country studies of South Korea, Taiwan, Indonesia, and China were prepared and analyzed. These studies informed the selection of variables in the econometric model and provided the depth of comprehension necessary to advance this field of inquiry. In particular, the country studies allow analysis of key marketization variables that are not easily quantified. The most important of these is assessing the populace's growing awareness of the market and its perceptions of barriers to entry. The qualitative studies also help correct the deficiencies of the econometric model in variable selection and sample size.

2   Adelman and Morris (1973) were among the first to suggest the use of this instrument and to discuss its strengths and weaknesses in a detailed fashion.

Part One

The Model

2

Theories of economic development and polity

In the second half of this century, two schools of thought arose within the economic development and polity debate. One group of scholars argued that the political institution dictates the type of market and, hence, the country's level of prosperity. Proponents of this view fall into two distinct camps: those who suggest that an authoritarian government can move a country toward prosperity and those who insist that only a democracy can accomplish the task. Both groups contend that it is possible for governments to successfully manipulate market type and prosperity level.

Rather than relying on political structure to determine market type, my research attempts to understand and predict future political trends in East Asia under the assumption that moves toward marketization in a country's economic system provide the underlying basis for democracy. A shift away from a centrally planned economy and a rise in the efficient allocation of resources increase general prosperity. Prosperity gives rise to the need for political self-determination and a way to ensure its institution. Perhaps more important, marketization fosters democratic "learning" by introducing citizens to concepts of choice, competition, and public accountability. Experiencing the benefits of economic freedom may increase citizens' desire for political freedom if to provide nothing more than protection of their newly acquired property. Preventing taxation without representation is a strong inducement for demanding political liberalization. Conversely, excessive constraints on the market limit the likelihood of a move toward a more democratic society.

The authoritarian model of economic development posits that authoritarian regimes can control the market and create optimal conditions for economic growth. Alternatively known as the "cruel choice" growth model, authoritarian theories reflect Bhagwati's sad statement that there may exist a "cruel choice between rapid (self-sustained) expansion and democratic processes."[1] The central theory is that authoritarian governments can spur the economy into higher and faster growth rates by forcing down consumption and increasing investment.[2] Authoritarian regimes do not allow the organization of public interest groups seeking income redistribution. Proponents of this model assert that without such pressures to transfer income from high-income families to low-income families (who usually have a lower marginal propensity to save), investment goals have a higher probability of being attained.

It has also been suggested that authoritarian regimes are less likely to be co-opted by the pressures of political lobbyists.[3] In a discussion of this literature, Przeworski and Limongi explain that, in a democracy, interest groups compete for benefits. The equilibrium "which results is inefficient both because lobbying is wasteful and because transfers of income that result from group pressures cause deadweight loss."[4]

Although this theory does not comment on the productivity of the investment, Marsh suggests that authoritarian regimes can also be more efficient than their democratic counterparts in allocating resources. Authoritarian regimes, without democratic checks and balances, can reorganize labor markets by moving portions of the population, decreasing or increasing wages, and directing labor to specific endeavors. They can also avoid specialization in primary production and limit their country's dependence on more advanced nations by controlling foreign investment.[5]

1   Bhagwati (1966), p. 204.
2   In an economy, all income is either consumed or saved. In a closed economy, saving = investment + consumption. Therefore, holding saving constant, investment must increase as consumption falls. A rise in investment leads to an increase in the capital stock that causes an increase in GDP.
3   Becker (1983).
4   Przeworski and Limongi (1993).
5   Marsh (1979). Huntington (1968, p. 8) wrote that "history shows conclusively that communist governments are no better than free governments in alleviating famine, improving health, expanding national product, creating industry, and maximizing welfare," but he did assert that authoritarian governments can "provide effective authority." There is also an extensive discussion in both Sirowy and Inkeles (1990) and Przeworski

The competing theory of polity and economic growth suggests that a democratic system has the means to promote long-term economic growth beyond the capabilities of an authoritarian regime. The economic-development/democracy model posits that self-government enhances freedom and provides the correct inducements for individuals to strive toward prosperity. Democratic models also rest on the weaknesses inherent in the authoritarian regime's concentration of influence. Such behavior leads to market inefficiencies associated with the arbitrary granting of economic rents and the exploitation of government office.[6]

Statistical analysis has moved the field forward to an extent, but the controversy among competing theories still remains. In 1990, Sirowy and Inkeles reviewed 13 studies that assessed the effect of democracy on economic development. Of these 13, three found the effect to be negative, six found no relationship, and four found a positive (albeit qualified) relationship.[7] Three years later, Przeworski and Limongi reviewed 18 studies that examined regime type as a determinant of economic growth. Nine of these studies had been included in the Sirowy and Inkeles report. Of the 18, eight found in favor of authoritarianism, four found no relationship, and six found in favor of democracy. With such conflicting results, the authors were left with the conclusion that "the impact of political regimes on growth is wide open for reflection."[8]

Continuing with this research, Robert Barro concluded that "on average, political freedom neither helped nor hindered growth."[9] Barro did suggest that although "democracy has, at best, a mixed record as a contributor to improved standards of living . . . enhanced political

and Limongi (1993) of how authoritarianism is thought to directly affect (positively) economic growth.

6   Essentially, politics will override sensible decisionmaking based upon economic and technical factors. Lindblom (1977, pp. 65–75) refers to authoritarian systems as having "strong thumbs, no fingers," lacking in the ability of rational calculation and economic choice. Without these assets, sustained productivity is impossible. According to the Solow growth model, technological advancement is crucial for a country's long-run growth. As the advancement of knowledge suffers most in a system that restricts free thought, contentions regarding the economic vitality of nondemocratic states become even more suspect. For a broader discussion of these issues, see Wade (1990) and Solow (1956).

7   Sirowy and Inkeles (1990).

8   Przeworski and Limongi (1993).

9   Barro (1993).

freedoms are more likely to follow prosperity than to precede it."[10] In 1997, Barro refined his model further but still found that the "net effect of democracy on growth is theoretically inconclusive." However, he found strong evidence supporting the Lipset hypothesis that growth and development increase democracy. The variables tested against Barro's cross-country dataset were the log of GDP per capita, schooling levels, life expectancy, urbanization rate, and an oil country dummy. All variables were significant except population, meaning that there was no evidence that country size determines regime type.[11]

The analysis presented here provides a clearer and more intuitive explanation of the relationship between regime type and economic growth than the authoritarian or democratic models discussed above. The present model is built on Lipset's traditional set of interrelated socioeconomic conditions necessary for democratic development (urbanization, high educational standards, and prosperity) and Kuznet's fundamentals of growth theory (the application of scientific thought and technology to industry and production), but it extends these theories by including a variable that measures marketization.[12] Unlike in Barro's 1997 model, prosperity was not found to be significant in this statistical analysis. As is discussed at more length in the following chapter, prosperity may have become insignificant with the inclusion of a marketization measure. Barro himself acceded to this point when he wrote, "It may be that the development of satisfactory theories for the determination of democracy would also suggest additional empirical linkages that ought to be explored."[13] By exploring the effect of marketization on regime type, my work expands on the theoretical models discussed.

Additionally, the qualitative country studies of Taiwan, Korea, Indonesia, and China contained in later chapters take this analysis

---

10   Barro (1993). Kohli (1986, p. 156) states that "systematic statistical evidence has failed to resolve the debate . . . [between the *authoritarian* and *democratic* models]. Three cross-national studies have supported the 'cruel choice' position by concluding that authoritarianism promotes economic growth, whereas one has found the reverse to hold. . . . Some scholars have even concluded that there may not be any systematic relationship between regime type and economic growth."

11   Barro (1997).

12   Lipset (1959); Kuznets (1956). For an in-depth discussion of the literature in the field, see Ravich (1996).

13   Barro (1993), p. 87.

one step beyond previous research in the field by examining how "democratic learning" arises in the populace. By looking at the effect of marketizing measures on different strata of society, this work attempts to explain how citizens arrive at the point where they not only desire more representation within their government but also can fashion effective associations to demand and win such concessions. The result of including these steps in the overall analysis increases the policy relevance of both development economics and growth theory.[14]

14   A good discussion of the limitations in both development economics and growth theory is contained in Rostow (1990).

3

The model

Building upon Lipset's classic work, the research described here explores the causal relationship between marketization and democracy. Figure 3.1 displays graphically the linkages between free markets and democracy, with the correlates of prosperity and technological innovation. Marketization—the process of moving away from a centrally controlled economy to a free market—provides the conditions necessary for fostering democracy and the means by which citizens can establish

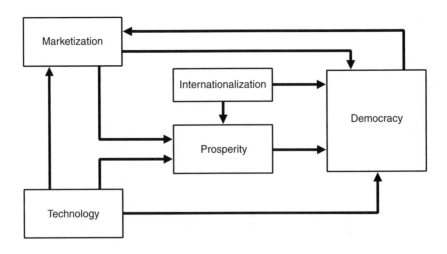

Figure 3.1. Linkages Between Free Markets and Democracy

12

this system of government. In moving toward a free market, society experiences the following phenomena: an increase in prosperity, an introduction to the concepts of competition and choice (greater individualism), a reduction in the level of corruption (public accountability), the rise of a private sphere able to balance the interests of the government, a forum for the exchange of ideas, and the desire for, and creation of, a process whereby citizens can protect their economic freedoms. In combination, these events provide the foundation for democracy.

An increase in prosperity

Open markets, through the efficient allocation of resources, move an economy to its optimal point on a production possibility frontier. Such a move maximizes both consumer and producer surplus and increases society's total welfare. The benefits of the open market rest on the assumption that consumers and producers act out of self-interest. When the market is open to all, and each trade is undertaken freely and without duress, an economically efficient outcome results. Under excessive government intervention, nonmarket failures occur from restrictions on the allocative function of markets and the creative functions of an economy (the ability to shift outward the entire production possibility curve). Restraints on the ability of an economy to reach both the optimal point on its production possibility curve and to push that frontier outward tend to depress the level of potential prosperity within a country.

Conversely, marketization expands an economy toward its optimal position. Charles Wolf, Jr., in his book *Markets or Governments,* discusses the "predictable shortcomings and miscarriages of government." He concludes that "as a general allocative mechanism, markets do a better job than governments, from the standpoint of both allocative (or static) efficiency (namely, realizing a higher ratio between outputs or products, on the one hand, and inputs or costs, on the other) and dynamic efficiency (namely, sustaining a higher rate of economic growth over time)."[1]

A country that achieves a level of wealth where a relatively small percentage of the population lives in real poverty stands a far better chance of creating and sustaining a participatory government than does a country with a large indigent population. Citizens need to overcome the

1 Wolf (1988, p. 153).

most fundamental of life's hurdles, such as obtaining food and shelter, before being able to intelligently participate in the exercise of self-government.

Democratic "learning"—an introduction to the concepts of competition and choice

Nonmarket economies replace the functioning of the market by a system that stifles creativity, innovation, and productivity by fostering an atmosphere of rent-seeking behavior among society's elite. Individuals fortunate enough to be well connected to the regime earn market privileges such as licensing rights and tax concessions. State-sponsored monopolies dominate the market and consumer welfare is at a lower level than under a competitive system. In contrast, competition brings numerous players into the market and forces the need for consumer choice. The populace is no longer presented with a single product. With an open market, products are tailored to particular preferences. As citizens become accustomed to selecting their own market basket, they experience greater prosperity. Marketization—the freeing of the commercial sphere from government constraints—provides potential benefits to society in addition to those associated with full employment and the efficient allocation of resources.

Free markets provide a foundation for the institution of democracy by introducing the concepts of competition and choice. Essentially, by applying the tools of microeconomics to the political arena, citizens experience democratic "learning" and recognize their ability to move to their optimal utility only under a system of competitive government. In both the marketplace and the government, competition increases society's total welfare by allowing citizens to select the goods, services, and political representation that give them the highest utility. Additionally, the concept of free choice is intricately bound to the development of the individual. Marketization, by placing the burden of responsibility upon the individual, strengthens the understanding of self-determination (acting out of self-interest). On free enterprise, Milton Friedman writes that "what we really mean is the freedom of individuals to set up enterprises. It is the freedom of an individual to engage in an activity so long as he uses only voluntary methods of getting other individuals to cooperate with him."[2] The evolution of humankind into a political animal, willing and able to act in accordance with rational self-interest, is quickened by marketization through a process of democratic "learning." Marketization increases citizens' competence to make rational, reasoned decisions.

Critics argue that the range of choice offered in the market actually fosters nondemocratic learning. The ability to "exit" a particular situation, transaction, or product choice teaches nonparticipation—one learns the ease of opting out. The cost of not voting is seen as marginal, encouraging some citizens to withhold their voice, thereby undermining participatory democracy.[3] The problem with this line of argument is the assumption that the boundaries of both market and ballot box are fixed. In reality, if the barriers of entry are low, those who exit the market can reenter it as a new competitor. Although voice creates marginal change within the existing system, the ability to exit allows for radical change to the system.

In addition to teaching the concepts of competition and choice, free markets teach the value of a system that operates through transactions that are intelligently entered into and voluntarily consummated. An individual who is allowed to act according to his own self-interest will produce and consume the appropriate amount of goods and services that directly or indirectly fulfills his wants. Given the ability to enter or not enter into any particular exchange, he will ensure that he reaches his highest possible satisfaction level. When an entire society acts in such a manner, not only does the amount of its output increase, but the allocation of its resources is accomplished efficiently. As with choice and competition, when citizens experience the benefits of free enterprise that arise under voluntary exchange, they will be more likely to push for informed and noncoercive elections within the public sphere.[4]

2 Friedman (1993, p. 4).
3 For further discussion of how excessive choice may prohibit a democracy from functioning optimally, see Bowles and Gintis (1986).
4 Diamond (1988) suggests that a democratic culture is a product of an effective democracy. Over time, citizens learn the value of participation, tolerance, and compromise. I do not disagree with Diamond; I only extend the foundation of this learning process. It is in the marketplace that citizens learn the value of these activities and apply them to their political lives.

A reduction in the level of corruption

Noncompetitive markets hamper efficiency by institutionalizing corruption. In a nonmarket economy, financial success is primarily achieved by the government doling out business licenses. Politicians must be kept in power, and in pocket, through "contributions." This system of favoritism denies equal participation within the society. A competitive market structure does away with industrial licensing systems. Marketization, by allocating wealth on the basis of productivity, demolishes the walls of corruption and levels the playing field.

The nefarious effects of corruption are being felt throughout Southeast Asia as the region suffers the lingering effects of the 1997 financial crisis. Indonesia provides the prime example of how closed markets institutionalize corruption and thwart the spread of democracy. For three decades, President Suharto manipulated the Indonesian economy to line the pockets of his family and friends. His children's business interests included sweetheart deals in cars, petrochemicals, shipping, and airlines. Relying on their political clout to bolster and enhance their economic prowess, the cronies of Suharto worked to keep both spheres closed to the average Indonesian.

Consider what occurred during the December 1996 deliberations over the country's first broadcasting bill regulating an industry that generates US$1 billion annually in advertising revenues. Late in 1996, Parliament passed the bill and sent it to the President for ratification. For the next seven months, Suharto took the bill under "advisement" and agreed to hear the arguments against the bill from an industry spokesperson. The spokesperson was Siti Hardijanti "Tutut" Rukmana, Suharto's eldest daughter. Her appointment to the position was not a surprise given that, together with her brother, she owned sizable chunks of four out of the five private television channels in the country. Late in the summer of 1997, the bill was sent back to the Parliament with revisions reflecting the industry's concerns.[5] When the financial crisis broke later that year, Parliament was still considering the law's revisions. The history of the people's revolution in Indonesia in the spring of 1998 is still to be written, but it is not too early to understand that the economy, and its lack of openness, fueled the fire that led to the ouster of Suharto.

5   McBeth (1997).

The corruption of governmental offices can be described using the principal-agent-client model. Civil servants will corrupt their offices when they perceive that the benefits of the transgression outweigh the risks (of being caught, prosecuted, and punished).[6] However, introducing the concept of competition into the system of government changes the nature of the agent-client relationship. Agents must compete on optimal service delivered, thereby decreasing the benefits of corruption. It is monopoly power, whether in the government or in the market, that leads to a reward based on coercive power rather than on the efficiency of a completed task.

In addition, an increase in the general standard of living provides civil service employees the prospect of employment outside of the government. This is necessary to ensure political competition and the ability for reforms to take hold. Without private opportunities for wealth, government officials will fight against any reforms that may remove them from office. Direct connections to a state-owned monopoly can generate enormous profits for the resourceful civil servant. The potential loss of such opportunity can provoke serious power struggles and can make regime modification and democratic advances unlikely. Such systematic corruption perverts a democratic system by reducing the process to a series of hostile takeovers and power plays where individual gain, more than the rational creation and implementation of efficient public policy, dictates the functioning of the state. Unlike statism, which exacerbates the tendency for bureaucrats to engage in corrupt behavior, marketization reduces the level of contact between government officials and profitmaking entities. With a separation of the two spheres, public officials must rely on their policy stances, rather than their success in soliciting bribes, as their means to stay in power.

A balance of power

A hallmark of a democratic system is its inability to coerce an individual into performing any action against his will. The likelihood of such coercion lessens as power is dispersed throughout the population. Friedman argues that the "preservation of freedom requires the elimination of [the] concentration of power to the fullest possible extent and the dispersal and distribution of whatever power cannot be elimi-

6 Klitgaard (1993, p. 21).

nated."[7] When the market is freed from the central control of the government, economic strength is separated from political strength and a more equitable balance of power is achieved between public and private domains.

A civil society, separate and distinct from the political sphere, must be created as a basis for a working democracy.[8] Such a society can flourish only in a system where economic power is dispersed throughout the society. Unlike political power, which tends to congregate in very few places with very closed circles, economic strength derived from a free market can (and does) arise without regard to geography, familial relations, race, creed, or skin color.

A more balanced distribution of power tends to facilitate an increase in democratic tendencies in two ways. First, under freer market conditions, private citizens gain economic autonomy. Economic autonomy provides for a fundamental level of political autonomy. Specifically, economic power increases the ability to raise capital to fund political opposition. In the absence of economic autonomy, the capital to fund a political march, candidacy, or leaflet campaign must come from the advocate's own resources or the sitting political authority (not a likely source to fund the opposition). Economic strength widens the entrance into the halls of political power. Citizens formerly denied a voice in politics because of their race, gender, or class are given one through economic autonomy.[9] Such a redistribution of power among citizens not only increases the ability to freely disseminate ideas but also smoothes the process of implementing those ideas.

The second way that market freedom promotes democracy is in its effect on the business sphere. As the strength of the private sector increases, so does the bargaining power of business firms when dealing with the government. In Taiwan and South Korea over the last decade,

7   Friedman (1962, p. 15).
8   For more information on the underpinnings of a civil society, see Huber et al. (1993).
9   Kohli (1986) writes that "the division into the public and private realms makes the sphere of legal and political equality somewhat separate from that of substantial social and economic [equality]. Separating political equality from economic inequalities not only lays the basis for legitimate elected governments in inegalitarian societies. It also opens up the hope and opportunity . . . of modifying inherited inequalities through the use of democratic state power."

the rising strength of private firms has enabled them to resist govern-ment direction. A private sphere that exists, separate and distinct from a public domain, erodes the ability of the government to exert coercive power over the populace.

A forum for ideas and a movement toward internationalization

The same market reforms that allow commerce to be conducted un-hindered also allow for the free exchange of ideas. In particular, the push toward internationalization permits entrance to the concepts of democracy. International businesses bring with them global networks, CNN, and MTV. A satellite dish makes the world a much smaller place and the forum for the exchange of ideas much larger. As former President Bush stated during the 1991 Most Favored Nation (MFN) hearings on China, "No nation on earth has discovered a way to import the world's goods and services while stopping foreign ideas at the border."[10]

Protecting one's economic freedom

As citizens begin to enjoy their wealth, they seek the political means to protect it. The United States was founded on Locke's principle that the state exists to protect the individual's property, a direct response to the taxation without representation suffered by the colonists at the hands of the British Parliament.[11]

The need for a stable market environment coupled with the wealth to organize may lead citizens to form business associations. This pro-gresses quickly to a forum of open debate and discussion—a corner-

10 Bush (1991).

11 To recoup its expenses from the French and Indian War, England's Parliament levied a series of taxes against the colonists including those in the Stamp Act of 1763. Opposition to the Stamp Tax revolved around the fact that it was the first time England had attempted to tax the colonists directly. Although a boycott of English goods and a subsequent protest by English exporters led to a revocation of the tax, a bitter taste was left in the mouths of the colonists. When, in 1773, the British Parliament allowed the near bankrupt British East India Company to im-port tea into the colonies without paying any tax, thereby hurting American importers who shipped tea in from Holland, rebellion oc-curred.

stone of democracy. Such assembly also promotes the creation of political groups to protect the rights of its members against the government. With the strengthening of the private domain, afforded to the populace through an increase in prosperity, governmental power can be restricted.

In addition to individuals' seeking to protect their economic and political freedoms, the marketplace, to ensure its ability to function efficiently, creates legal institutions. A rule of law arises naturally to facilitate business transactions and protect property. A formal definition of property rights, to clearly apportion income, risk, and responsibility, is necessary to sustain economic development.[12] Ultimately, such bureaucratic systems, by decentralizing the decisionmaking process, erode the power of authoritarian regimes.

Technology

As a result of the groundbreaking work of Simon Kuznets in the 1950s through the 1970s, the world now readily accepts that technological innovation is a major source of growth per capita product over and above what is provided through labor and capital inputs.[13] Increases in the advancement of knowledge (technology) cover both technological advancements and positive changes to managerial and organizational skills. An increase in this "knowledge" is predicated on a rise in education, investment as a percentage of GDP, R&D as a percentage of GDP, and income distribution. As a country's access to technology rises, so does its ability to become more productive and increase GDP. If GDP increases and the population remains constant, prosperity per capita will increase.

12   Weimer (1997, pp. 9–10) argues persuasively that private property rights contribute to the strengthening of democracy. In addition to many of the arguments presented in this chapter, Weimer discusses property rights and democracy in terms of the social choice rule. Building off Arrow's 1963 work, Weimer asserts that in the case of "unrestricted majority rule voting over alternatives with multiple dimensions, for example, 'chaos' results in the sense that, in all but trivial cases . . . any alternative can be defeated by some other alternative preferred by a majority." Institutional constraints, such as property rights with "constitutional status," can "reduce the risks of democratic instability."

13   Kuznets (1956, 1971).

Beyond its contribution to prosperity, however, technology (in particular, technological innovation in the realm of telecommunications) can contribute to an increase in democracy. Information entitles citizens to become active participants in the workings of their society. Telecommunications advance this process by allowing a greater flow of information to reach the populace and increase the speed of its dissemination. An augmentation in this technology (phone to fax to modem to teleconferencing) also networks people in ways never before thought possible, increasing the available forums for discussion, debate, and the free exchange of ideas.

The widespread use of these new technologies increases the ability to associate and to form alliances with the goal of altering public policies. Governmental participation takes on greater depth when a citizen can sit at a computer terminal and email the White House, or fax in his stance on a congressional bill up for a vote.[14] In addition, societies with highly developed technologies promote communication of preferences among competing groups, thereby allowing groups with shared preferences to organize, combine their resources, and successfully implement their desires.

THE FOUNDATION AND REQUISITES FOR DEMOCRACY

Democracy is often seen as an elusive concept and one that is frequently assessed more in its absence than its presence. To analyze the depth and breadth of democracy in a society, it is necessary to somehow create a fixed scale upon which one can measure the presence of the essential aspects of a competitive system of government. The following sections provide both a brief exposition of the historical definitions of democracy and those conditions that must exist for a society to realize democracy. Although the Freedom House/Gastil index is used to measure democracy within the econometric model described here, the conceptual framework developed below provides the analytic foundation for the study of democracy within the qualitative country studies.

---

14 Pitroda (1993) stated, "As a great social leveler, information technology ranks second only to death. It can raze cultural barriers, overwhelm economic inequalities, even compensate for intellectual disparities. In short, high technology can put unequal human beings on equal footing, and that makes it the most potent democratizing tool ever devised."

A theoretical definition of democracy

Kenneth Bollen writes that "providing a definition of political democracy that everyone accepts is impossible."[15] His solution, one that is adhered to in this study, is to settle for providing a working definition of democracy. This is accomplished by first presenting the distilled essence of democracy and its essential components, then uncovering the conditions and processes that enable the theory to become a reality. On the basis of this recipe, it is proposed that the most fundamental requirements of democracy are participation and political competition.

It is through participation, the process of making one's will known to the government, that democracy is achieved. Unlike totalitarian regimes, in which the individual is of little consequence, democracies survive by assuming the worth of the individual. Through the individual's contribution to the creation of government, the system ensures that the government derives its authority from the populace.[16]

Competition, and its by-product political choice, is the second key component of democracy.[17] A market is viewed as competitive if it has enough buyers and sellers so that no single buyer or seller has a significant effect on price. In the political sphere, we can view competition similarly. To ensure that the will of the people is accurately reflected in the policies of the government, a competition of ideas (and the candidates who support those ideas) must exist. As in a competitive market, where the exercise of monopolistic powers is prevented, a competitive government safeguards against the extreme concentration of political power.

15   Bollen (1990, p. 7).
16   Rostow (1971, p. 268) suggests that a basic proposition of a democracy is that "governments [must] take their shape legitimately only from some effective expression of the combined will and judgments of individuals." Participation, then, as the act of this expression, underlies this proposition.
17   For an excellent discussion of this, see Schumpeter (1942). In his treatise, Schumpeter attests that "the democratic method is that institutional arrangement for arriving at political decisions in which individuals acquire the power to decide by means of a competitive struggle for the people's vote."

The necessary conditions of a democracy

Representative government. In defining democracy, clarification of certain basic terms is required. The first common misconception to dispel is that for a democracy to exist, each individual citizen must be involved with each aspect of the government at all times. In a post-tribal world, this method of government is insupportable. Sheer numbers alone would make functioning impossible. In addition, if we conclude (as we will later) that a population must make informed decisions in the determination of policy to promote democracy, absolute self-government would topple what it set out to achieve. The only type of meaningful democracy that can exist today is a representative one.[18]

Electoral rights. Because individuals cannot wield their will directly over policymaking, voting for a representative has become the most appropriate proxy for direct participation. When a citizen enters a voting booth, he or she influences the country's direction.[19] It is understandable that to many, voting rights are synonymous with competitive government. Since voting is one of the most important proxies in the measurement of democracy, questions such as "Who gets to vote and how many times?" "Is voting mandatory?" and "Are the ballots secret?" must be raised and answered.

The above relates to the "breadth of democracy"—the percentage of the population eligible to vote and the percentage of the population who exercise this right. At first blush, one may be tempted to say that every citizen should be able to vote. However, a democracy survives only if it comprises a thinking, reasoning electorate. It is inevitable, therefore, that some citizens' ability to participate in government will be constrained. We must be extraordinarily careful in classifying the type of citizen denied enfranchisement. In times past, women, people of color, and those who did not own property were restricted from voting. In regard to the landless, Thomas Jefferson made the observation, "I may . . . say that I have not observed men's

---

18 For an excellent primer on democratic rules, procedures, and norms, see Cohen (1971).

19 The 1994 U.S. congressional races provided a telling example of this proposition. A Connecticut race was decided by a handful of votes, and the electorate ousted a significant number of incumbents and rewarded the GOP with the House of Representatives.

honesty to increase with their riches."[20] Jefferson believed that general
suffrage was a goal the country should strive to attain. Although he
conceded that not all of humanity is endowed with the same riches or
genius, he thought that this should have no bearing on the right to
participate in government.

The second issue involving the right to vote is the necessity of equality among voters. Plural voting—the concept that some members of the
community are "fuller" members than others and consequently should
have more votes—is a scheme that in certain instances may seem rational. Lani Guinier, professor of law and former nominee for the top
civil rights position in the Clinton Justice Department, argued that in
certain situations, to ensure a functioning democracy, plural voting
should not only be accepted but actively advanced. She theorized that
in certain districts of the country, where historical barriers prevent
minorities from exercising their civil rights, weighted-voting schemes
balance the scales.[21] In an interview with the *Los Angeles Times,*
Guinier stated that the Civil Rights Act was passed in 1965

> because the Constitution, which had been amended after the Civil War,
> presumably to guarantee blacks the franchise, was never vigorously en-
> forced. . . . The Voting Rights Act as a result was passed with the idea
> and understanding that it wasn't enough simply to declare that we are a
> free society, that we are a democracy, that everyone should register and
> vote. The Voting Rights Act was passed with the understanding that the
> law had to monitor beyond simply a rhetorical declaration, the actions of
> some of these jurisdictions who were determined not to have blacks regis-
> tering, then not to have blacks voting, then not to have blacks electing
> people to office.[22]

Despite Guinier's accurate portrayal of the abuses suffered by black
Americans, the question remains: Can the breadth of democracy be
increased in the long run by placing clearly undemocratic regulations on
the electorate in the short run? Three main reasons dictate rejection of
such cumulative voting plans. First, weighted voting tends to shut out
challengers, making the race far less competitive and denying the needed
forum for a working democracy. Second, protected incumbents,
without the real threat of a challenge, become removed from the electorate. Representation diminishes and democracy suffers. Last, such

20   Jefferson (1959 edition).
21   "The Guinier Battle: Where Ideas That Hurt Guinier Thrive" (1993).
22   Terry (1993, Section B, p. 7).

dangerous departures from the precepts of democracy easily lead to a slippery slope in which a country's many minorities demand a weighted vote. In summary, the costs of setting a portion of the populace on a higher level of involvement in society whereby they can enshrine their holdings or expand their power far outweigh any benefits to the interested parties.

To answer the question, Can voting be mandatory? it is necessary to explore free and fair elections—the buzzwords in the post–Cold War world. Free and fair elections are often linked with pictures of armed guards stationed in front of polling places in South Africa, Cambodia, and Haiti. Although an obvious requirement is that coercion not be used to direct the vote (if it is not a vote by choice, how could it be called self-government?), the effects of compulsory voting on a democracy are less apparent. Debate exists over the effect of an apathetic electorate and the outcome on society when only a minority of citizens elect to vote. Many argue that a democracy *works better* when a majority of its citizens participate, but mandating involvement contradicts the premise of the ideal that voting is meant to represent. In addition, if those who do exercise their right to vote are an accurate sample of the eligible population, full representation of the population can be achieved. Unfortunately, if the sample group contains certain attributes not found in the population at large, the outcome can deviate from the true will of the people. Since it is reasonable to assume that those who do vote have specific agendas not found in the general pool of voters, democracy declines with the reduction in voter turnout. As the sample size approaches the size of the population, a more representative result occurs.

Electoral processes. Three other aspects of the electoral process must be explored in the search for a measure of democracy: the ability of a citizen to run for office, the dictum of majority rule, and citizen oversight over elected officials.

Candidacy. Many of the same arguments used above to discuss the categories of citizens eligible to vote also apply in the discussion of the eligibility to serve in government. Sanctioned restrictions (age and residency stipulations) may exist to ensure experience and the honest intentions of the candidate, but laws meant to exclude certain segments of society restrict democracy.

Other constraints to a free electoral process are nepotism and the system of favoritism often used by political machines. This arbitrary assignment of "additional rights" destroys what is best about a representative government—the ability to produce, as Thomas Paine once remarked, "the wisest laws, from collecting wisdom where it can be found."[23]

Majority rule. Majority rule is the decisionmaking principle that ensures the implementation of the people's will in government. Not only does the rule apply to the election of the candidate who has gained the support of the majority of the electorate, but it continues into the policy realm by the acceptance of the decision of the majority when the opinion of the representatives is divided. John Locke, in his *Second Treatise of Government* (1690), wrote

> For when any number of men have, by the consent of every individual, made a community, they have thereby made that community one body, with a power to act as one body, which is only by the will and determination of the majority; . . . it being necessary to that which is one body to move one way, it is necessary the body should move that way whither the greater force carries it, which is the consent of the majority; or else it is impossible it should act or continue one body, one community.

Although the will of the majority determines the course of government, the views and opinions of the minority must be allowed to enter the public forum. By disseminating its ideas on the free market, the minority has the potential to sway enough minds and convert its weak position to a stronger one. Through this process, each individual possesses the means to influence the government despite an initial position of weakness.

Citizen oversight. As the rules that allow government to govern are necessary to society, so too are the constraints upon government that

---

23   Paine (1993, first published in 1791). Paine extended his argument against hereditary powers by asserting, "Experience, in all ages and in all countries, has demonstrated that it is impossible to control nature in her distribution of mental powers. She gives them as she pleases. . . . It would be as ridiculous to attempt to fix the hereditaryship of human beauty as of wisdom. Whatever wisdom constituently is, it is like a seedless plant; it may be reared when it appears, but it cannot be voluntarily produced. There is always a sufficiency somewhere in the general mass of society for all purposes; but with respect to the parts of society, it is continually changing its place. . . . As this is in the order of nature, the order of Government must necessarily follow it, or Government will, as we see it does, degenerate into ignorance. The hereditary system, therefore, is as repugnant to human wisdom as to human rights; and is as absurd as it is unjust."

protect the people from the abuse of power. Without certain limitations, the environment needed to perpetuate self-government quickly erodes. The ability of the voting public to directly affect legislation and choose representatives as the need arises ensures the continuing process of democracy. Whereas formal elections can be held at infrequent intervals, thereby diminishing the power of the people to influence the acts of government, referendums and initiatives serve to preserve community involvement. The ability to impeach a public official safeguards the basic tenet of democracy that government, ultimately, is answerable to the people.

In sum, by expanding on Daniel Webster's famous statement, a working definition of democracy emerges: a government *for the people* is instituted by means of free and fair elections and the concept of majority rule; a government *by the people* is monitored through the process of regular elections and a referendum/initiative process; and a government *answerable to the people* is one in which citizens maintain the right to remove their representatives from office through the electoral or impeachment process.

The sufficient conditions of a democracy

Aside from the basic tenets of democracy elucidated above, a number of sufficient conditions must exist to maintain a democratic system. They provide an answer to the question, What actions of, and protections by, the government are needed to ensure that each citizen is able to fully participate in the act of governing? These conditions can be thought of as the pillars of democracy. They are the fundamentals needed to provide the correct climate for democracy. Without them, self-government collapses. Although the electoral process operationalizes democracy, the pillars described below are integral in creating and sustaining a democratic society. Many provided the backbone of the American Declaration of Independence, were later codified in the Declaration of the Rights of Man (issued by the French National Assembly in 1789), and were included in the American Constitution as the initial amendments.

Democratic liberties. The enshrinement of the liberties enumerated below assists in ensuring full participation in government.

- Freedom of speech—the ability of citizens to propose and oppose, to debate, and to argue.

- Freedom to disseminate information (freedom of the media)—the ability to have access to information ensures the participation of a reasonable, rational populace. Therefore, not only must the media be *allowed* to exist, it *must* exist. Independence of the media from the government is also necessary if the media is to be a free and public forum for debate, as well as a means of relaying information.

- Freedom of travel—the ability to journey outside the borders of one's country is necessary for the intellectual growth of citizens.

- Freedom to emigrate/freedom from forced emigration—as democracy is based upon the free will of the individual, denial of movement (or conversely, forced relocation) is in direct contradiction to this principle. In addition, forced relocation minimizes the *process* of democracy: the ability to vote or participate in government.

- Freedom of the person under the rules of habeas corpus—citizens must be allowed to exercise the rights listed above without fear of unjust governmental reprisal. A citizen not protected from illegal confinement would be unable to pursue his involvement in government in a free and open manner.

- Freedom to own property—without this right, a government can exert undue power over its citizens by the actual or threatened taking of a person's property.

- Protection of the rights of the minority—without a real opposition to the empowered elite, there would be few constraints on authority. Democracy rests on the ability of those *not in power* to have a voice in the creation of public policy.

Economic independence and social welfare. Although not fundamental in conceptualizing political democracy, certain economic conditions strengthen the likelihood of democratic success. The provision of free education by the government is of paramount importance. A system of government that relies on the participation of the population cannot survive in the long run without educating its people. To self-govern, one must understand the issues of the day, as well as the needs of tomorrow. Lipset, in reviewing a number of research surveys on democracy conducted in the 1940s and 1950s, concluded that "*the most important single factor differentiating those giving democratic responses from others has been education.* The higher one's education, the more likely one is to believe in democratic values and support democratic practice" [emphasis in original].[24]

Analogous to the importance of education in helping the electorate understand its representatives' recommendations is the need for people to achieve a level of economic well-being that allows them to think beyond the confines of the individual to the broader realm of the community. A person who is starving or who lacks basic shelter cannot fully participate in his government. And although pervasive poverty may not eliminate democracy (India provides the perfect example), it weakens the breadth and depth of self-government. For just as the law comprehends that a starving man *will* steal a loaf of bread despite the illegality of his action, so too must we recognize that the same man will allow his vote to be purchased for the price of a meal. To ensure democracy, subsistence must be achieved.

In a different capacity, a citizen's economic situation must have no bearing on his ability to participate in government. The rich should have no greater say in the process of government than the poor. This is exemplified by the one person, one vote rule. This also applies to the workings of a governmental bureaucracy. If bribery is the accepted means of government participation, democracy will be severely hampered. The effect of the cost of an American political campaign on universal participation in government is less clear. If it is impossible for a candidate to win without significant media exposure, and the cost of such advertisements prices him or her out of the race, democracy is ill served. Even if we believe that the free market will fund the candidates who have the "largest expected return" (probability for success), this does not mitigate the harm done to democracy from the elimination of the candidate with no chance of winning but whose platform gives voice to a specific minority.

In summary, the above describes a concept of democracy and the fundamentals needed for democracy to be created and maintained. The essence of democracy is embodied in the right to vote (free and fair elections), the concept of majority rule, the availability to influence government between elections by means of the referendum and initiative, and the ability to supervise government via the impeachment process. These rites of democracy would cease to exist if society did not have the rights of free speech, free press, free movement across borders, and habeas corpus.

24   Lipset (1959, p. 79).

4

————————————————————————————————

Quantitative analysis of democracy

Since Lipset first systematically explored the relationship between economic development and democracy, a number of researchers have attempted to expand and refine his model using more sophisticated analytic techniques and more valid measures. The earliest attempts[1] relied exclusively on correlation analyses and often used dichotomous measures of democracy. Later studies[2] employed single-equation ordinary least squares (OLS) models, with no attempts made to analyze the interrelationship and endogeneity of the constructs. Consequently, results from these early studies were often contradictory. The three main causes of such confusing results are model misspecification, omitted variable bias, and the assessment of the relationship at single points in time, rather than as trends.

The model presented here builds upon the work of previous researchers by using cross-sectional, time-series data to understand the interrelationships among democracy, marketization, prosperity, technology, and internationalization. Rather than focusing exclusively on economic development, this model broadens modernization research by incorporating a theory of marketization. Economic development may be a precondition of democracy according to Lipset, but marketization provides the foundation of democracy by introducing choice, competition, and public accountability. These concepts, first introduced to the people through the marketplace, are then transferred to their political lives. Made better off by market competition—more choice at better

1 Lipset (1959); Cutright (1963).
2 Feierabend and Feierabend (1972); Dick (1974); Huntington and Dominguez (1975); and Marsh (1979).

prices—citizens demand to see the same sort of competition within their system of government. Of equal importance, marketization assists in the maturation of the *individual* as a political unit. In reference to China in the mid 1980s, Thomas Gold said that "privatization of activity had a counterpart in privatization of values. Increasingly, Chinese opted out of Party-led political activity." This in turn decreased the power of the state.[3] In Korea and Taiwan, each with its own history of military rule and authoritarian control, markets bolstered a private sphere separate and distinct from the state, thereby contributing to the creation of a democratic opposition.

To strengthen and advance the field of modernization research, which assesses the social prerequisites for a country to develop into a modern economy as opposed to a feudal or mercantile economy, this work includes both the construct of prosperity (the more traditional focus of economic development) and marketization and analyzes how each affects democracy. The time period 1976 through 1992 has been chosen not only because of data limitations on earlier years but because these two decades span an especially interesting time within East Asia. In China, the Cultural Revolution was drawing to an end after the September 1976 death of Mao; in Taiwan, the country was taking its first significant steps toward a market economy with the organization of the "First Nation-Wide Economic Conference," which brought together leaders from both the private and public spheres to discuss the future of the Taiwanese economy; and in Thailand, the military overthrew the civilian government in the bloodiest coup in Thai history. The use of pooled cross-sectional, time-series data and fixed effects specifications for seven East and Southeast Asian countries, needed to estimate a simultaneous-equations model, provides added confidence in the parameter estimates.

THEORETICAL MODEL AND EMPIRICAL IMPLEMENTATION

The formulation and testing of a system of equations for a dataset consisting of seven East and Southeast Asian countries (1976–1992) allows examination of causal relationships among the constructs: *democracy, marketization, prosperity, internationalization,* and *technology.* The basic model of the relationship between the socioeconomic factors under consideration and democracy takes the following form:

3   Gold (1990, p. 203).

$$democracy = f(marketization; prosperity; internationalization;$$
$$technology) + \mu$$

However, to explore the pathways of causality, a more detailed model must be constructed around the above framework. Figure 4.1 graphically depicts the interrelationships among the constructs. Each construct is circled, and the measures for these constructs extend off the circles in rectangles. The measures *stock*, *edu*, and *urban* serve as instruments to identify *marketization* and *prosperity* within the *democracy* equation.

Based on the above, the structural equations of the model become:

democracy:

$$demscale = \beta0 + \beta1(mtwo) + \beta2(lgdpcap) + \beta3(fdigdp) + \beta4(open) +$$
$$\beta5(trate) + \beta6(tele) + \beta7(invest) + \beta8\text{-}\beta13(country\ dummies) +$$
$$\beta14(time) + \mu \qquad (1)$$

marketization:

$$mtwo = \beta0 + \beta1(demscale) + \beta2(tele) + \beta3(invest) + \beta4(stock)$$
$$+ \beta5\text{-}\beta10(country\ dummies) + \beta11(time) + \mu \qquad (2)$$

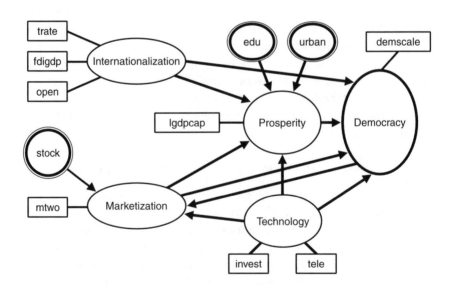

Figure 4.1. Detailed Model of Democracy

prosperity:

$$lgdpcap = \text{ß}0 + \text{ß}1(mtwo) + \text{ß}2(tele) + \text{ß}3(invest) + \text{ß}4(fdigdp) + \text{ß}5(open)$$
$$+ \text{ß}6(trate) + \text{ß}7(urban) + \text{ß}8(edu) + \text{ß}9\text{-ß}14(country\ dummies)$$
$$+ \text{ß}15(time) + \mu \qquad (3)$$

The system is estimated using a two-stage least squares (2SLS) regression technique. A more comprehensive discussion of the 2SLS estimation procedure used in this examination is presented in Appendix A. *Democracy*, as well as the variables constituting the vectors of the socioeconomic constructs, is discussed below. A complete codebook for the variables is given in Appendix B.

Democracy is measured by *demscale*, a variable that takes values between 0 and 1 (0 representing the absence of democracy; 1 representing a full democracy). The variable is a combination of the political rights and civil liberties indices created by Freedom House over the last three decades.[4] Transforming the composite of these two scales linearly is acceptable, since the correlation between the two indices is above 0.90.

Prosperity is measured as *lgdpcap*, the log of real per capita gross domestic product in current U.S. dollars, converted through purchasing power parity. Per capita GDP was transformed logarithmically to meet the assumptions regarding a normal distribution, since bivariate plots suggested that the relationship between GDP per capita and democracy was curvilinear. Transforming GDP per capita logarithmically allows a linear model to capture a nonlinear relationship.

Marketization is measured by *mtwo*, currency plus demand and time deposits as a percentage of GDP. The measure *mtwo* assesses whether or not the financial system is "repressed," or, in other words, whether the financial market is *adequately allocating resources*. A key component of a market system is the ability for internal savings to be channeled into productive investment. The size of the formal financial intermediary sector can be used to measure financial sector development. As financial development deepens, the efficiency of capital allocation increases, thereby spurring economic growth. Through a more efficient allocation of resources the breadth of the market increases. Although *mtwo* serves as a useful tool for measuring marketization, it may not be equally useful as a policy lever. It may, actually, distort the phenomena it attempts to measure. Consequently, further study should be directed

4   Finn (1994).

at linking the measurement with an appropriate tool.[5] Further study should also be directed at finding a stronger empirical measurement device, since *mtwo* does not accurately reflect whether the average individual can enter the market or the involvement of the government in the economy. The share of GDP taxed and spent by the government would be a useful secondary measure, as would the distribution of capital ownership, but unfortunately the data for these variables are not available for many East Asian countries.

Technology is measured by two proxies: *invest* (real investment as a percentage of GDP) and *tele* (telephones per 100 inhabitants).

Internationalization is measured by three proxies: *fdigdp* (foreign direct investment/GDP), *open* ((imports + exports)/GDP), and *trate* (international tariffs/(imports + exports)).[6] Three variables have been included to reduce specification error, since past research has indicated their importance as determinants of internationalization.

Because the structural parameters have two right-hand-side endogenous variables (*mtwo* and *demscale*), the question is raised whether there is sufficient information available to estimate the structural parameters from the reduced form. Three variables are included in the model to identify the *democracy* equation. The variables *edu* (gross educational enrollment of all ages/children in the appropriate age group) and *urban* (percentage of population residing in major cities) are highly correlated with *prosperity* but not with the *democracy* equation error term. Excluding these two variables from the *democracy* equation identifies the effect of *prosperity* within the *democracy* equation. The variable *edu* can be interpreted as human capital formation which contributes to rising incomes. According to the World Bank, "the economic rate of return to investment in schooling is high, frequently well above that of physical investment."[7]

Although education is often correlated with democracy in large cross-national databases, the justification for inclusion within an East Asian subset is less valid. The Confucian and Buddhist cultures of East Asia have a history of stressing the importance of education while at the same time, until recently, spurning democracy. O'Donnell makes the

---

5   See King and Levine (1993); Adelman and Morris (1973); and McKinnon (1993).
6   Note that the share of exports and imports to GDP may be affected by the absolute size of GDP. Future research should consider this possibility.
7   World Bank (1980, p. 97).

valid claim that modernization research often falls prey to the "universalistic fallacy"—that since "some positive correlation between socioeconomic development and political democracy can be found, it may be concluded that this relationship holds for all the units included in that set."[8] A more plausible theory in regard to East Asia is that although increasing amounts of education raise the per capita GDP of the country, education does not, in and of itself, produce the individualistic character necessary to create and sustain democracy.

Urbanization, by bringing the factors of production closer together, leads to increases in wealth that tend to promote a more moderate citizenry likely to develop and sustain a stable democratic form of government. The direct linkages between urbanization and democracy, especially in this age of telecommunications, are less obvious.

The variable *stock* (stock market capitalization in millions of U.S. dollars) is included in the model to identify the effect of *marketization* within the *democracy* equation. Stock markets encourage free markets in a number of ways. First, by providing a screening and monitoring function, stock markets help entrepreneurs raise capital they may not be able to obtain otherwise. Second, stock markets allow firms to achieve an efficient mix of debt and equity, thereby increasing their chances of success. Finally, capital markets allow investors to diversify and reduce their risk exposure, which, ultimately, lowers the overall cost of capital. These functions increase the market's level of efficiency and expand its breadth. Although concern exists that Asian markets suffer from inefficient pricing mechanisms, manipulative operations, and often cumbersome listing practices, capital markets in the region nonetheless succeed in directing savings into productive economic ventures, thus promoting growth and development. It can be argued that a functioning capital market, through its role in expanding the free market, also increases choice, competition, and public accountability, giving citizens the skills and desires for economic independence. However, there is no theory suggesting that stock markets, in and of themselves, lead citizens down the path of democracy. Consequently, there is prima facie validity for excluding *stock* from the *democracy* equation.

The propositions arising from the theoretical framework laid out in Chapter 3 were tested empirically by using the Freedom House index to measure political democracy between 1976 and 1992 for China,

---

8   O'Donnell (1973, p. 6).

Indonesia, Korea, Malaysia, Singapore, Taiwan, and Thailand. The framework can be used to derive explicit hypotheses regarding the effect of certain socioeconomic factors on the level of democracy within a country. It was hypothesized that a positive relationship would exist between the dependent variable—*democracy*—and the independent variables measuring economic development and marketization. The hypotheses tested within the empirical model are as follows.

1. A positive relationship is hypothesized to exist between *democracy* (*demscale*) and *marketization* (*mtwo*). (H0: B1 < 0; H1: B1 >= 0)

2. A positive relationship is hypothesized to exist between *democracy* (*demscale*) and *prosperity* (*lgdpcap*); however, increases beyond a certain level of economic well-being are not correlated with any additional increases in democracy—a positive curvilinear relationship. (H0: C1 < 0; H1: C1 >= 0)

3. Countries with closer ties to the world—*internationalization* (*fdigdp, open, trate*)—are expected to have higher levels of *democracy* (*demscale*). (H0: D1 < 0; H1: D1 >= 0); *trate*, reflecting the level of tariffs as a percentage of imports plus exports, is expected to have a negative relationship with *democracy,* since higher tariffs suggest fewer open ties to the world. (H0: D1a > 0; H1: D1a <= 0)

4. Countries with higher levels of *technology* (*invest, tele*) are expected to score higher on the *democracy (demscale)* index. (H0: E1 < 0; H1: E1 >= 0)

SUMMARY STATISTICS

Tables 4.1 and 4.2 present summary statistics for the variables included in the model. The value of *demscale* ranges from a low of zero (China) to a high of 0.75 (Korea, 1987 through 1992; Thailand, 1976). The mean score of the *democracy* index is 0.39. The standard deviation, which measures how widely individual countries are dispersed around the average, is 0.18. Assuming a normal distribution, nearly two-thirds of the countries lie within the range of 0.21 to 0.57, with all but 5 percent of the observations falling between 0.03 and 0.75. Although the pairwise correlation matrix takes into account only bivariate relationships, it serves as a useful indicator of which variables may be significant in predicting the value of *democracy* within a regression equation and detecting whether multicollinearity may be a problem (this does not appear to be the case). The heuristic employed for determining a correlation coefficient calculation for significance is 2/square root of N. In this dataset, the calculation yields a value of 0.18. Reviewing the matrix, *lgdpcap, tele, open,* and *mtwo* appear to be significant. Although *stock* appears to be highly significant with r = 0.46, theory informs us that a stock market affects a country's movement toward democracy through greater marketization rather than as a direct influence. We assume that any effect of *stock* on democracy will dissipate once other variables are controlled for within a regression model.

Reviewing the summary statistics, it is apparent that many variables contain values in both the very high and very low ranges. In part, this is due to the length of the time period studied (during the 20 years, many of the countries modernized, opened stock exchanges, and promoted education), but country differences must also be recognized. For instance, the variable *urban* ranges from 15.5 percent of the population to 100 percent, with a standard deviation of 29.15 Because China, a country of over 1 billion citizens, and Singapore, a city-state, are both represented in the sample, such a wide divergence in values is expected.

Summary statistics provide a basic understanding of the data, but they do not shed light on how countries within the region vary along the dimensions of the variables and across time. Figures 4.2 through 4.10 supplement the summary statistics by graphically displaying these

Table 4.1. *Summary statistics*

Variable	No. of Obs	Mean	Std. Dev	Min	Max
demscale	119	.3928571	.1825558	0	.75
lgdpcap	119	3.461917	.3698866	2.595496	4.223652
edu	119	55.67269	19.80776	20	91
urban	119	49.10924	29.14648	15.5	100
invest	119	26.42815	6.37782	15.2	41.5
tele	119	12.83067	14.70236	19	48.6
fdigdp	119	1.71764	3.198705	0	14.32841
open	119	95.62052	76.73577	8.306862	306.5715
trate	119	3.929253	2.383385	.1795802	10.44379
mtwo	119	58.41489	30.0858	15.0182	170.5076
stock	119	20007.34	36700.8	0	237012

Table 4.2. *Correlation matrix*

	demscale	lgdpcap	edu	urban	invest	tele	fdigdp	open	trate	mtwo	stock
demscale	1.0000										
lgdpcap	0.5270	1.0000									
edu	0.0938	0.5959	1.0000								
urban	0.1807	0.7773	0.7264	1.0000							
invest	0.1790	0.6318	0.4745	0.6688	1.0000						
tele	0.3339	0.8397	0.7390	0.9099	0.5540	1.0000					
fdigdp	0.1067	0.5636	0.1811	0.6451	0.5844	0.5911	1.0000				
open	0.1912	0.6807	0.2921	0.8003	0.6980	0.6612	0.8804	1.0000			
trate	-0.0082	-0.6257	-0.4119	-0.7250	-0.6067	-0.6482	-0.5301	-0.6406	1.0000		
mtwo	0.1840	0.6521	0.3927	0.5134	0.1117	0.6247	0.3292	0.3748	-0.3506	1.0000	
stock	0.4633	0.5814	0.4831	0.3543	0.2763	0.5745	0.0659	0.0949	-0.2681	0.5280	1.0000

trends. Figure 4.2 displays the democracy index (*demscale*) for the seven countries during the 1972–1992 time period. As shown, both Korea and Taiwan have made remarkable progress in altering their political systems over the last two decades. Both countries began the early 1970s in the lowest third of the democracy range, well below Malaysia and Singapore, yet ended the period with functioning democracies. Malaysia experienced a curtailment of democratic freedoms as Islamic law replaced British law within the country's judicial system. As the summary statistics show, there is great variation in Thailand, a country in which 19 military coup attempts occurred between 1932 (when the Thais overthrew their absolute monarchy) and 1994.

Indonesia stayed constant during the 1970s and early 1980s, moved down in the mid 1980s, reflecting the annexation and brutal repression of Timor, saw a brief resurgence in freedom in the late 1980s (when Suharto made motions that he would retire at the end of his 1993 term), and then dropped back to lower levels in the early 1990s, reflecting Suharto's confirmation that he would seek another term of office.

The most apparent trend shown in Figure 4.2 (*demscale*) is that of China. Falling well below the other countries in the sample, China was

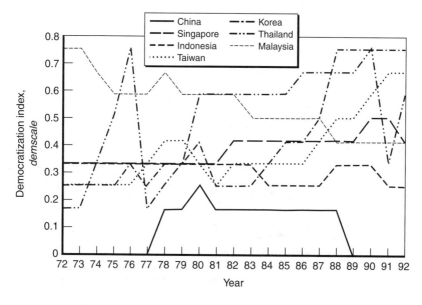

Figure 4.2. Democratization Trends: 1972–1992

ranked as having no freedom for most of the 1970s. From 1976, following the death of Mao, through the late 1980s, China gradually
opened its market to foreign investment and private initiative. Market
reforms, and a concomitant political liberalization, occurred in the mid
1980s, reflected in an increased ranking on the freedom scale. The period from 1977 to 1989 marks the beginning of China's economic and
political transition and is discussed at length in the China chapter. In
June 1989, Chinese authorities executed a brutal crackdown on the pro-
democracy protesters in Tiananmen Square. Freedom House adjusted
its ranking accordingly. What the chart does not portray, yet the
econometric model elucidates, are the contributing factors that influence
a country's movements toward democracy. Although 1989 will forever
be remembered by Chinese and Sinologists as the year of Tiananmen
Square, it is also the year when prices rose over 30 percent in the major
cities and the general economy was in upheaval. Understanding the in-
terplay between economic and political factors is essential in fashioning
appropriate foreign policies.

In the *marketization* graph (Figure 4.3), Taiwan stands out as having
deepened its financial system dramatically throughout the 1980s. Yet
the region's other democratic leader, Korea, hovers with one of the lowest percentages. This may be explained, in part, by the structure of the

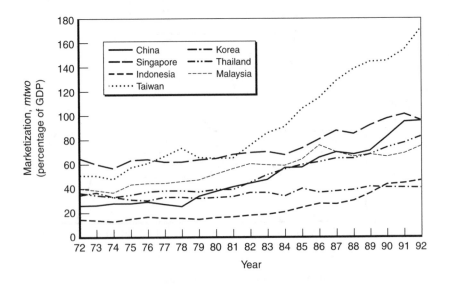

Figure 4.3. Marketization Trends: 1972–1992

countries' economies. Taiwan is fueled by small to medium-sized firms, and Korea's economy is controlled by the chaebol (large conglomerates). The ability of the chaebol to do business outside institutionalized channels is notorious (as evidenced by the recent prosecutions of former presidents Chun and Rho), and their need for financial depth is less imperative than it is for the business sector in Taiwan. Discussion on the different paths taken by Taiwan and Korea, both in the creation of a modern market and in the march to democracy, is contained in the specific country chapters.

The trust that Indonesians put into their banking system, as measured by *mtwo,* went through two distinct growth phases. The first occurred between 1967 and 1972 when M2/GDP increased from 3.8 percent to 13.0 percent. Following directly on the heels of Suharto's ascendance, and the conclusion of the Year of Living Dangerously, the New Order Regime instituted a wide range of banking reforms.[9] To ensure that these reforms would be accepted by the populace, the technocrats in government embarked on a public relations campaign to enlist public involvement in the reform process. For many Indonesians, this was their first personal, and positive, contact with their government. The second phase of development of the financial system occurred between 1983 and 1990, when *mtwo* rose from 18.9 percent to 40.1 percent. During this time, credit and interest rate ceilings were removed and restrictions on the entry and expansion of banks were relaxed.

China's financial intermediaries, as measured by *mtwo* as a percentage of GDP, have been growing stronger over the last two decades. Starting at 25 percent in 1972, by 1992 China had rates nearly identical to Singapore's (95 percent). The question remains: What will this financial liberalization mean in terms of the country's system of government? Will the ruling elites in China, like those in Singapore, be able to control the process—allowing free markets without a counterpart in the political sphere? Or will China follow its cousins across the strait and witness a democracy movement emerge from a business sphere in need of property rights and fuller marketization? The beginning of an answer to these questions is contained within the model and the accompanying country studies.

Figures 4.4, 4.5, 4.6, and 4.7, displaying *lgdpcap, invest, tele,* and *open,* show little other than the variables trended upward over time.

---

9   Cole and Slade (1996).

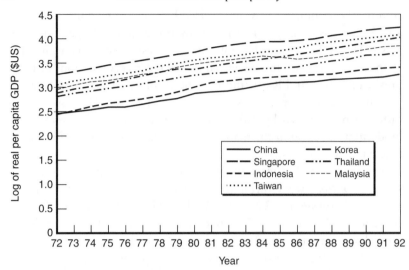

Figure 4.4. Trends in Real Per Capita GDP: 1972–1992

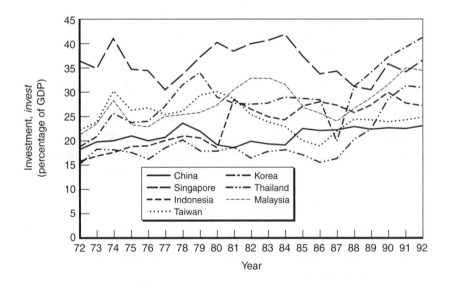

Figure 4.5. Trends in Real Investment: 1972–1992

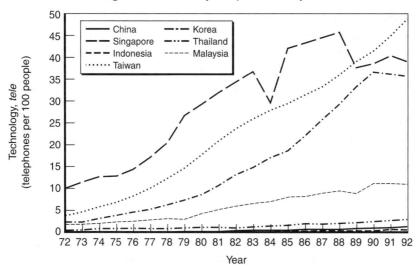

Figure 4.6. Technology Trends Measured by Telephones per Inhabitant:
1972–1992

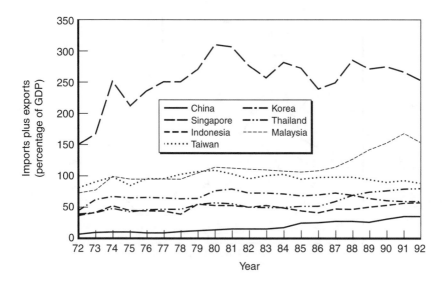

Figure 4.7. Trends in Imports and Exports: 1972–1992

Figures 4.8, 4.9, and 4.10, however, displaying *trate, fdigdp* (both measures of *internationalization*), and *stock,* show higher levels of variation. Although tariff levels have declined over time, China stands out as having raised tariffs as a percentage of imports plus exports in the mid 1970s, the early 1980s, and again in 1989 in an attempt to reduce significant deficits in its balance of payments account. Figure 4.9, which presents foreign direct investment (FDI) as a percentage of GDP, shows most of the countries clustered between 0 percent and 2.5 percent. However, the values for Singapore range between a low of 2 percent during the recession of 1976 and a high of nearly 14 percent. The extremely high level of FDI as a percentage of GDP occurred because the Singaporean government, under the leadership of Prime Minister Lee Kuan Yew, established itself as an independent port for transit trade, enticing foreign companies to locate their offshore manufacturing base on the island as a way to counterbalance the country's large and chronic deficit in its merchandise trade account.

In the case of *stock,* the standard deviation is greater than the mean, signifying the vast amount of dispersion within the data. This comes as

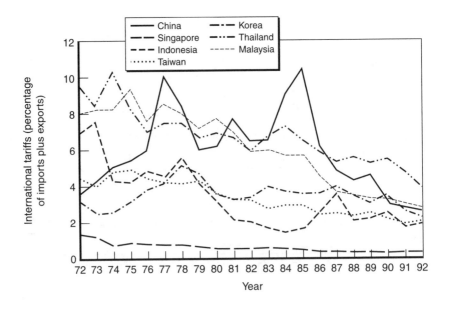

Figure 4.8. Trends in Tariff Rates: 1972–1992

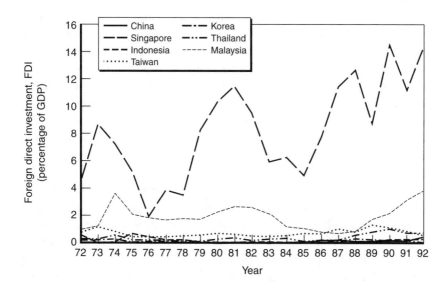

Figure 4.9. Trends in Foreign Direct Investment: 1972–1992

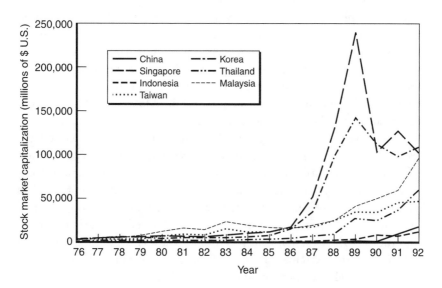

Figure 4.10. Trends in Stock Market Capitalization: 1976–1992

little surprise, since the histories of the individual markets are vastly different. Taiwan's market was established in the mid 1950s and is dominated by private investors involved in short-term transactions. The modern infrastructure of Korea's market, in contrast, was established in the early 1970s and has remained relatively small over the last two decades. By the early 1990s, Korea's exchange was roughly the size of Thailand's and Singapore's. Unlike Taiwan, Korea's market has been actively promoted by the government to assist companies with high debt ratios and to privatize several large national companies including Korea Electric Power, the National Bank of Korea, and Korea Telephone and Telegraph.[10]

The Malaysian and Singaporean stock exchanges were officially separated in 1965, when parity between the two countries' currencies ceased. Although dual listings of Malaysian and Singaporean firms on both countries' markets continued until 1989, the listing practices of the countries and the makeup of those listings differed substantially. Most of the Singaporean listings are dominated by family-controlled businesses that hold the majority of stocks with little intention of selling. By the early 1990s, Singapore's exchange was second in performance in East Asia (behind the Hong Kong exchange). Malaysia's market has been distinguished by the strong governmental role in shaping the market. After the ethnic riots of 1969, the government embarked on a policy to create a more even distribution of capital. By 1990, 30 percent of corporate capital was to be owned by indigenous Malaysians. To implement this policy, the government not only guided the development of the investor population but promoted the public listing of targeted firms. Unlike its Singaporean neighbors, the Malaysian exchange suffers from lack of liquidity and high volatility.

Indonesia's exchange was established in 1976 and remained extremely small until the latter half of the 1980s when it enjoyed a period of rapid growth. Still, the Jakarta exchange remains quite immature despite the government's active involvement in its development through periodic reform measures. The newest exchanges in the region are those in China. The Shanghai exchange was established in December 1990 and the Shenzhen exchange in July 1991. The limited number of observations and the extreme volatility of these markets upon their opening add to the level of dispersion in the overall dataset.

10 Long Term Credit Bank of Japan (1994).

Moving beyond simple correlation and graphical displays, the present econometric model estimates three equations simultaneously. The results from these regressions are presented in the next section.

EMPIRICAL EVALUATION

A regression model of *democracy* was estimated using pooled cross-sectional, time-series data for seven East and Southeast Asian countries for the period 1976 through 1992. The model includes a number of co-variates to control for explanatory factors contributing to democracy that have been suggested in the literature. These include measures for internationalization and technology. In estimating the regression equation for *democracy,* three alternative approaches, each with two variations, were analyzed. The results of these equations are presented in Table 4.3. The first approach employs a 2SLS technique, with and without a time trend. The second approach also employs a 2SLS technique, yet corrects for serial correlation. A discussion of the procedure used for this correction is presented in Appendix C. Although serial correlation does not affect the unbiasedness or consistency of the estimators, it does affect the efficiency of the estimators (the standard errors will be biased downward, leading to inappropriate rejection of the null). The correction procedure, however, may raise more problems than it solves. Because of the limited number of observations for each country (n = 17), the correlation coefficient is estimated on an extremely small sample size. The second approach, with or without the time trend, is, therefore, highly suspect.

The third approach estimates the regression equation by ordinary least squares. As discussed above, this method fails to take into account the endogeneity of *marketization* and *prosperity.* The Hausman test for simultaneity confirms that OLS is not an appropriate technique. The null hypothesis that *mtwo* is not exogenous is rejected at the 1 percent level. When *lgdpcap* is also assumed to be endogenous, the null hypothesis that the predicted values of *mtwo* and *lgdpcap* are both equal to zero can be rejected at the 10 percent level, with an F statistic of 2.89. The discussion below focuses on the preferred estimation technique (Models I and II).

The first regression model, estimated by 2SLS without a correction for serial correlation, explains 50 percent of the variance in outcome. When a time trend is included, the amount of variation explained, adjusted for degrees of freedom, falls from 54 percent to 47 percent.

Table 4.3. *Democracy regressions*

	Model I	Model II	Model III	Model IV	Model V	Model VI
Method	2SLS	2SLS	2SLS w/correction	2SLS w/correction	OLS	OLS
Marketization:						
mtwo	.007 (.003)**	.007 (.003)**	.001 (.002)	.001 (.002)	-.000 (.000)	.000 (.000)
Prosperity:						
lgdpcap	-.283 (.252)	2.078 (1.37)	.137 (.065)**	.134 (.07)*	.163 (.104)	.521 (.250)**
Technology:						
tele	.007 (.031)**	.000 (.006)	.005 (.004)	.005 (.004)	.008 (.002)***	.007 (.002)***
invest	.011 (.035)**	.002 (.008)	-.000 (.898)	-.000 (.004)	.003 (.003)	.002 (.003)
Internationalization:						
fdigdp	-.007 (.010)	-.004 (.010)	-.000 (.008)	-.000 (.008)	-.005 (.008)	-.004 (.008)
open	-.001 (.001)	-.001 (.001)	-.000 (.000)	-.000 (.001)	-.002 (.000)**	-.002 (.00)*
trate	.045 (.017)***	.017 (.019)	.004 (.011)	.004 (.011)	.025 (.010)**	.019 (.011)*
Country Dummies:						
Indon	.583 (.138)***	.175 (.246)	.118 (.045)***	.118 (.045)**	.289 (.057)***	.230 (.068)***
Korea	.580 (.168)***	-.719 (.726)	.130 (.052)**	.130 (.052)**	.225 (.073)***	.018 (.150)
Malaysia	.564 (.127)***	-.770 (.766)	.141 (.046)***	.141 (.047)***	.448 (.091)***	.423 (.166)
Singapore	.597 (.263)**	-1.47 (1.16)	.044 (.115)	.041 (.123)	.493 (.199)**	.125 (.306)
Taiwan	.193 (.103)*	-1.43 (.912)	.137 (.053)**	.137 (.055)**	.199 (.082)**	-.084 (.197)
Thai	.608 (.109)***	-.323 (.543)	.180 (.040)***	.1811 (.041)***	.442 (.061)***	.298 (.109)***
[China]						
Time Trend		-.101 (.056)*		-.000 (.002)		-.018 (.011)
Cons	.091 (.587)	-5.29 (3.2)	-.57 (.055)***	-.155 (.059)**	-.54(.292)*	-1.35 (.593)**
N	119	119	119	119	119	119
Adj R^2	0.543	0.471	0.551	0.547	0.715	0.719
F	15.11	12.33	12.16	11.19	23.74	22.53

NOTE: The coefficients and the standard deviations, in parentheses, are presented for each variable.
***Significant at the 1 percent level.
**Significant at the 5 percent level.

Figures 4.11 through 4.17, which show the predicted versus actual values of *democracy* for each of the seven countries over the time series, corroborate that, overall, the model performs extremely well. The figures are based upon Model I.

However, the model failed to predict the path of democracy during the mid 1980s in Korea and the late 1970s in Thailand. This is due to the oftentimes serendipitous nature of politics. In reference to Korea, few would have predicted the rapidity with which political reforms occurred in 1987. In January 1987, a student protester died while in police custody, escalating the already simmering tensions between the populace and the government. After President Chun picked Roh Tae Woo as his successor, more violent protests erupted. Unlike his predecessors, who dealt with student protests through military crackdowns and martial law, Roh took the world by surprise by announcing direct presidential elections and a restoration of civil liberties. Sooner than anyone would have thought possible, Korea had moved toward political liberalization.

Thailand's severe curtailment of political rights and civil liberties in the late 1970s had as much to do with external as internal factors. The 1975 Communist takeover of Vietnam, Laos, and Cambodia brought

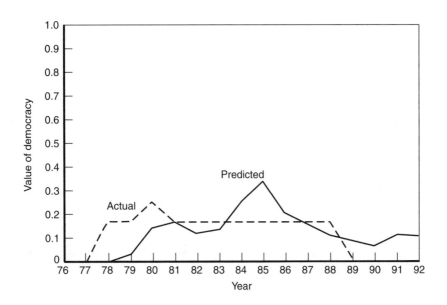

Figure 4.11. Predicted versus Actual Values of Democracy for China

Marketization and prosperity

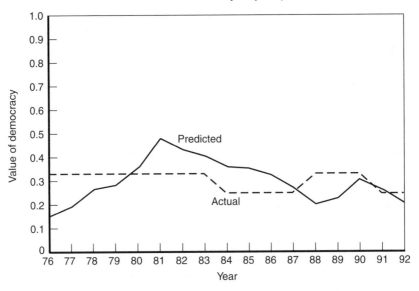

Figure 4.12. Predicted versus Actual Values of Democracy for Indonesia

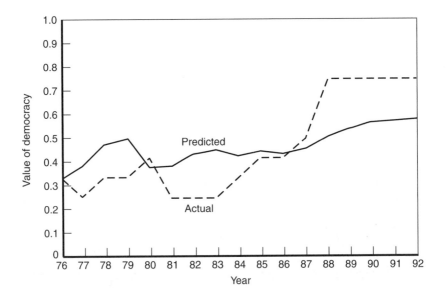

Figure 4.13. Predicted versus Actual Values of Democracy for Korea

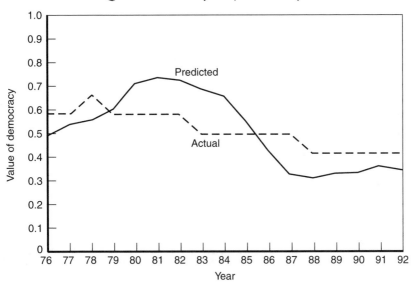

Figure 4.14. Predicted versus Actual Values of Democracy for Malaysia

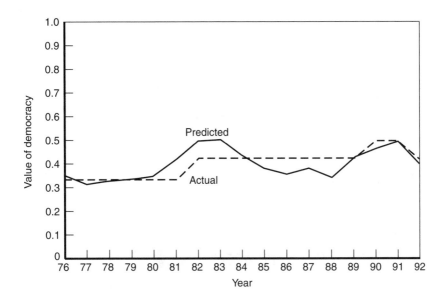

Figure 4.15. Predicted versus Actual Values of Democracy for Singapore

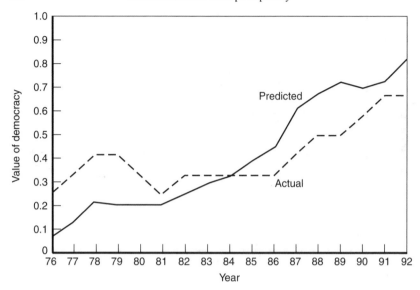

Figure 4.16. Predicted versus Actual Values of Democracy for Taiwan

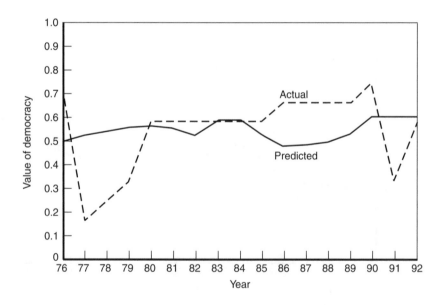

Figure 4.17. Predicted versus Actual Values of Democracy for Thailand

immense pressure to bear on the civilian government, leading to a loss in popular confidence. The democratic civilian period of the previous three years was brought to a bloody halt by a brutal military coup in October 1976. Despite this, the lessons learned in the period of political liberalization, and the continued modernization of the country's economy, allowed Thailand to slowly restore freedom over the next few years, as shown in Figure 4.17.

As discussed in Chapter 3, a positive relationship is hypothesized to exist between *democracy (demscale)* and *marketization (mtwo), prosperity (lgdpcap), internationalization (fdigdp, open, trate),* and *technology (invest, tele)*. Interpreting the coefficients of Model I, as seen on Table 4.3, three of the nondummy variables are significant at the 5 percent level (*mtwo, tele,* and *invest*) and one at the 1 percent level (*trate*). Using the means of the actual data for both the left- and right-hand-side variables, we can estimate elasticities. The coefficient on *mtwo* is +0.0066, which translates as a 10 percent increase in *mtwo*/GDP and leads to a 9.8 percent increase in the *democracy* index. Increasing *mtwo*/GDP by 50 percent increases *democracy* by 49 percent. Using Freedom House rankings, such an increase in *marketization* could raise the level of political rights and civil liberties within Indonesia closer to those in Malaysia and could lift Malaysia to Taiwanese levels of democracy. In practical terms, this could mean a freer press in Indonesia (something akin to that of their neighbor Malaysia) and the freedom to organize political parties in Malaysia (as seen in Taiwan).

The other variables of significance are *tele, invest,* and *trate*. Both *tele* and *invest* are measures of *technology* and both have signs in the expected (positive) direction. The model suggests that with a 10 percent increase in the number of households with telephones, *democracy* increases by 0.07 point (on a 0 to 1.0 scale). This finding is statistically significant, but its practical value is less clear, since an increase in *democracy* of 0.07 point may be meaningless. As investment increases by 10 percent, *democracy* increases by 0.11 point.

The sign on *trate* is opposite to what is suggested by the literature. As can be seen in Figure 4.8 (the trend of tariff rates across time), aside from Singapore, which started out with extremely low rates, most of the nations had falling rates through the 1980s, with the exclusion of China and Indonesia, both of which had wide variations as a result of their hesitant steps toward freer markets. Both China and Indonesia drastically lowered rates to entice foreign investment into their export-oriented sector and then increased rates unexpectedly to counter the ill effects that large amounts of imports had on their balance of payments. When a time trend is included in the regression (Model II), *trate* is no longer significant. Neither *fdigdp* nor *open* was significant, suggesting the possibility that they are inappropriate measures of *internationalization*. Future research should explore alternative measures.

As shown in Table 4.3, four of the six models found *lgdpcap* to not be significant in predicting democracy. In that many previous studies exploring the relationship between development and democracy have found this relationship to be significant (as discussed in Chapter 2), these regression results require further analysis. Rerunning Models I through VI without the *mtwo* and *stock* variables found *lgdpcap* to be significant at the 1 percent level in Models III and IV (2SLS with a correction), significant at the 5 percent level in Models II and IV (2SLS with a time trend and OLS with a time trend), and significant at the 10 percent level in Model V. *Lgdpcap* remained nonsignificant in Model I. The biggest changes were in Models II through V, which showed *lgdpcap* becoming significant with the omission of *mtwo*. This suggests that prior work in the field, which included a prosperity but not a marketization construct, may have suffered from omitted variable bias.

With the exception of Taiwan, the estimated country effects are significantly different from the level of democracy in China (at the 1 and 5 percent levels). Jointly testing the country effects for each model (an F test) found the results to be significant at the 1 percent level. These results suggest that country variations explain some of the differences in the trends toward democracy. In the qualitative country studies, sociopolitical environments are examined to determine their effect on providing the initial conditions for democracy.

To better understand the interrelationship among *democracy, marketization,* and *prosperity,* the entire three-equation system, as depicted in Figure 4.1, should be analyzed. Tables 4.4 and 4.5 present the regression coefficients for both the *marketization* and *prosperity* equations, duplicating Models I and II (henceforth referred to as Models Ib and IIb for *marketization* and Ic and IIc for *prosperity*). In Model IIb, there are no significant direct effects of *democracy* on *marketization,* although when the time trend is excluded, there is a significant negative feedback, as seen in Ib. This may suggest that there is not enough variation in the excluded variables intended to identify the equation.

Table 4.4. *Marketization regression*

	Model Ib	Model IIb
Method	2SLS	2SLS
demscale	−89.813 (32.1)***	16.659 (21.9)
tele	1.516 (.357)***	−.4727 (.287)
invest	−.3483 (.404)	−1.383 (.276)***
stock	.0002 (.000)***	.00015 (.000)***
indon	−11.86 (8.41)	−28.91 (5.49)***
korea	−24.07 (10.1)**	−9.509 (6.65)
malaysia	26.75 (12.8)**	7.455 (8.18)
singapore	−2.85 (12.6)	49.10 (9.45)***
taiwan	20.454 (8.7)**	51.46 (6.32)***
thai	33.45 (14.6)**	−11.299 (9.88)
time		3.2705 (.307)***
cons	71.617 (10.2)***	40.625 (7.04)***
N	119	119
Adj R^2	0.7249	0.8879
F	34.46	86.57

Table 4.5. *Prosperity regression*

	Model Ic	Model IIc
Method	2SLS	2SLS
mtwo	−.0025 (.003)	−.0011 (.001)
tele	.00368 (.002)	.0036 (.000)***
invest	.0053 (.003)	.0037 (.001)***
fdigdp	.046 (.012)***	.0029 (.003)
open	−.00084 (.001)	−.0004 (.000)
trate	−.0389 (.017)***	.0066 (.004)
urban	.0363 (.008)***	.0033 (.002)
edu	−.0006 (.002)	−.0013 (.000)**
indon	−.185 (.157)	.107 (.039)***
korea	−1.066 (.342)***	.4324 (.077)***
malaysia	−.0576 (.613)	.532 (.051)***
singapore	−2.455 (.572)***	.634 (.182)***
taiwan	−1.276 (.283)***	.574 (.118)***
thai	.509 (.060)***	.384 (.023)***
time		.042 (.003)***
cons	2.47 (.239)***	2.37 (.084)***
N	119	119
Adj R^2	0.9266	0.98
F	109.77	745.2

NOTE: The coefficients and the standard deviations, in parentheses, are presented for each variable.

***Significant at the 1 percent level.

**Significant at the 5 percent level.

*Significant at the 10 percent level.

In both Models Ib and IIb, the coefficient on the variable *stock* (stock market capitalization, expressed in millions of dollars) is positive and highly significant, although the elasticities are 0.07 and 0.05, respectively. As China's stock market matures (it began operating in 1990), this relationship may change. Keeping close watch on stock market capitalization rates is one possibility for future research in the area of marketization and democracy. A surprising finding (and one contrary to the literature) is that *invest* is negatively associated with *mtwo*. Few of the results from the *prosperity* model are of interest, possibly reflecting a misspecification.

CONCLUSION

As data-collection methods improve in East and Southeast Asia, better measurement devices will be found to estimate the constructs of *democracy, marketization,* and *prosperity*. Since its inception in the early 1960s, Freedom House's *Comparative Survey of Freedom* has had its critics. Its methods were attacked as lacking rigor, its judgments as personal, and its rankings as too reflective of sensational media coverage. Although there is no doubt that the rating system developed by Freedom House cannot be analogous to a similar exercise performed by the hard sciences, over the decades since its institution, Freedom House has earned a reputation for objectivity and accuracy. Nonetheless, as Freedom House continues to improve its survey methods and ranking review process, better measurements of democracy will become available.

A more accurate measure for marketization would be to quantify the amount of GDP produced by the private sphere as opposed to the public domain. At first blush this seems possible to obtain from government spending and revenue statistics. Unfortunately, in many of the countries under study, such figures are used for political purposes, include categories that make their totals incomparable, or are highly affected by measurement error. Other important measures that reflect the breadth and depth of the market include the distribution of resources within the business sector.

The importance of Model I is that it shows that marketization, and not simply economic development (as measured by prosperity), may provide a country with the smoothest pathway to political liberalization. Within the econometric model presented here, the measurement for the construct *prosperity* was found not to be significant yet became

significant when *mtwo* was omitted, suggesting possible model misspecification in earlier research. A more valid model specification would
have to include measurements of *marketization*.

Marketization assists in the development of the individual, which is
vital for citizens' ability to create and sustain democracy. Policymakers
hoping to develop the type of environment conducive to democracy
should look at ways to promote marketization. Assisting in the liberalization of the financial system would be one such method. If the financial market is allowed to adequately allocate resources, funds can be effectively channeled toward productive investment. Through this, the
private sector can flourish and individuals can become economically
autonomous. To safeguard their new positions, citizens will be more
apt to demand a voice in government. Of equal importance, promoting
marketization may be more politically palatable than promoting prosperity, which is often seen by the recipient country as a means to bolster
the existing elites. Although an increase in GDP per capita may not
show the underlying inequalities of income distribution, true marketization stands a better chance of creating economic autonomy for a broad
section of the populace by giving citizens a functioning market in which
to participate.

Some policymakers express skepticism that financial liberalization
will lead to political liberalization in China. They cite the Freedom
House survey of 1993–1994 which reported that although "ordinary
Chinese now face less intrusion by the government than in the past, the
regime does not tolerate dissent, lacks effective judicial safeguards, and
has one of the worst human rights records in the world."[11] However,
with the success of the special economic zones and the movement toward freer enterprise, millions of Chinese have become independent
from the state-owned enterprises and the concomitant system of state-
rationed privileges. This loosening of the bonds to the state has resulted
in a weakening of the authority of the Chinese Communist Party. If we
discount the past few years, as less of a reflection of the true political
environment and more as a backlash against the horror of Tiananmen,
and instead focus on the political environment of the mid 1980s, we
may be able to make certain predictions. Although still brutally repressive, China in the mid 1980s was beginning to experiment with rural
representation and a less-intrusive government structure. At a Freedom
House ranking of 0.167 (on a 1.0 scale), China was considered one of

11 Finn (1994, p. 201).

the least free countries in the world. Nonetheless, according to the model, a 59 percent increase in M2/GDP could create the type of environment that would allow China to move slowly toward Indonesia's kind of freedom. The average Indonesian still lacks most of the basic rights associated with democracy, but his political rights and civil liberties far outrank those of the average Chinese citizen.

The econometric model sheds light on how best to move a country toward democracy, but many questions remain unanswered. For instance, What in the socioeconomic environments of Korea and Taiwan has allowed these countries to marketize? Can those same reforms be used to advance political liberalization in Indonesia or China? How does internationalization affect a country's political regime? Although it was not significant within the econometric model, does internationalization create an environment conducive to the formation of a democratic opposition?

The quantitative model suggests that increases in financial liberalization and technology increase democracy, but without a fuller conceptualization of the particular socioeconomic environments of the countries in question it is doubtful that U.S. policymakers can effectively use these suggestions to create viable foreign policy. Part Two of this book examines four countries (Korea, Taiwan, Indonesia, and China) within the rubric of the theoretical hypotheses laid out in the beginning of this chapter. The specific question of whether increases in prosperity, marketization, internationalization, and technology increase democracy is analyzed. The country studies enrich the conclusions reached through the econometric analysis by providing a deeper understanding of the mechanisms through which marketization imparts "democratic learning" to the populace, raising people's awareness of their political lives and providing the means to effectively transform their systems of government.

Part Two

Qualitative Comparative Historical Studies:
Korea, Taiwan, Indonesia, and China

Qualitative comparative historical studies

This work employs a bifurcated research agenda—relying on both quantitative econometric modeling and qualitative cross-country comparative studies. This dual approach is different from other research in the field of democracy and development that relies exclusively upon one or the other method. Combining both types of examinations allows for a deeper understanding of events. Rigorous statistical analysis is used to explore trends over time and to make connections between dependent and independent variables, and the country studies investigate the complexities and nuances of these relationships. In addition, the qualitative work pays particular attention to the social and political structures that fashion and continuously influence these variables.

By analyzing the modern economic and political trends of Korea, Taiwan, Indonesia, and China, further insight into the relationship between marketization and democracy can be gained. The questions of how and why a country moves toward political liberalization are more likely to be answered by a fuller understanding of a country's historical sequences.

In determining model type, one must consider the research objectives, the independent and dependent variables, and the availability of data. The econometric model empirically tested the relationships between *marketization, prosperity,* and *democracy,* with the additional explanatory variables of *technology* and *internationalization.* The regressions suggested that increases in *marketization* and *technology* lead to increased *democracy.* The constructs of *prosperity* and *internationalization* were not found to be significant. Given the extensive literature (cited in the previous chapter) linking these two constructs with *democracy,* the findings of nonsignificance are quite surprising. One goal of integrating qualitative, comparative country studies with quantitative, cross-national research is to obtain a better understanding of the empirical outcomes. For policymakers to use these findings effectively, a deeper understanding of the particular sociopolitical environments of the specific countries is needed. Not only will detailed examinations reinforce and enrich the findings of the quantitative model, they will enable policymakers to transform the analytic findings into viable foreign policy levers.

5

———————————————————————————————

Korea: A balancing of power

Understanding the conjunction of events that usher a country along the path of democracy requires looking past blunt assessments of historical happenings to the more subtle undercurrents occurring within a society. Nicholas Eberstadt writes that in

> the four decades between 1949 and 1987, the Republic of Korea experienced not a single peaceful and orderly transfer of political power. One president was turned out of office by riots; another came to power in a *putsch* and ruled until he was assassinated by a trusted aide; a third consolidated his position after leading what came to be called a "constitutional coup." . . . Such notions as impartial authority, equality before the law, respect for private property and the integrity of the person, rights of the minority, and due process have yet to make their way into the everyday routine of Korean political life.[1]

The main problem with the above is that it focuses on wholesale changes in regime structure rather than gradual movements within the broader society. By ignoring the trends and patterns of the private sphere and the marketplace, Eberstadt fails to comprehend Korea's steady increase in political self-restraint. Authoritarianism gave way to popular elections not through any fundamental epiphany on the part of citizens but by incremental steps. This chapter attempts to place those steps within the context of a coherent pathway that stretches toward democracy. Although the journey to full participatory government is by no means accomplished, one cannot ignore how far the Republic of Korea (ROK) has advanced toward its goal of political liberalization.

1   Eberstadt (1991, p. 267).

In an insightful article that examines Korea's political transformation, Gaston Sigur identifies a number of characteristics that were essential to the country's democratic transition.[2] Within Korea:

- Democratic reforms had a broad base of support within the citizenry;

- The people viewed the democratizing process "as legitimate and effective in design";

- The process was allowed to reach its natural conclusions without stipulations regarding the eventual outcome;

- There was a general acceptance of the results of democratic decisions—elections, mandates, laws, etc.;

- Reconciliation, accommodation, amnesty, compromise, and acceptance became the watchwords of the new order; and

- Democracy had support from abroad.

Although these properties were vital to the rise of Korean democracy, Sigur ignores one very important factor—marketization. The balancing of power between the public and private sphere, achieved through marketization, played a fundamental role in Korea's transition to democracy, as did the strengthening will of the people to protect their economic freedoms. Numerous attempts were made to launch democracy between 1948 and the mid 1980s, but democracy succeeded in 1987 largely because of the calls of the business sphere for economic and political liberalization. The independent private sphere, strengthened by education, urbanization, modernization, and the expectations that occurred as a result (leading to the creation of activist and interest groups), broadened the base of power and ultimately forced the regime into accepting democratic reforms.

The premise of this book is that marketization provides citizens with the desires and ability to create and sustain democracy. Marketization teaches the lessons of choice and competition and spurs *democratic learning*. Marketization fosters internationalization, which brings new ways of thinking into the country. Marketization, through the wide distribution of economic power, allows market access to the previously disenfranchised. This last point, however, seems to be refuted by Korean history. Consequently, one goal of this work is to explain how

2   Sigur (1993).

democracy took hold in a country where there is an extreme concentration of economic power—a country where 75 percent of private land is owned by 6 percent of the population.[3] Part of the answer lies in the shifting of economic power from the public to the private domain. The growth of the business sphere permitted a formidable challenge to the authoritarian regime. Coupled with the loss of legitimacy suffered by the government from a faltering of the Korean economy in the late 1970s, pro-democracy forces were able to coalesce and push through reforms by the mid 1980s.

Within this chapter, a broad overview of Korea's political transformation, along with the underlying mechanisms that led to this change in polity, is presented and examined. In particular, three essential elements that arose in Korea during the years preceding democratization are analyzed. These elements—marketization, prosperity, and internationalization—solidified in the 1980s to provide the springboard for democracy. The evolution of these elements within the political chronology of the Republic of Korea is traced below.

KOREAN DEMOCRACY

The roots of Korean democracy stretch back to 2300 BC and the philosophy of Hong-ik In-gan ("Devotion to the Welfare of All Mankind"). Startlingly modern for its time, this philosophy stressed that humans, by nature, are born equal and that politics is a means to the ultimate end of guaranteeing freedom to the populace. Despite this grounding in democratic theory, it took another 4,300 years for democracy to become a reality in Korea.

During much of the Choson Period (1388–1910),[4] Korea experienced a relatively stable social structure. This changed with the appearance of Japanese ships on Korean shores in 1876.

For the purpose of this research, the extent of Japan's contribution to the emergence of an industrial Korea can remain largely unexamined. Although Japan abolished slavery, established a cash-based taxation system, and codified the civil law of Korea, the unspeakable atrocities committed by Japan on the Korean people left the country fractured and demoralized. It is important to note that although 94 percent of industrial capital in 1940 was in Japanese hands and reverted to Korean

3   *Mini Dragons: South Korea* (1991).
4   The Yi dynasty.

control through nationalization a few years later, by the late 1960s most of Korea's GDP came from sources unconnected with the Japanese occupation.[5] By 1972, it had become inaccurate to view Korea's economic development as simply a natural outgrowth of the foundation laid by Japanese colonization.

At the conclusion of World War II, South and North Korea gained their separate independences. Partition between the two countries was arbitrarily drawn at the 38th Parallel, about 30 miles north of Seoul. Although the United Nations called for freely held elections in both the North and South, only South Korea complied. On May 10, 1948, a Constituent Assembly was voted into office. Syngman Rhee, recently returned from the United States and well into his 70s, was elected speaker and then president. On August 15, 1948, the Republic of Korea was officially born.

PROGRESS AS AN IDEOLOGY: THE FIRST REPUBLIC

The defining event of the First Republic was the Korean War. On June 25, 1950, Communist forces invaded South Korea. United Nations forces came to the aid of the South, and Communist China backed the North. The war lasted three years and claimed six million victims. One out of every ten North Koreans was killed in the conflict. Destruction of the South's infrastructure was nearly complete. Seoul lost 80 percent of its industry and public works. Three-quarters of the office buildings and one-half of the residences were destroyed.

In many respects, the war marked ground zero in the ROK's march toward democracy. It ushered in a generation of military dominance and stymied the country's economic development, leaving the populace with a siege mentality. The presence of a hostile neighbor was inimical to South Korea's democratic transition. Paranoid, perhaps with good reason, of the North and the encroachment of communism, the ruling elite exerted considerable effort in its constant vigilance of actual and perceived leftists. This quickly escalated into the suppression of any dissent against the state. In 1948, in the first blush of independence, the peasants of Cheju took to the streets to revolt against the state. To quell the protests and disabuse the populace of the notion that public protest would yield results, opposition leaders were rounded up and assassinated. Elections that followed shortly thereafter were

5   Choi (1971).

manipulated at every level by the state's machine. Corruption and cynicism pervaded the moral fabric of the new country.

Although Korea does not have an ancient military heritage, the Korean War created a new generation of professional warriors. The armed forces quickly evolved into a training program for the future political and business elite of the country.[6] These students became ardent supporters of technological innovation and solid bureaucratic structure—two ideologies that shaped the future of Korea, no doubt helped along as these young officers advanced into the elite of the policy and business circles.

In 1953, at the conclusion of the Korean War, the military guided the country back from the brink of disaster. The assumption of this leadership role by the military was appropriate. With the infrastructure of Korea in shambles, the Korean military was the only sector able to effectively organize the rebuilding of the state and efficiently manage a large bureaucracy through its modernization. Whatever the original understanding as to the tenure of the military leadership, the command of the military over the political and economic structure of Korea did not decline at the conclusion of the restoration. Rather, the military took on a significant, and often surprising, role in moving Korea toward political liberalization and affecting the balance of power between state and market.

The creation of Korea's formidable military machine was made possible through the active support of the United States. The end of the Korean War, with the subsequent partitioning of North and South into Cold War camps, transformed South Korea into a test case of U.S. foreign policy. Not only was the ROK to serve as a line of defense against communism, it was to become a democratic nation under the tutelage of the United States. In a request for aid before Congress in 1953, President Truman wrote that "Korea has become a testing ground in which the validity and practical value of the ideals and principles of democracy which the Republic is putting into practice are being matched against the practice of communism which has been imposed upon the people of North Korea." Truman backed up his words with money and troops. Over the next 40 years, the United States would keep a constant troop presence of nearly 50,000 servicemen on Korean soil. Although there is little research on the effect that these Americans had on Korean society, there is little doubt

6   For a discussion of the roots of the Korean military, see Cotton (1991).

that some portion of American culture accompanied the soldiers to the overseas bases. Visions of American life, through movies, newspapers, and discussions with off-duty servicemen, most likely increased Korean awareness of Western culture and American democracy.

The military and restorative aid that flowed into Korea during and after the war affected nearly every aspect of Korean life. With the first wave of the North's invasion into South Korea in 1950, the ROK embarked on an era of complete reliance on foreign assistance. From 1945 to the late 1950s, foreign aid constituted nearly all sources of foreign capital, and over 70 percent of all imports into Korea from 1953 to 1960 were paid for by foreign assistance.[7] Such a course may have been necessary after the havoc of the war, but the inflow of dollars was inefficiently allocated and largely misspent. A system of cronyism sprang up around the allocation of the foreign assistance. In addition to the distribution of U.S. aid to administration favorites, select firms also received subsidized loans, tax exemptions, and an allocation of hard currency to import scarce resources.

From the time of independence, the state played an activist role in Korea's industrialization. Whether it was due to the recognition that an industrialized country is better able to defend itself from aggressive neighbors (i.e., North Korea), or a vow to never again allow Korea to be humiliated by a foreign power (i.e., Japan), a unique partnership was created between the public and private spheres that helped Korea create one of the strongest economies in the world. The Korean model of state intervention into the private sector was based on five mandates: key industries would be targeted with government assistance, wage increases would remain lower than the rate of productivity, the growth of the chaebol would be encouraged to foster economies of scale, all available resources would be devoted to industrialization, and the government would maintain control over the planning and operation of investment.

The success of such massive government intrusion flies in the face of traditional economic theory. Alice Amsden explores why Korea's initiative rested with the state as opposed to the entrepreneurial private sector. She reasons that the state had an overview of the entire economy that the private corporation lacked and that "the initiative to diversify, particularly into more capital intensive investment projects, tend[ed] to fall to the state because these projects require[d] more

7   Il Sakong (1993, p. 96).

comprehensive incentive packages to make them financially attractive to private firms."[8]

Others have explored the paternalistic relationship that existed between the state and the market in Korea. From the 1950s, the Korean government encouraged the entrepreneurial sector to grow by reducing the risks and uncertainties of new ventures. Like a parent who guides a child toward productive habits, the Korean government coaxed business interests (with the aid of economic incentives, bribes, and threats) to forgo short-term, rent-seeking activities in favor of longer-term, more socially optimal ones. And, like a child, as the business sector matured, it desired independence from the influence of the parent. The movement of the private sector away from the intrusive controls of the state played a pivotal role in laying the groundwork for Korean democracy.

As businesses create a separate and powerful sphere of influence, distinct from the state, a foundation is laid for democracy. Specifically, a powerful business sphere erodes both the coercive and legitimate power of the state, making room for competing ideas and opposition candidates to come to the fore. Coercive power stems from the state's ability to punish; legitimate power stems from the acceptance of a social contract based upon common values. In the contract, the state agrees to provide for the citizenry and maintain the social order in return for the populace accepting the state's legitimate right to influence. The basis for legitimate power is often the acceptance of the social structure. If the political system fails to provide this social structure, pressure to change the system will prevail.

In Korea, the dominant ideology of the late 20th century was rooted in economic expansion and modernization. In particular, the Korean people believed strongly in progress as a virtue.[9] The Rhee regime instilled in citizens the desire for progress and held out the government as the rightful leader of this advance. The state as patriarch, ruler, and economic guide continued throughout subsequent regimes. As long as the government performed its role, its authority remained absolute. When it became apparent that progress was being stymied by government intervention, Koreans began to question the government's role in their lives. Such questions ultimately led to the de-legitimization

8   Amsden (1989, p. 85).
9   Bennett (1991).

of the state. Although the seeds of dissent may have been planted as early as the Rhee regime, the challenge itself would take over 30 years to materialize.

The strong governmental hand in economic affairs paralleled the repression of political rights and civil liberties. Rhee, followed by subsequent regimes, resorted to a variety of techniques to silence criticism and co-opt the opposition. Such tactics included compulsory union membership in government-sponsored union federations, mandatory security clearances as a precondition for study abroad, frequent purges of faculty members who criticized the government, restrictions on the import of publications, formal prohibitions on the formation of opposition groups, preventive detention without trial, and death or severe penalties for broadly defined treason.[10] Despite these sanctions, Korean pro-democracy forces were never completely silenced. Opposition parties pressed their claim for three decades before finally succeeding. A large part of their eventual success was due to the rise of an authority strong enough to challenge the legitimacy of the government and organized enough to consolidate the pro-democracy forces into a coherent opposition—the private sector.

Most Korea watchers of the time agreed that the elections of 1952 were rigged.[11] The opinions on the elections of 1956 are split. There is little doubt that Rhee manipulated the electorate, but there was enough of an opposition vote to win Chang Myon the vice-presidency. Although the 1956 elections may have been an improvement over 1952 in terms of electoral misconduct, the elections of 1960 were a major setback for pro-democracy forces. The cynical heralding of the election as "free and fair" by the administration led to student demonstrations on April 18 and 19, 1960. Its own ranks split over the controversy, the Korean military refused to quell the protests. Lack of military support, in conjunction with the broad dissatisfaction of the people with the autocracy, the lack of fiscal and economic management, and the extreme corruption, led to the fall of the Rhee regime. Economic discontent, and a fear that the government was not leading the society toward *progress*, not only played a major role in the collapse of Rhee's government but served as a harbinger for the events of the 1980s. In both instances, the call for greater political rights and civil liberties served as the catalyst for the political action, but protection of one's

10   Pae (1992, p. 253).
11   Steinberg (1989, p. 53).

economic livelihood widened the scope of the protest from a gathering of elites to a mass demonstration.

DEMOCRATICALLY ELECTED AND SHORT LIVED: THE SECOND REPUBLIC

Prime Minister Chang Myon and President Yun Po-son of the Democratic Party were elected to office in July 1960. Despite intentions to reform a corrupt and mismanaged government, the new administration could not rid itself of the baggage left by Rhee. Within the year, 500 major demonstrations by students and 45 by trade unions erupted in the streets of Korea protesting the new government.

Political demonstrations are not uncommon in a country's first hesitant movements toward democracy. Long-simmering frustrations, uncertainty over the future, and a desire to test the limits of new freedoms often lead to societal upheaval and instability in post-authoritarian regimes. Such was the case in Korea in 1960, and, in some ways, this foreshadowed the pains the republic would suffer in the 1980s. Opposition political groups needed to test the limits of repression, radical forces intensified confrontation, and conservatives called for backlash. When the door was opened slightly, pent-up unrest surfaced.

PARK CHUNG HEE: THE THIRD REPUBLIC

In 1961, the military actively intervened in South Korean politics. Upon his election, democratically elected Prime Minister Chang Myon promised middle-ranking and senior military officers that those responsible for prolonging Rhee's dictatorship would face sanctions. When Chang failed to deliver on his promises, the military retaliated with the May 1961 coup. Leading the military action was Park Chung Hee, who promised the people that he would create a strong, self-reliant, morally based regime unshackled from undue foreign influence.

Park's agenda revolved around economic revitalization and moral discipline. To accomplish the first task, Park established the Economic Planning Board in 1961 and began work on the first Five Year Economic Development Plan (1962–1966), a master program governing the functions of the entire economy. The Korean Central Intelligence Agency (KCIA), created under the auspices of Colonel Kim Jong Pil, was to provide the moral backbone for the country. Under the guidance of the KCIA, the functions of the judicial and executive branches were consolidated into one organization, thereby eliminating the checks and balances inherent in a separation of powers. Surprising many, from their original position of upholding the authoritarian rule of Park, the KCIA would, over the next three decades, become integral to Korea's transition to political liberalization.

In 1963, Park formed the Democratic Republican Party and launched his first bid for the presidency. In elections of that year, Park defeated Yun Po-son. Despite his administration's claims of democratic legitimacy, Park's Third Republic never achieved such a goal. Park Chung Hee was well on his way toward shaping his country to his liking when he again defeated Yun Po-son in 1967. This time, however, Park won with only the slimmest of majorities—51.4 percent of the vote. The small margin attested to the growing intolerance of the populace for Park's financial and legal malfeasance. In 1965, Park decreed that exports would be the salvation of the Korean economy and, to that end, mandated specific export levels in the private sector. Although this discipline certainly assisted in Korea's industrial expansion, such a clear example of economic authoritarianism was not favored by the private sector. Using the discontent of the urban class, and the quieter rumblings of the business sphere, as the foundation for their voter appeal, the opposition began preparing for the National Assembly vote of 1971.

In April 1971, in a watershed election, Park nearly lost his presidency to a young opposition congressman. Park succeeded in retaining his presidency, but opposition forces won more than one-third of the seats in the National Assembly. Recognizing his eroding power base and the weakened position of a less than two-thirds majority, Park declared martial law on October 17, 1972. The Korean constitution was suspended.

MARTIAL LAW: THE FOURTH REPUBLIC

The coup in office by Park Chung Hee in 1972 was made possible by strong support from the military. In exchange for their fealty, the armed forces were given an even greater role in the country's decisionmaking process. The opposition's strength, as evidenced in the 1971 elections, was characterized by Park as a loss of moral discipline. To save the country from such turpitude, Park announced the Yushin constitutional reforms late in 1972. The reforms were a bifurcated strategy to strengthen the economy and instill discipline in the citizenry.

Economic expansion would be achieved through massive industrial and military investment as well as an aggressive search for Middle East construction contracts to earn hard currency and ensure Korea's oil supply. The societal reforms included prohibiting debate on the constitution, completely censoring the press, forbidding criticism of Park, and disbanding local governments. Article 30 of the Supplementary Rules to the Yushin Constitution stipulated that "local councils under this Constitution shall not be formed until the unification of the fatherland shall have been achieved."[12] The threat of the North was never far from Park's mind. By feeding the paranoia of the country, Park hoped to solidify his control.

Under the Park regime, current and former military officers accepted high-level positions both in the government and within private businesses. These military officers-cum-bureaucrats built up extensive networks between the public and private domains, working long-standing relationships into lucrative business deals. Nam describes the ties between Korean business and the state as a relationship of "mutually exchanging continued favors between unequals at the expense of collective goals of the community or the organization to which both the patron and the client belong."[13] The governmental favors were often repaid in the form of large contributions to election funds.

President Park maintained his discipline over the private sector by closely watching even the smallest details of the economy and by backing up his decrees with harsh sanctions. A 1984 World Bank report listed the attendants at a typical trade promotion meeting in 1976. A portion of the list is shown below:[14]

President Park
11 economic and political staff of the President
18 cabinet ministers
Ambassadors to Kuwait, Saudi Arabia, and the U.A.E.
18 assistant economic ministers
8 representatives of commercial and government banks
5 representatives of private and government research institutes
39 business and trade association representatives
11 firm representatives

12   Pae (1992, p. 225).
13   Nam (1994, p. 197).
14   Rhee, Ross-Larson, and Pursell (1984).

In Park's monthly meetings with business leaders, the state of the economy was reviewed in detail, and future monthly export and production targets were set. To effect such compliance, Park doled out economic incentives. For those who failed to reach the agreed upon targets, credit lines were curtailed or revoked and public humiliation and censure awarded to the unfortunate firms' presidents. In reviewing the modern economic history of Korea, it becomes clear that although state intervention may have fostered the dynamism of the Korean economy, as the power and experience of the business sphere increased, the costs of government involvement began to outweigh the benefits. As the business sphere actively sought to limit state control and increase the role of the free market, more interest groups arose to challenge the status quo. Figure 5.1 shows that as the state decreased its influence in the market (here measured as public enterprise's share of gross domestic fixed capital formation), the number of political parties increased.[15] The government was no longer in a position to moderate the conflicting goals of these new groups. To sway people to their cause, interest groups relied on publicizing their message to get attention. As a result,

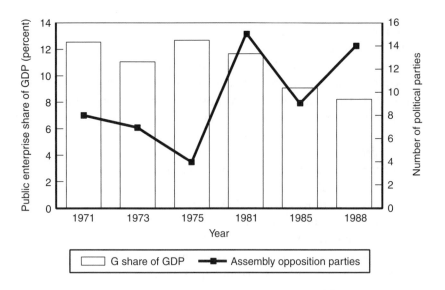

Figure 5.1. Government Spending and Political Parties in Korea

15   Pae (1992); Summers and Heston (1991).

more citizens were made aware that options existed outside of the menu presented by the regime.

Movements toward a reduction in government control over the economy began with the introduction of Korean treasury bills in 1977. Coupled with further deregulation, the ratio of financial assets to GNP rose from 89.3 percent in 1965 to 252.4 percent in 1980. In addition, the ratio of the change in financial assets to total capital formation increased from 96 percent in 1965 to 185 percent in 1980. These statistics show that people began saving their money in financial form, a signal that they were less fearful that their savings would be spent on nonmarket investments.[16] The mission of financial reform was to reduce automatic approval of bank credit to government-sanctioned investment. During the Park years, Korean banks did little more than serve the government's will. In essence, the banks became rationing agents for state-sanctioned credit. As a consequence, the economy experienced severe market distortions.

Under the new guidelines, market transactions would determine the appropriate way to funnel investments. Such reforms would not only increase the efficiency of the investment but would disperse the concentration of capital and assets away from a few large organizations. However, in the late 1970s, policy loans still accounted for nearly 80 percent of incremental domestic credit extended. Restrictions on lending led many firms to seek out the curb market and pay extortionate rates[17] (Table 5.1). On April 17, 1979, stabilization and liberalization measures were announced by the government. They included deregulating commodity prices and improving the commodity distribution system.

Much of the pressure for this economic liberalization came from the United States. During the 1950s and 1960s, the United States believed in promoting democracy in Korea through a holistic approach. This "open diplomacy" included formally protesting against the Korean government when democratic institutions and processes were jeopardized and accompanying these strong demands with threats of economic sanctions. In a specific action, the United States was instrumental in pushing the Park government toward land reform. Aid from the United States was tied to specific programs that would pay

16 For a broader discussion, see Lau (1986).
17 Il Sakong (1993).

Table 5.1. *Interest rates on bank loans in the ROK*

		Policy Loans		
Year	General Loan	Export	Machinery Promotion	Curb
1971	22.0	6.0	n.a.	46.4
1972	15.5	6.0	n.a.	37.0
1973	15.5	7.0	10.0	33.4
1974	15.5	9.0	12.0	40.6
1975	15.5	9.0	12.0	41.3
1976	18.0	8.0	13.0	40.5
1977	16.0	8.0	13.0	38.1
1978	19.0	9.0	15.0	39.3
1979	19.0	9.0	15.0	42.4
1980	20.0	5.0	20.0	44.9
1981	17.0	5.0	11.0	35.3

landowners for government takings and then resell the land to the peasants at low interest loans.

Open diplomacy was replaced by quiet persuasion in the 1970s. Some observers place part of the blame for the imposition of martial law in 1972 on the change in U.S. policy. Park may have taken his cue from the lack of U.S. objection to martial law in the Philippines only three weeks before the Korean event. Although in the late 1970s U.S. diplomacy may have quieted in terms of political liberalization, economic openness was the new watchword. In response to U.S. pressure on Korea to open its markets, and the recognition that future progress would depend on international credibility, Korea began a pre-announced import liberalization schedule in 1977. The Ministry of Trade and Finance promised to gradually liberalize Korea's import market by increasing the number of goods granted automatic approval from 691 in 1971 to 9,991 in 1991. Figure 5.2 shows the increasing amount of imports into Korea between 1972 and 1991.[18]

In addition to the pressure brought to bear on Korea's imports, the tools of exchange rate management, budgetary discipline, institutional flexibility, technological innovation, and labor absorption were also employed. Direct foreign investment into Korea increased dramatically

18   Korea's Ministry of Finance, various years.

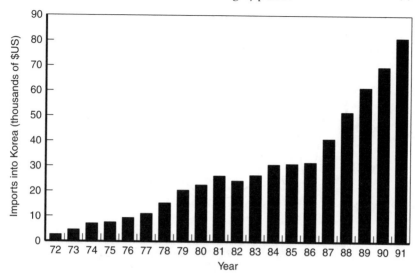

Figure 5.2. Imports into Korea: 1972–1991

between 1965 and 1985. Figure 5.3 shows the rise of foreign direct investment, measured in current dollars and as a percentage of GNP.[19]

The incremental opening of Korea's markets corresponded with a general liberalization in both the economic and political realms. This is not a surprising occurrence. International businesses bring with them new ideas. Global networks, organized to facilitate business, also increase contact with the world. Korea imported not only Western clothes and technology, but also Western ideals and political philosophies.

Although those in the business sphere continued throughout the 1970s and 1980s to amass power and consolidate their strength in direct opposition to the government, a broad distribution of economic power failed to materialize. During the Park regime, the 46 largest chaebol grew at an annual rate of 22.8 percent, whereas the nation's GDP grew at only 9.9 percent. Manufacturing, which accounted for roughly 60 percent of the chaebol's value added during the 1970s, grew at 17.2 percent for the general economy and 24.4 percent for the top 46 chaebol. By 1984, the ten largest groups accounted for 67 percent of total sales in the economy. In 1989, the top four accounted for nearly

19   Korea's Ministry of Finance, various years.

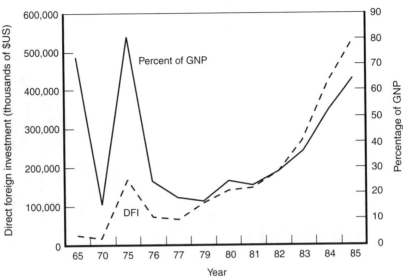

Figure 5.3. Direct Foreign Investment in Korea: 1965–1985

one-half of GDP. Such statistics show that the concentration of power continued unabated during democracy's formative years. In 1970, roughly 40 percent of all shipments from the manufacturing sector originated under competitive conditions—where the market share of the top three producers is less than 60 percent. In 1982, only 31 percent of all shipments were produced in competitive markets.

Theoretically, the severe concentration of economic power should work against the common good and act as a stumbling block to democracy. James Madison, in *The Federalist Papers,* wrote that economic factions should be kept small and diverse so as to be "unable to concert and carry into effect schemes of oppression."[20] If this is correct, how can we explain the Korean situation? One explanation lies in the difference between the economic distribution of power *within* the private sector and the distribution *between* the public and private domains. In Korea, democratic learning occurred in a more societal context than it did in Taiwan. In Taiwan, where the majority of businesses are small and medium-sized firms, the lessons of the market were choice and competition. Mom and Pop stores cannot survive without competitive pricing strategies and wide selections of marketable goods. Under-

20   Madison (1961, p. 80).

standing that these factors contributed to the success of their businesses and their prosperity, the Taiwanese people translated the lessons of choice and competition into their political lives. Competing ideas on public welfare, international relations, and Taiwanese independence would produce the most effective and efficient policy options. In Taiwan, the lessons of the market, and their analog within the political sphere, were taught on a very personal level.

By contrast, in Korea, the land of the conglomerate, where economies of scale and monopoly pricing were the obvious lessons of the market, the driving ideology was *progress*. As long as the government could produce the most efficient results, it retained legitimacy. But as the 1970s drew to a close and the oil crisis threatened Korea's expansion, the Korean people voiced their discontent with the government's system of resource allocation. The state had made wrong choices by investing in heavy industry and promoting import substitution well beyond legitimate usefulness. Many of these investment decisions countervailed the direct advice of Korea's business leaders. As the state lost its legitimacy, the business sphere rose to replace it. With this shift in the balance of power, new interest groups arose to ensure Korea's progress. These new groups challenged the traditional social structure and weakened the authoritarian regime. Although protection of economic freedom played a vital role in the transition to democracy in both Korea and Taiwan, different contributing factors led to regime change in the two countries. In Korea, the balancing of power between state and market played a much more prominent role than in Taiwan. In comparison, the importance of individualism, learned through the market concepts of choice and competition, was much stronger in Taiwan than Korea.

There is little doubt that the increasing citizen disapproval of government actions led to the October 26, 1979, assassination of President Park by the KCIA. Ironically, the very organization created by Park to enforce his decrees realized that Korea's future depended on a reconciliation with the opposition. Park, the KCIA believed, would never accept a compromise. KCIA Director Kim Jae Kyu justified the assassination on the grounds that Park violated the "constitutional principles of peaceful transfer of power and [instituted] a series of executive emergency decrees depriving tens of thousands of democracy-aspiring citizens and leaders of their basic freedom and rights."[21]

21   Pae (1992, p. 303).

On December 6, 1979, Choi Kyu Ha became the interim president. For a week after Choi was elected, it appeared as if authoritarianism was retreating. Nearly 70 dissidents were released from prison and a total of 687 anti-government politicians were politically rehabilitated. Unfortunately, this groundswell of freedom was short lived. Park's assassination threw the economy, already suffering under the weight of Park's ill-advised investments into heavy industry and a major failure of the rice crop, into turmoil. Korea's exports, a driving force behind the country's economic expansion during the previous two decades, were sharply curtailed by the worldwide tightening of demand caused by the second oil shock. After averaging 9.6 percent from 1967 to 1971 and 9.2 percent from 1972 to 1976, the GNP growth rate declined significantly for the next four years, turning negative by 1980[22] (Figure 5.4).

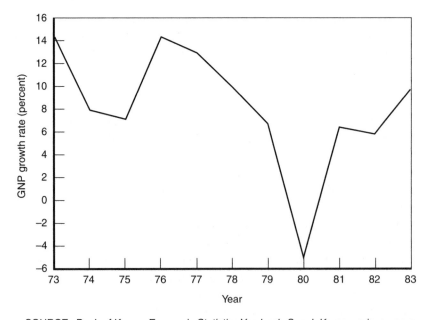

SOURCE: Bank of Korea, *Economic Statistics Yearbook*, Seoul, Korea, various years.

Figure 5.4. Growth of GNP in Korea: 1973–1983

22   Economic Planning Board, various years; International Monetary Fund, *IFS Yearbook*, various years.

Both the peasants and the urbanites felt the pinch of recession and blamed their plight on the central government's loss of command. At this point, Chun Doo Hwan of the Defense Security Command claimed control. A military coup ensued, martial law was again declared, and General Chun was appointed Director of the KCIA in April 1980. The banking and financial reforms instituted before Park's death were halted. On May 17, 1980, the citizens of Kwangju (the southwestern provincial capital) demonstrated against the imposition of martial law. The military was called upon to dispel the protesters. Civilian riots ensued, the military stepped up its use of force, and when the Martial Law Command finally retook the streets of Kwangju, 200 protesters were dead. Within days, the leaders of the opposition (including Kim Young Sam, Kim Dae Jung, and Kim Jong Pil) were tried in a rigged military tribunal and sentenced to extended prison terms.

CHUN DOO HWAN: THE FIFTH REPUBLIC

Nearly nine months after the coup, Chun Doo Hwan took the presidency. Five years of state censorship, political suppression, and economic repression were to follow. Chun's guidelines for the country included handing back an orderly nation to the people at the appropriate time. Like Park before him, Chun saw his mission as disciplining an unruly nation. Despite his strong-arm tactics, the Korean people would not forget the Kwangju incident.[23] The victims and the imprisoned leaders became a focal point for further protests, hunger strikes, and general civil disobedience. Despite the increased pressure for public accountability from the government, no change in regime doctrine seemed imminent until powerful business interests joined forces with the opposition in calling for reforms.

Beginning in 1982–1983, as a direct result of influential meetings between business and government leaders, a new round of liberalization measures was announced. Pressure from a strengthening business sector, as well as a United States intent on liberalizing Korea's market,

23   In December 1995, Chun Doo Hwan was arrested for mutiny and treason (graft charges were later added). On August 26, 1996, Chun was sentenced to death by Korea's lower court. It is unlikely that the sentence will be carried out, but the arrest, trial, and sentencing of Korea's former leader serve as a testament to Korea's desire to fully realize a democracy in which even the highest officials are not above the law.

began to erode the state's influence over the economy. In a short span of time, power devolved from the government's elites into the hands of both the business sector and the labor unions.

Through a broad coalition of interest groups, the Korean people informed the government that the time had come when any further state intrusion into the affairs of the private economy would be seen as anti-progressive. In answer to the people's demands, the Korean Development Institute (KDI) was charged with the task of drafting public enterprise reform regulation. The main goals of the legislation were to make enterprises efficient in achieving given objectives by providing better incentives to upper and middle tier management. The scope and breadth of government involvement in the private sector would also be severely curtailed. The liberalization measures included:

- The adoption of the Monopoly Regulation and Fair Trade Act in 1981. This measure was to promote fair competition and wean the government from direct intervention;

- The privatization (between 1981 and 1983) of government-held shares of nationwide commercial banks;

- The relaxation of internal management of banks and lending practices (banks were allowed, within an acceptable range, to vary interest rates depending on clients' credit standing);

- The gradual admission of nonbank financial institutions into the market, breaking the stranglehold of the banking sector;

- The passage of an anti-trust law that prohibited firms from controlling more than 40 percent of the assets of their subsidiaries;

- The enforcement of credit controls that set limits on debt/equity ratios;

- A ban on large firms entering into industries designated for small and medium-sized firms; and

- A ban on certain upstream integration.

The growing independence of private firms from their strong-willed government sponsor was not always greeted with encouragement. The *Far Eastern Economic Review* reported in 1988 that Kukje, a large business concern, was split up and the owner was forced to sign over his stock to creditors. The Federation of Korean Industry believed that the state's action was a punishment for Kukje's refusal to contribute the appropriate amount to quasi-governmental organizations.[24] As businesses continued to consolidate their base of power, their confidence in challenging the legitimate authority of the state increased. Beginning in the early 1980s, the private sphere stepped up its attacks on the official state practice of government strong-arm tactics meant to elicit large campaign donations from private corporations using the threat that donations not deemed appropriate would be repaid with economic sanctions.

The labor movement also made significant advances in the mid 1980s toward attaining market wages. As Korea prospered and marketization increased, labor differentiated. The new system was represented by grass roots labor organizations. The new labor leaders abandoned their predecessors' pro-government and pro-management leanings in favor of a stronger, more strident stance demanding higher wages and better working conditions. The unions' new attitude struck a responsive chord among the workforce. Table 5.2 highlights trends in union membership between 1980 and 1990.[25]

Growing participation in the labor movement came as a surprise to many Korean scholars. Active involvement in public affairs, whether in a workplace democracy or in a government voting booth, was not a traditional part of the urban Korean's psyche. In a study of the 1980 presidential elections, Benjamin reports that urban Koreans voted less frequently than their rural counterparts. He asserts that Koreans "will vote when and where it is least costly to do so. . . . Higher social class and more urban Koreans . . . prefer to "exit" thereby reducing their costs, presently associated with the virtually meaningless choices

Table 5.2. *Trends in ROK union membership*

Year	Thousands of Members	No. of Unions
1980	945	n.a.
1987	1,267	4,086
1988	1,707	6,142
1989	1,932	7,883
1990	1,887	7,698

24 Clifford (1988).
25 Korea Labor Institute (1992).

afforded by nonvoting electoral participation."[26] Benjamin argues that "exiting" was a rational response to the situation. This notion of the rational actor is useful in understanding how the market may have contributed to "democratic learning" in Korea and encouraged political participation.

Korea's traditional roots in agriculture fostered a group-think mentality. Dependency on the community was essential if all were to survive. With the rise of the industrialized marketplace in Korea, the traditional sectors of employment were displaced. People migrated into the urban areas to take advantage of the growing industrial sector[27] (Table 5.3).

In 1963, 63 percent of Koreans were employed in the agricultural sector. However, nonfarm employment grew at an annual average rate of 6.9 percent between 1963 and 1982. By 1988, only 20.7 percent of Korea's labor force was employed in agriculture.[28] In the traditional agricultural world, the importance of the group outweighed the desires of the individual. This philosophy was challenged in the marketplace. As the urban class became more vested in the market, and in Korea's economic progress in general, it became increasingly wary of the government's intrusion into the private sphere. By the mid 1980s, the urbanites had joined the broad coalition of pro-democracy forces calling for mass political and economic liberalization.

A country's movement toward fuller democracy depends, in great part, on citizens' ability to participate in the creation and administration of their government. After 30 years of authoritarian rule, the Korean

Table 5.3. *Changes in ROK urban and rural population: 1946–1980*

Year	% of Urban Population	% of Rural Population	Total (millions)
1946	14.6	85.4	19.3
1955	24.5	75.4	21.5
1960	28.0	72.0	24.9
1970	41.4	58.9	31.4
1975	48.5	51.5	34.6
1980	57.2	42.8	37.4

26   Benjamin (1980, p. 33).
27   *South Korea: A Country Study* (1992).
28   Kim and Park (1985, p. 14); Bedeski (1994, p. 89).

people finally experienced political liberalization in 1987. A motivating factor in becoming politically active is often the citizen's wish to protect his economic freedom and hard-earned gain. Of course, if there is little prosperity, there is little motivation. Such was not the case in Korea. Since the early 1960s, Korea has achieved a remarkable rate of economic growth. Between 1972 and 1991, real GDP per capita increased from US$1,845 to US$7,251. Unlike in many other developing countries, income was broadly distributed throughout the society[29] (Table 5.4).

The increase in wealth experienced by the populace, in conjunction with its broad distribution, greatly affected the way Koreans participated in their government. When at first it appeared that any protest would be futile, the mass of urbanites refused to vote. As incomes continued to rise, and a level of economic security was obtained for the majority of Koreans, political participation increased. People wanted political rights to accompany their wealth.

In addition to an increase in prosperity providing an impetus toward the transition to democracy, technological advancement and its linkages with internationalization encouraged the wish for political liberalization. Like most of the economic policy changes adopted in Korea from 1948 to 1988, the ideology of *progress* lay behind the creation of the Office of Investment Promotion (OIP) in 1966. The OIP's mission was to help the country adapt and assimilate foreign technology. In a 1976 World Bank survey of 113 Korean firms, 54 percent ranked foreign private institutions and firms as important and very important sources of technology.[30]

Table 5.4. *Income distribution in Korea*

Year	Lower 20%	Lower 40%	Upper 20%	Upper 10%
1965	5.9	19.3	41.8	25.8
1970	7.3	19.6	41.6	25.4
1976	5.7	19.9	45.3	27.5
1980	5.1	16.1	45.4	29.5
1985	6.1	18.9	42.7	28.3
1988	6.4	19.7	42.2	27.6

29   Economic Planning Board, various years.
30   Rhee, Ross-Larson, and Pursell (1984, p. 107).

The importance of creating a Korean technological base quickly became a priority for the private sector. The expenditures on research and development rapidly increased throughout the 1980s. In yet another signal of the increasing autonomy of the market in dictating the channels of investment, R&D funding from the public sphere decreased in relation to the amount from the private sector as the 1980s continued[31] (Table 5.5). The technological revolution of the 1960s through the 1980s helped fuel Korea's phenomenal growth.

Technological growth as an economic priority increased Korea's exposure to the ideology and processes of liberal democracy through expanded contact with the West. Korean scientists and business leaders visited international expositions, attended conferences, paid site visits to overseas facilities, and were eager to hire young Koreans who were educated in the sciences at foreign universities. During the early years of the Park regime, a surprising number of Koreans were educated abroad. This changed abruptly with the adoption of the Yushin Constitution in 1972. With the demise of Park, Koreans once again traveled overseas to be educated, and, as Figure 5.5 shows, the number of students abroad climbed steeply in the late 1980s.[32]

By the early 1980s, Koreans realized that future progress depended on a fuller integration into the world economy. As Korea became increasingly wedded to the international economy during the 1960s and 1970s, democratic ideas and processes were introduced to the people of Korea. In the 1985 National Assembly election, the New Korea

Table 5.5. *Korean expenditures on R&D*

Year	R&D/GDP	Source of Funds (%)		
		Public	Private	Foreign
1980	0.58	49.8	48.4	1.8
1983	1.01	27.3	72.5	0.2
1985	1.48	19.3	80.5	0.2
1986	1.68	19.0	80.9	0.1
1987	1.78	20.3	79.6	0.1
1988	1.90	17.7	82.3	0.0
1990	1.92	17.1	82.9	0.1

31   Korean Industrial Research Institute.
32   United Nations, *Statistical Yearbook,* various years.

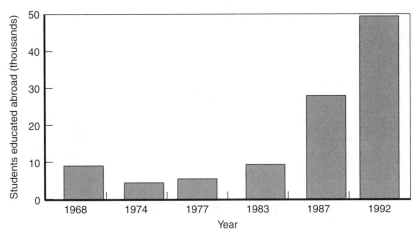

Figure 5.5. Number of Koreans Educated Abroad: 1968–1992

Democratic Party (NKDP), led by Kim Young Sam and Kim Dae Jung, emerged as the strongest opposition party. The NKDP called for the abolishment of the indirect electoral college system in favor of direct presidential elections. A full-scale investigation of the Kwangju incident was also demanded. The pro-democracy forces were coming together in unprecedented numbers. An all-out campaign was launched for ten million signatures on a petition calling for a constitutional amendment on direct elections. The Chun administration became entrenched in an escalating war of words. In 1985, there were 3,877 on-campus demonstrations.[33]

On January 19, 1987, a student protester died while in police custody, raising the stakes in the battle for governmental control. Tension between the government and the opposition (now including members from all walks of life) continued to escalate. To forestall a popular coup, President Chun agreed to overhaul the government, "civilianize" politics, and step down at the end of his term in February 1988.

In June 1987, Roh Tae Woo became the ruling party candidate and announced an eight-point reform plan including direct presidential elections, removal of media control, and a new constitution ratified by popular referendum. Some veteran Korea watchers have claimed that

33   Steinberg (1989, p. 61).

Roh's move occurred at the military's instigation.[34] In a line of reasoning not dissimilar to the one that led to Park's assassination, the Korean military backed Roh's proclamation to ensure their own removal from the political sphere and the professionalization of their corps.

The pressure for deregulation by the business sphere continued throughout the 1980s and reached its apex only months before the first democratically held elections in Korea in 30 years. On May 3, 1988, Koo Cha Kyung, chairman of Lucky-Goldstar group, called for fuller economic autonomy by asking the government to end tight control over business loans and foreign currency supplies.[35]

ROH TAE WOO: THE SIXTH REPUBLIC

We the people of Korea . . . having assumed the mission of democratic reform and peaceful unification of our homeland and having determined to consolidate national unity with justice, humanitarianism and brotherly love, and to destroy all social vices and injustice, and to afford equal opportunity to every person and to provide for the fullest development of individual capabilities in all fields, including political, economic, civic and cultural life by further strengthening the basic free and democratic order conducive to private initiative and public harmony . . .

The Constitution of the Republic of Korea
(as amended in 1987)

In December 1988, Roh Tae Woo was elected president in the first direct election in 16 years. Capturing only 37 percent of the total vote, it was hardly a sweeping victory, yet the transition of power was essentially nonviolent and corruption-free. The watchword of the 1988 election became compromise. Coalition building became the hallmark of the new Korean democracy.

Upon election, Roh immediately restored the free press, curbed police power, and permitted assembly and political protest. At his presidential swearing in, President Roh pledged that "everyone, not just a single person . . . [would] have a say in what is good for the country."[36] Democracy seemed, at last, to have gained a foothold in Korea. A Sixth Republic Constitution was ratified. Some of the main principles in-

34   Plunk (1991, p. 108).
35   *Korea Times*, May 4, 1988.
36   Plunk (1991, p. 106).

cluded: the armed forces staying politically neutral, a restoration of habeas corpus, an end to the licensing of media, the establishment of minimum wage and the right to unionize, the imposition of term limits on the president to one five-year tenure, and the reformation of the process by which lower court judges were appointed. In the past, all lower court judges had been chosen solely by the Chief Justice. Under the new constitution, lower court judges would be chosen with consent of the entire upper court.

Roh made good on many of his promises to break with the Fifth Republic. Within his first year, Roh replaced many of Chun's men still in the administration and began investigations into the Kwangju incident and government corruption.[37] The 1988 Assembly elections proved to be a high-water mark in Korea's political transition. The Democratic Justice Party (DJP) lost majority control of the Assembly for the first time in 30 years. Perhaps more astounding was the fact that in eight short years, the three Kims (Kim Jong Pil, Kim Dae Jung, and Kim Young Sam) went from being political pariahs, silenced by the Chun administration, to controlling members of the Assembly. Kim Jong Pil's New Democratic Republican Party (NDRP) won 35 seats, Kim Young Sam's Reunification Democratic Party (RDP) captured 59 seats, and Kim Dae Jung's PDP won 70 seats.

On January 22, 1990, Kim Young Sam and Kim Jong Pil reached an accord with Roh's ruling party to form the Democratic Liberal Party (DLP) coalition. Despite these compromises, and the movements toward democracy, it would be naive to argue that Korea solved all of its problems. Although by law there was a more even distribution of power between the branches of government, "authoritarian pluralism" and "a one and a half party system" remained catch phrases that described the power that still resided in the executive branch.[38] Nonetheless, measured on a continuous scale, it is clear that the changes enacted in 1988 moved Korea well down the path toward full democracy. It is also clear that without the backing of a powerful and

---

37 Ironically, it would be Roh Tae Woo and Chun Doo Hwan who would be arrested for corruption charges (mutiny and treason charges were added later). Roh was found to have amassed hundreds of millions of dollars in illegal campaign funds during his time in office. Roh was sentenced to 22 years in prison and ordered to pay a fine of US$350 million.

38 *Korea to the Year 2000* (1986, p. 13).

independent business sphere, the change in regime would not have occurred.

In the 14th National Assembly elections in 1992, the DLP lost nearly half of its seats. Party infighting and economic mismanagement were at the heart of the public's discontent. Kim Young Sam was elected the new President of the ROK in a peaceful transition of power.

THE FUTURE OF KOREAN DEMOCRACY

Reviewing its modern economic and political history provides a clear roadmap as to the direction Korea took in achieving democracy. Although the road to political liberalization was a bumpy one (Figure 5.6), a number of forces coalesced in the late 1980s to finally bring about the change in regime.[39] Marketization instilled the importance of a separate and distinct private sphere, as well as the necessity for public accountability, to a society previously operated under the communal agrarian mode. Prosperity allowed for a level of economic security that provided the self-confidence to challenge the existing social structure. Internationalization brought to Korea the fundamental ideas, as well as the procedural mechanisms, of democracy.

Few will argue that Korea's progress in government reform in the last decade has been anything short of remarkable. Nonetheless, the tangle of relationships between industry and government built up over the last

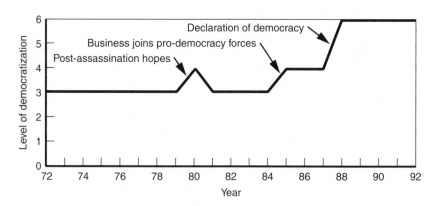

Figure 5.6. Democratization in Korea: 1972–1992

39   Finn (1994).

30 years remains in place and threatens to stymie further democratic reform. However, in the last few years there have been signs that both the leaders of the government and the chaebol realize that the future stability of the country depends on increasing citizens' market access. One such signal was sent on May 10, 1990, when the ten largest chaebol announced their intentions to liquidate a large portion of their real estate holdings. In that same year, a resolution to take the chaebol out of small and medium-sized businesses and to continue "efforts to make the [chaebol] publicly owned and to promote management by professional businessmen, realizing that business should be publicly owned" was developed jointly by the President, the Ministry of Trade and Industry, and the Korean Federation of Businessmen.[40]

Still, many laborers feel shut out of the process that brings inordinate wealth and power to a few family-run businesses. Although the ability to form unions and protest unfair working conditions was a major step in the broader economic liberalization of the mid 1980s, the strikes and work stoppages that resulted may produce unanticipated outcomes. For example, in 1989 President Roh threatened a national emergency if the violent protests by students and workers did not cease. During the first few months of 1989, 331 manufacturing companies were subjected to strikes and stoppages amounting to $3.5 billion in lost production and $877 million in forgone exports.[41] However, both work stoppages and violent protests seem to be declining as labor and management learn the language of negotiation. Down from a peak of 7 million work days lost in 1987, only 1.4 million were lost in 1994 and a minimal 22,000 in the first four months of 1995.[42]

Yet, on December 26, 1996, the labor movement embarked on a series of violent, countrywide protests demonstrating against the signing of a labor reform bill making it easier to fire workers and to hire seasonal and temporary replacements. The bill was passed during an extraordinary pre-dawn parliamentary session of which opposition MPs were not informed. Although the new reforms were in keeping with the entrance requirements of joining the Organization for Economic Co-operation and Development (OECD), and most likely will help Korea advance its economy, the way the bill was passed and the lack of any

40   Bedeski (1994, p. 88).
41   Oh (1994, p. 5).
42   "Not So Militant" (1995).

retraining or social safety net provisions within the legislation are deplorable.

There is little research on the opinions of the broader society regarding the labor strikes besetting the country. Quite possibly the populace is of a split mind. Progress and economic stability have been the watchwords of Korea for the last 40 years. Consequently, if the chaebol can co-opt the middle class urbanites into categorizing the protesters as a radical fringe, responsible for degrading the Korean economy, the strikers may lose any chance of gaining a wide acceptance. Yet, there is growing evidence that citizens resent the powerful elite and are demanding change and further economic liberalization.

To ensure open political competition and societal stability, the Korean economy must broaden the scope of its economic liberalization measures. Perhaps more important, the chaebol cannot stand in the way of these reforms. Recent pledges by the chaebol to foster the growth of small and medium-sized firms, which generate roughly 44 percent of GNP and 40 percent of Korea's exports, suggest that the elites may be recognizing this fact. Korea's petition to enter the OECD may also encourage greater market liberalization, although with concomitant labor reforms of the type that led to the December 1996 labor riots.

As the events of 1997 unfolded, however, it became increasingly clear that the decision of whether or not to cooperate may have been taken out of the hands of the chaebol. The financial crisis of 1997, the subsequent International Monetary Fund (IMF) bailout package, and the election of opposition leader Kim Dae Jung to the presidency may have created a momentum for economic and political liberalization that even the chaebol cannot contain.

Kim Dae Jung of the National Congress for New Politics was elected to the presidency on December 18, 1997, as the first opposition candidate ever to rise to that office. It had been a long climb from his roots as an outspoken critic of the regime and a jailed dissident. The Koreans, mired in the midst of an economic collapse, had decided that business as usual no longer worked. Kim was elected as the consummate outsider and heralded as the kind of leader that could help resuscitate Korea. After an initial faux pas (that was quickly rectified) in which Kim's remarks that the IMF bailout package was too stringent sent the won to 1,962 to the U.S. dollar (half of its value from two months earlier), the international investment community lined up behind Kim as well. To back up their confidence, the Group of Seven Industrialized Nations advanced the ROK US$10 billion on Christmas Eve, 1997, and bankers in both the United States and Japan agreed to bankroll billions of dollars of short-term debt. This helped alleviate the pressure on businesses lacking credit because of the depreciation of the currency.

The foundation for both the domestic and international confidence rested on two aspects of Kim's background. First, Kim Dae Jung had made his career by defending the rights of the country's laborers. He would need the support of those same workers to pass the difficult labor laws that the IMF was demanding in exchange for the US$57 billion bailout package. Yim Ch'ang-yol, Deputy Prime Minister and Minister of Finance and Economy, explained in his position paper on market opening, that an "inflexible labor market not only encroaches upon the competitiveness of companies with surplus manpower, but it even blocks other companies from utilizing labor, causing a two-fold harm on the entire economy." He continued that although the new laws permitting employment adjustment and flexible work hours would cause hardship in the short run, they would ultimately strengthen the market, for "one must realize the stark fact that if it is difficult for companies to lay people off, they will hesitate about hiring."[43] Only the good will of the labor unions, earned by years of protesting in their behalf, would allow Kim to avoid massive protests in response to the new laws.

The second reason for the vote of confidence in Kim was the perception that, as an outsider accustomed to challenging authority, he would be able to tackle the problem of reforming the chaebol system and breaking the inappropriate relationship between government and business. In his first address as the 15th term ROK president-elect, Kim Dae Jung remarked that "democratic politics have been sacrificed for a long time under the authoritarian rule. In fact, politics in which everything was sacrificed for the sake of economic development have continued. As a result, erratic and distorted trends took the lead in overall society. This phenomenon is seen from politics-business collusion, government-ruled economy, and persisting irregularities and cor-

---

43   "Full text of letter to people by the Ministry of Finance and Economy" (1997).

ruption. Sacrificing small and medium-sized enterprises has continued and the rights of common people have not been protected."[44]

To eradicate such ties, Kim's government will need to implement the IMF demands to reform its foreign exchange system, capital flow controls, and highly regulated direct foreign investment market. By increasing marketization in this manner, Koreans can take a more active role in determining the direction of their lives and country and in ensuring the continuation of progress.

There remains one large wild card in such planning, however. The North, its leadership and its intentions, weighs heavily on the minds of South Koreans. Complete economic or political collapses of North Korea are very real prospects. Civil breakdown could either catalyze a peaceful reunification process or spark a hostile confrontation. As of June 1997, military strategists around the world viewed the situation with a growing sense of unease. The U.S. chairman of the Joint Chiefs of Staff, General John Shalikashvili, remarked in May 1997 that of all the potential dangers in Asia, "first and most threatening is the unpredictable regime in Pyongyang."[45] Whether the North will try to take advantage of this time of economic and political restructuring in South Korea is unknown.

Nonetheless, the South Koreans have little choice but to continue their march toward greater liberalization and integration with the world's trading systems and hope that the situation in the North will not escalate into a time of devastation not seen for five decades.

44   Address by Kim Dae Jung (1997).
45   Landay (1997).

6

——•—■—■•—■—■•—■——•—■——•—■—■•—■——•—■——•—■——•—■—■•—■——•—■——•—■——•—■——•—■•—■—

Taiwan: The bringing in of new elites

In a 1993 speech before the Taiwanese 14th National Congress, President Lee Teng-hui declared:

> Today we stand at a turning point in history. Over two thousand years ago, the Chinese had such democratic thoughts as "the people rank higher than the nobility" and "the people are the foundation of the state." In recent years, we in Taiwan have successfully adopted the Western political philosophy of government of the people, for the people and by the people, and created on Chinese soil the first ever democratic society based on party politics. This achievement, unprecedented in Chinese history, marks the beginning of a new historic era.[1]

President Lee's words capture the Taiwanese sense of accomplishment in converting their society from a repressive authoritarian regime to a functioning, albeit "Taiwan styled," democracy. This chapter analyzes the building blocks of Taiwanese democracy and discusses whether or not the lessons learned from the transformation of the island's political system can be transferred to other East Asian nations.

In Taiwan's movement toward participatory government, five stages can be delineated: the early years of the Kuomintang (KMT) on Taiwan,[2] the concentration of economic and political power in the hands of the KMT in the 1950s and 1960s, the government's limited steps toward economic liberalization in the late 1970s and early 1980s, the transitional period of Taiwanese politics during 1986–1987, and the

---

1 From a speech delivered at the opening of the 14th National Congress of the Kuomintang on August 16, 1993, in Hu (1994, p. 4).

2 In this chapter, the name Taiwan is used interchangeably with the Republic of China on Taiwan and the ROC.

current consolidation of institutionalized democracy hallmarked by a normalization of politics and a solidifying of the multi-party system.[3] As these stages of political evolution progressed, so did Taiwan's economic, political, and social development. Citizens, on the whole, became richer, more educated, and more civic minded. These changes were most apparent in the rising middle class. Before the 1980s, middle class citizens in Taiwan were essentially apolitical, fighting only for their economic freedom. As the 1980s progressed, they became aware that they could use the power of their purse to pursue other issues on their agenda, such as environmental concerns. They also became aware that they could field their own slate of candidates and minimize their reliance on the entrenched political elite.[4] Andrew Brick, writing in the *Asian Wall Street Journal,* commented that the "locomotive that drove Taiwan's commercial development made the old politics obsolete. There actually was political subversion by economic development. . . . The commercial cadres demanded the same accountability from their government as was demanded of them by their business colleagues."[5] Increased prosperity led the Taiwanese to press for a reduction in the political corruption that threatened their economic gains. The opportunities for political corruption also declined as marketization increased the privatization of Taiwan's state-owned enterprises, separating policy-makers from profitmaking entities.

In the following country study, the five stages described above form a basic structure for analyzing the importance of marketization and internationalization as the primary building blocks of Taiwanese democracy. By understanding this process of economic liberalization, we are better able to gauge the effect of market transformation on Taiwan's burgeoning democracy movement. Preceding the fall of authoritarianism by a decade, marketization gave a voice to a previously disenfranchised people and, ultimately, brought about the rise of political liberalization. The lessons of choice and competition taught by the market to the thousands of small entrepreneurs increased the "democratic learning" of the nation. Applying the precepts of the marketplace to their political life, the Taiwanese began to call for more competition in the political process. This chapter explores the societal and economic underpinnings that strengthened the foundation of this political transition.

3   Rigger (1994).
4   Lu (1991, p. 40).
5   Brick (1992).

In comparison to the evolution of economic and financial liberalization in the Republic of Korea, Taiwan's experience can be seen as more diffuse (the pressures for transformation had a much broader base within the general population). However, it is inaccurate to represent the pressures for transformation as rising only from the populace and not being influenced and, in great part, directed by key members of the political elite. In particular, no history of Taiwanese liberalization can be written without careful scrutiny of the role of Chiang Ching-kuo. Both as Premier (1972–1978), and later as President (1978–1988), Chiang Ching-kuo was essential in Taiwan's conversion to both a market economy and a fledgling democracy. Although his guidance and direction were necessary for the country's liberalization, would it have been sufficient without the tidal forces of the broader society? Indeed, would Chiang Ching-kuo have permitted, and in many instances instigated, these radical economic and societal changes without extensive pressure from below? For the purpose of this work, clarification of whether Chiang Ching-kuo was the "hero that contributed to the shaping of current events" (tsao-shih-shih chih ying-hsiung) or the "hero that was created from current events" (shih-shih so-tsao chih ying-hsiung) can remain vague. It is enough to recognize that the transformation of Taiwan occurred through a confluence of events, some originating within the government, most arising from the will of the people. These events and actions can be seen as the determinants of Taiwan's democracy. This chapter attempts to identify these building blocks with an eye toward further study of whether the same blocks can be assembled in China and elsewhere in East Asia to create a basis for democracy.

THE ROOTS OF MARKETIZATION AND DEMOCRACY IN TAIWAN

Taiwan's modern history began not on Taiwan but on mainland China in the early years of the 20th century. It was there that a Cantonese Christian doctor named Sun Yat-sen organized the National People's Party and wrote the texts that became the bases for the economic and political systems of the Republic of China. Sun's political party (the Kuomintang, or KMT), supported by peasants and small capitalists, arose to fill the power vacuum left by the fall of the Ch'ing dynasty in 1912. Politically, the KMT's ideology centered on Dr. Sun's Three Principles of the People, or San Min Chu-I: nationalism, the people's livelihood, and political tutelage. Sun's philosophy entailed steering a course between the incentive-stifling communist ideology and the excesses of the capitalist system of the West (Figure 6.1).

Sun's economic development plan was presented in his book, *The International Development of China* (c.1922). Sun wrote that

> industrial development in China should follow two distinct lines: private enterprises and government enterprises. All those that could be entrusted to the private sector, or those for which private operation is more appropriate than government operation, should be open to the private sector, encouraged by the state and protected by law. In order for private enterprises to develop in China, the hitherto suicidal tax system should be immediately eliminated, the monetary disorder should be immediately corrected; bureaucratic barriers should be removed and, most important, communications and transportation systems should be improved.

Sun's economic precepts regarding marketization, distribution of economic power, and technological advancement not only helped create Taiwan's economic miracle but laid the foundation for democracy by giving citizens the desire and ability to influence their government. Prybyla lists the following as essential ingredients in Taiwan's economic boom: a flexible price mechanism, which quickly eliminates occasional resource misallocation; minimal structural disruption during the transition to an industrialized economy; restructuring the ownership of Taiwanese enterprises from government to private hands; and an equitable distribution of the economy's resources.[6] Taiwan's remarkable success, measured on these indicators of performance, is founded upon

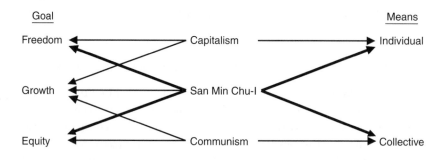

SOURCE: Adapted from Clark (1989).

Figure 6.1. Guiding Principles of the Kuomintang

6   Prybyla (1991, pp. 50–55).

Sun's original economic vision. However, it took nearly six decades after Sun penned those words for the ROC to blossom economically and an additional ten years for his ideas of "political tutelage" to produce a quasi-democratic system of government.

Sun died in 1924 before his writings would shape a nation but after he had reorganized the KMT along Leninist lines, following the advice and guidance of the Communist International. The legacy of this early relationship with Leninist ideology created a powerful party with a strong central decisionmaking arm. Yet, the powerful Nationalist army kept the central, and oftentimes more conservative, political structure somewhat fragmented and unable to exert the influence wielded by other Leninist regimes.[7]

After Sun's death, his military commander, Chiang Kai-shek, took control of the KMT and, in the 1st KMT Congress in January 1924, helped adopt Soviet organizational principles. This system vested Chiang Kai-shek, and the future leadership of Taiwan, with extensive powers by consolidating most of the party's (and the state's) decision-making ability in the central command structure.[8] Soon after the 1st Congress, the on-again, off-again battle between the KMT and the Chinese Communist Party (CCP) erupted. Outnumbering the CCP forces, both in sheer manpower and in trained forces, the Nationalists won a decisive defeat over the CCP by the beginning of 1928. The KMT quickly established a Nationalist government on Mainland China. Whether or not Chiang believed that the Republic of China would eventually evolve into a constitutional democracy (per Sun's writings), the chaos left by the civil war provided a ready excuse to establish an interim military regime—one that would restore stability and inculcate the values of "democracy." The KMT's defense of authoritarianism as political tutelage would serve as a harbinger for the future of Taiwan.

In name the KMT ruled China during the late 1920s, but in actuality the nation remained factionalized and controlled by rival warlords. By the early 1930s, large portions of the country began to fall into Japanese hands. As the economy of the country declined, the KMT saw its original base of support among farmers, small capitalists, and laborers erode. The KMT exacerbated its troubles by stepping up harassment of labor unions, which it accused of being in league with the Communists, thereby losing another potential ally. Mid 1937 brought

7   See Moody (1992) for a broader discussion of these forces.
8   Scalapino (1993, p. 72).

a full-scale invasion by the Japanese and briefly reunited the KMT and the CCP.

At the conclusion of World War II, with the Japanese army vanquished, tensions between the KMT and the CCP reemerged. Nationalist forces moved their headquarters onto Taiwan and continued to battle the CCP on the mainland. The defeated Japanese had left Taiwan in economic chaos. Resources were depleted during the war and the island was subjected to heavy U.S. bombing that destroyed three-quarters of the industrial base, two-thirds of the utilities, and one-half of the transportation network.[9] The arrival of the Nationalist army onto the battle-scarred island was at first met with enthusiasm from the native Taiwanese (Chinese who had immigrated to Taiwan as far back as the 17th century) who believed that after decades of subjugation at the hands of outsiders, Chinese would finally govern Chinese.

Unity between the Mainlanders and the Taiwanese did not materialize. The Taiwanese were shocked at the illiteracy and backwardness of their mainland brethren. Although the Taiwanese had inherited the Japanese social system, derived originally from ancient China, the fleeing KMT army was schooled in the corrupt ways of early 20th century China. To many Taiwanese, members of the KMT, in comparison to the Japanese, were ignorant bullies. Initial Taiwanese enthusiasm for KMT rule faded as the native population recognized the cultural gulf that separated them from the Mainlanders. Bitterness from the locals against the KMT surfaced in an islandwide revolt in 1947, which sent many Taiwanese nationalists to jail, exile, or death. Fueled with an excuse to seek revenge on the Taiwanese whom they believed to have collaborated with the Japanese, the KMT's military (commanded by Ch'en Yi) executed a brutal response to the crisis. In what later became known as the 2-28 Incident, Ch'en Yi's military massacred close to 20,000 Taiwanese civilians.

Civil war continued to consume China for the next two years. In the winter of 1949, after a crushing defeat by the Communists in a battle north of the Yangtze, the Nationalists fled to the island of Taiwan, where they hoped to regroup and retake the mainland. The KMT's impression that Taiwan was little more than a staging ground, coupled with the intense hatred spawned by the 2-28 Incident, wreaked havoc on hopes of Taiwanese unity. Political action became a life-threatening endeavor, one in which few Taiwanese chose to participate. After see-

9   Ranis (1979, p. 209).

ing their leaders slaughtered by the Mainlanders, the Taiwanese decided to withdraw from the political arena. It would take four decades of cautious actions before the Taiwanese people would feel safe enough to venture back into the political waters.

It was an inauspicious beginning to the KMT's rule on the island of Taiwan and solidified the schism between the Mainlanders and Taiwanese. Mutual distrust and animosity between the two groups were major factors in keeping democracy at bay for so many years, contributing to the instability that could still threaten the country. For 40 years, the Mainlanders were a minority ruling over a hostile majority. Although martial law was imposed, ostensibly to contain the threat from the People's Republic of China (PRC), it applied equally to a threat from the Taiwanese upon the KMT's preeminence. The next sections of this chapter explore the pressures behind the KMT's increasingly moderate position, arrived at over two decades. It appears likely that as the Taiwanese accumulated economic power, the KMT was forced to concede economic and then political reforms to retain its powerful position.

THE KMT ON TAIWAN: THE EARLY YEARS

In 1949, the KMT concluded its final exodus from the mainland and prepared for its rule over Taiwan. Chiang Kai-shek, elected as the nation's president in April 1948, resigned from the office in January 1949 after the KMT's final defeat on the mainland. Yet he continued to control the political situation and charged his son, Chiang Ching-kuo, with the responsibility of ensuring stability on the island. To that end, Chiang Ching-kuo became head of Taiwan's new security organization, the Political Action Committee, and director of the General Political Department of the Ministry of Defense. In these new capacities, he invoked those passages of the 1947 Constitution that read: "For reasons of averting an imminent crisis, maintaining social order, or advancing the general welfare" individual rights and liberties could be abridged. On May 19, 1949, the KMT passed into law the "Temporary Provision Effective During the Period of Communist Rebellion." Martial law, which would last until 1987, had officially begun.

Ironically, despite the imposition of martial law, the KMT permitted the continuation of local elections. In part, Dr. Sun's teachings of "Rule by the People" forced the KMT's authoritarian regime on Taiwan to hold these elections, but more than likely the KMT hoped that not only would the local elections restore the people's faith in the KMT after the February 28, 1947, massacre but they would legitimize the KMT's claim to the whole of Mainland China.[10] Never one to lose an opportunity to consolidate power, the KMT, and especially Chiang Ching-kuo, used the local elections to create a system of highly loyal grass-roots organizations throughout the country. Since opposition parties were severely restricted, the threat of political loss was nil. The creation of mass organizations, such as agricultural societies, youth corps, and women's organizations, was typical of an authoritarian regime. These organizations were cultivated by Chiang Ching-kuo and became central recruiting grounds for his future aides.[11]

The KMT organized the new ROC government on Taiwan around the five branches of government originally proposed by Sun Yat-sen in the early 1920s (Figure 6.2). The branches were the Executive Yuan, the Legislative Yuan, the Judicial Yuan, the Control Yuan, and the Examination Yuan. The President, who was indirectly elected, was the top political official and appointed the leaders of three of the five branches. The most important appointment was the Premier of the Executive Yuan, who functioned as the Prime Minister. Members of the Legislative Yuan would be elected through direct elections, although for most of the period of martial law, the Legislative Yuan acted as a rubber stamp on the wishes of the President. Like the evolving Chinese Communist Party, the KMT quickly developed into an autonomous institution where the party, for all intents and purposes, became the state. Yet two factors kept the KMT from becoming the all-encompassing authoritarian regime the CCP became on the mainland. The primary reason, which will be discussed in greater length below, was the bifurcation of political and economic power, with the Mainlanders controlling the public sector and the Taiwanese dominating the private sphere. The second factor was the way the Taiwanese economy evolved. Unlike those of many other developing countries, Taiwan's economic resources and factors of production were broadly distributed. Consequently, the traditional tool used by bureaucratic authoritarian regimes, politically motivated confiscations from key elites in the opposition, could not easily occur on Taiwan—economic power was too diffuse.

10   Huang (1991, p. 102).
11   For a good discussion, see Winckler (1993, p. 72).

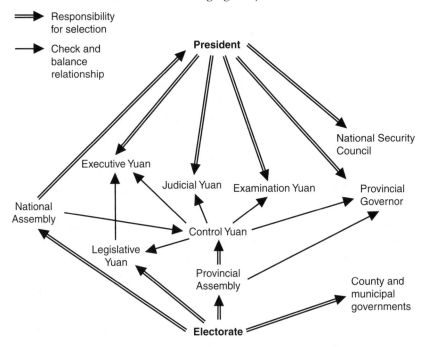

SOURCE: Adapted from Clark (1989).

Figure 6.2. Government Structure of the ROC

In the first few decades of the ROC on Taiwan, nearly all important policy decisions were made at the national level, and most were made by a single individual, Chiang Ching-kuo. Following the example set by his father, he continued to consolidate power in the hands of the KMT's central authority. As Winckler writes, the "institutionalization of personal leadership was partly through constitutional provisions and ministries, partly through extraconstitutional enactments and agencies, and partly through informal political alliances and personal networks."[12] Over three decades, Chiang Ching-kuo built a power structure that wielded enormous influence over Taiwan. It is logical to assume, therefore, that the economic and political reforms that transpired during his leadership could not have occurred without his support. Yet it is also reasonable to assert that Chiang Ching-kuo's active role in curtailing

12   Winckler (1993, p. 111).

the activities of the government in the mid 1980s was influenced by a broad push for such reforms from the populace. Without the growing strength of the Taiwanese market sector, and their increasingly vocal protests over economic and political repression, reformation would not have occurred. Nevertheless, it is extraordinary to consider that Chiang Ching-kuo, as the head of an authoritarian regime, set in motion a transition that eventually broke his party's hold over the state and allowed power to devolve from the party elite to a broader segment of the bureaucracy. It is a testament to his foresight in recognizing that change was inevitable and that his choices were whether reform would occur sooner (with perhaps violent repercussions) or later (after a slow process of evolution).

The KMT ended the 1940s fully entrenched in its seat of power and unfettered by any serious opposition. The Taiwanese elite had been murdered or coerced into silence, and the peasants had yet to organize in calling for land reform. The ROC on Taiwan, consequently, became the personal property of the KMT, or, more precisely, of the Chiang dynasty.

To the ire of the KMT, throughout 1949 and 1950 the United States continued to woo the PRC, culminating its sales pitch with the official U.S. statement of the "United States Policy Toward Formosa" issued in January 1950. In the statement, the United States reiterated its assertions that Taiwan was part of China and that the United States would discontinue its sale of military supplies to the KMT. The statement sent Taiwan and its U.S. backers into the deep freeze. North Korea's invasion of the South in 1950 microwaved the U.S.-Taiwan relationship. Overnight, Taiwan became Free China—the bastion of anti-communism in East Asia. The United States became the official champion of the ROC in its fight to retain the China seat in the United Nations. In January 1950, the PRC demanded Taiwan's expulsion from the United Nations. For two decades the United States and its allies kept the PRC at bay through a variety of tactics, including arguing that the PRC did not meet the U.N. requirement of a "peace-loving state" and was ineligible for membership.

Aside from providing moral and political support, the United States became the major benefactor of the ROC's economy by providing massive military and nonmilitary aid. The aid played a fundamental role in promoting Taiwan's economy, and the announcement of the aid's termination served as the catalyst for Taiwan's transition from a stagnating import substitution strategy to a more viable export promotion policy. The change in direction fueled Taiwan's economic growth in the 1970s and 1980s and mitigated much of the hardship caused by the two worldwide oil crises.

CONSOLIDATION OF POWER: THE 1950s AND 1960s

The KMT entered the 1950s in a position of extreme dominance. Despite this, the KMT leadership recognized that without a strong base of support among the peasants, their tenure in office would be limited and their dream of posing a united front against the Communists doomed to failure. The KMT leadership understood that the carrot and the stick needed to be used in tandem. As a result, severe curtailment of civil and political liberties coincided with a revamping of the party by Chiang Kai-shek. Chiang offered the carrot originally promised by Sun Yat-sen: that the KMT would uphold the precepts of nationalism, democracy, and people's livelihood. With this in mind, and the constant reminder of the 2-28 Incident as an ever-present Achilles' heel, the government undertook a vast reform of land control including rent reduction, public land sales, and the passage of the influential land-to-the-tiller program, which vested property rights in the peasantry.

In 1953, Taiwan launched its first Four Year Economic Development Plan and created the Economic Stabilization Board (ESB). Although in general the ESB became an unwieldy, regulation-prone bureaucracy that stifled the economy, the agency was extremely successful in its agricultural policy. Beginning in 1954, under the auspices of the ESB, the government of Taiwan embarked on a large-scale land reform. Land reform was originally begun on the mainland before the exodus of the KMT and continued in limited form during the first few years of the ROC on Taiwan. The more cynical critics of the KMT suggest that the Nationalists were finally able to achieve their desired land reform only when firmly ensconced on Taiwan because none of the ruling elite owned any land on the island. On the mainland, the KMT had been prevented from instituting land reform because of political infighting and the power of provincial landlords.[13]

Another possible motive for land reform was the ability to use the resettlement of the tenant farmers as a wedge to break up the power

13   Cumings (1987) reviews the history of this period.

structure of the Taiwanese landholding elite—a group over which the KMT held little influence. What the KMT did not envision at the time was that the small-scale farmers, powerless in the 1950s, would organize during the next 20 years into a serious political opposition.

The land reform of the 1950s was accomplished in three stages. The first stage reduced land rental rates throughout the countryside, ensuring the farmers a livable income. The second stage transferred large tracts of land from the government and state-owned enterprises (SOEs) to private ownership. The third and final stage was the institution of the influential land-to-the-tiller program, which limited landlords' ownership to three hectares of field and compensated the owners 70 percent in kind and 30 percent with shares of four recently privatized SOEs producing cement, paper products, machinery, and agricultural products.[14] The effect of the land-to-tiller program can be seen in Figure 6.3, which shows the net percentage gain in peasant income from land reform.[15] The income gain from rent reduction and land redistribution

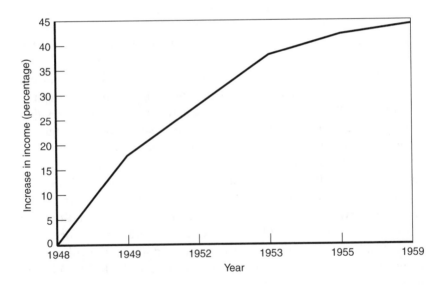

Figure 6.3. Increase in Peasant Income Resulting from Taiwan's Land Reform: 1948–1959

14   Yu (1985, p. 5).
15   Ho (1978, p. 169).

was calculated to determine the countrywide net gain from the land reform policies.

The rise in income was due, in large part, to the expansion in owner-cultivated land, which increased from 55.88 percent in 1948 to 82.78 percent in 1953.[16] As a result of the land-to-the-tiller program, the life of the peasant dramatically changed. Living conditions vastly improved; the tenant farmers gained a large measure of autonomy from the landlords (in many cases being given title to the land) and found a political voice in a plethora of new organizations designed to encourage participatory government.[17]

The U.S. role in the promotion of Taiwanese land reform, and the economic and political changes the reform spurred, cannot be ignored. Apart from the military aid given to the Taiwanese as a tool to promote U.S. security against the threat of hostile Communist forces, U.S. aid agencies hoped to find a way to raise the Chinese standard of living without de facto support of the rightist KMT regime. Financially assisting the land-to-the-tiller program and funneling loans to small-scale entrepreneurs seemed the way to achieve this goal. However, when a Taiwanese entrepreneur told a U.S. Mutual Security Agency official that there was "no free enterprise on Taiwan . . . and that there was not equal treatment for all, or freedom of action in business," U.S. aid officials realized that without a strengthening of the private sphere, land reform would collapse.[18] The four recently privatized SOEs would not be able to survive without a competitive enterprise economy, and the panic from a bankruptcy could discredit the entire land-to-the-tiller program. Recognizing these facts, the United States increased pressure on the KMT to liberalize the economy.

The three basic land reform policies begun in the early 1950s grew by the end of the decade to encompass education, agricultural management, improvements to the marketing system of produce, and the creation of a farm credit market. Land, as the sacred family property, became a transferable commodity, and the traditional small family farmer began to link his interests to the ongoing government reforms. Prosperity, and the desire to protect it, forced the farmer to take a more activist role in civic affairs. Yet, it was clear that the small farmer posed no serious threat to the regime. It would take until the early 1980s for

16 Directorate-General of Budget (1987).
17 Ting Tin-yu (1991, p. 76).
18 Barrett (1988, p. 142).

the farmers' movement to gain countrywide support and effectively influence the pricing and marketing of agricultural products. Still, the increase in rural wealth and the closer relationship with market forces brought about by land reform and the industrialization of the country created a groundswell of support for democracy. As market forces continued to sweep Taiwan, the ruling elite was forced, out of necessity, to invite technocrats and administrators into the government Many of these new recruits were from outside traditional mainland circles and many were educated in the United States.

Another consequence of land reform was the breakdown of the traditional family structure and the beginning of the gradual migration of the younger generation into the cities (Figure 6.4).[19] As in Korea, these first-generation city dwellers, without a strong support network, were less likely to question the authoritarian regime. And also as in Korea, the second- and third-generation urbanites, with fewer ties to the old traditions, felt more comfortable challenging the status quo and the authoritarian regime. Residing in the cities, with access to the "marketplace of ideas," these challenges would grow into a formidable pro-democracy movement.

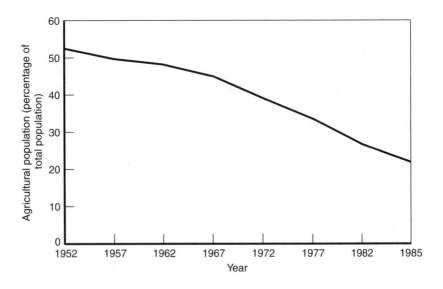

Figure 6.4. Decrease in Taiwan's Agricultural Population: 1952–1985

19   *Taiwan Statistical Data Book,* various years

Of these early migrants, many were co-opted into supporting the KMT through the party's strong push in the early 1950s to bring Taiwanese into lower levels of authority within the government. Although the top positions of the KMT remained in the hands of Mainlanders, Taiwanese were encouraged to fill administrative posts. In August 1950, Chiang Kai-shek established a Central Reform Committee to redesign the KMT with the mission of repudiating bad elements within the party (a quiet nod to the 2-28 Incident) and broadening its base of support by opening its ranks to native Taiwanese. Since the takeover of the island by Nationalist forces, native Taiwanese had been systematically excluded from the political power structure.

Despite the lack of political clout, the Taiwanese controlled the economic resources of the country. The rise of these competing political-economic factions was due to the particular events of the 1945–1954 period. When the KMT fled the mainland, most Chinese business owners refused to accompany them, disillusioned with the Nationalists after years of high inflation caused by the civil war. The majority of those who moved to Taiwan were government officials and members of the military, untrained and unsuited for the business sphere.[20] More violent reasons kept the Taiwanese from entering public service. Most of the politically minded Taiwanese were driven underground or exiled during the Japanese colonization. Many of those who remained on the island were killed during the violence of the 2-28 Incident. Despite this background, the two elites, Mainlander and Taiwanese, may have developed relationships if the economic and political spheres had been freed from constraints. Under such a scenario, linkages between the two groups may have formed. As it was, the Mainlanders and Taiwanese had no natural setting in which to form alliances. As a result, both the economic sector and the state bureaucracy suffered. The reforms proposed in the early 1950s were an initial attempt to remedy this segregation.

The broad economic policy measures enacted, in conjunction with the increasing Taiwanization of the KMT and the introduction of economically liberal technocrats into the government, widened the circle of elites operating within both the public and private sectors and set the stage for greater economic and political liberalization. Still, it would be decades before the Taiwanese would have a substantive role in their

20   See Winckler (1988) for a broader discussion of the ROC's early years on Taiwan.

government. In the intervening years, a native Taiwanese identity would arise. Although the ancestral roots of the Taiwanese reached back into Mainland China, the schism that arose after the 2-28 Incident continued to widen the gap between the Mainlanders and the Taiwanese. What began as mistrust over cultural differences grew into hatred by the Taiwanese of the brutally repressive Mainlanders represented by the KMT. The mutual animosity hardened, over the next 30 years, into two entrenched camps with competing ideas of nationalism. The Mainlanders considered Taiwan part of the Republic of China, nothing more and nothing less than a province. The Taiwanese, most having severed their roots with the mainland centuries before, considered Taiwan a separate and distinct nation from the one across the strait. Kept in check by the KMT until the 1980s, ideas of nationalism and Taiwanese cultural identity would be a driving force for political liberalization.

In the 1950s, national identity was little discussed. Economic advancement and military security were the primary goals of the KMT. In addition to agricultural reform, the other major economic policy initiative of the 1950s was the establishment in 1955 of the China Productivity Center. The agenda of the center was to promote import substitution, a very popular development strategy at the time. The theory behind the strategy was that import substitution helped economize on foreign exchange spending, allowing infant industries to develop and stabilize prices. The means for achieving import substitution were high tariffs and other protectionist controls. The strategy built up Taiwan's nascent industries, but it also limited contact with the outside world and entrenched the power of the state through its capacity to limit credit to private enterprises. Nonetheless, the reforms begun in the 1950s to structurally shift the base of the economy away from agriculture and toward industry were a remarkable success, as can be seen in Figure 6.5, which shows the breakdown of GDP by sector.[21]

Although programs such as land reform, Taiwanization, and import substitution improved economic life on Taiwan, the social structure remained under the control of a repressive government. On June 10, 1951, the Executive Yuan ordered licensing restrictions for newspapers and in 1955 limited news publications to six pages per issue.[22] The crackdown on the media, a traditional tool of authoritarian regimes,

21 *Taiwan Statistical Yearbook*, various years.
22 Hu (1994, p. 479).

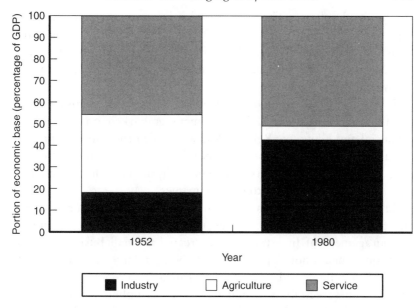

Figure 6.5. Shift in Taiwan's Industrial Structure from Agriculture Toward Industry: 1952–1980

may have had an ulterior motive beyond the simple curtailment of liberty. Lei Chen, chief editor of the *Free China* magazine and veteran member of the KMT, had begun to speak out vociferously against the KMT's one-party rule. Silencing his medium would presumably silence the man. Lei Chen did not agree. In the fall of 1960, he tried, unsuccessfully, to organize the Chinese Democratic opposition party. The KMT, in its first major political crackdown since the 2-28 Incident, accused Lei of Communist espionage and sentenced him to 10 years in prison. The rest of the 1960s would see a continuation of such abuses. Yet even during this time of purges, political assassinations, and unjustified jailings, there were signs of hope.

That hope stemmed from a small, but growing, coalition of business owners and entrepreneurs. Unlike in Korea, where the economic power of the private sector resided in the hands of the chaebol, in Taiwan, tens of thousands of small and medium-sized business owners influenced the economy. This powerful coalition of small business owners, which began to take shape in the early 1960s, was instrumental in introducing the lessons of choice and competition, learned in the marketplace, into the political sphere. The coalition also became an economic power separate and distinct from the state. This power would eventually buttress the challenge to the authoritarian regime by the pro-democracy movement. Table 6.1 highlights the effect that small and medium-sized firms had on the Taiwanese economy by 1985.[23]

It was at the instigation of the small and medium-sized business owners that in 1960 the KMT government embarked on its 19-Point Financial and Economic Reform Program, which encompassed privatizing a number of SOEs, providing tax relief to private firms, easing foreign exchange requirements to promote export growth, and granting low-interest start-up loans to new companies.

In conjunction with this program, the government also encouraged the funneling of private savings into investment (the Statute for Encouragement of Investment) and created a Small Business Administration. The economic policies came about, in large part, to offset the loss of U.S. military aid announced to Taiwan in 1965. Such a blow to the Taiwanese economy would have been crippling without careful precautions. Total U.S. aid to Taiwan from 1950 to 1968 equaled US$1.5 billion.[24] Such aid allowed the KMT to run its hugely inefficient military regime without facing the true economic consequences. The elimination of U.S. aid forced Taiwan to look for outside sources of capital, foreign exchange, global credit, and technological experience, if it hoped to build a dynamic, export-oriented economy.[25]

Table 6.1. *Share of small and medium-sized enterprises in total industry sales, ROC, 1985*

Industry	Sales Value (%)
Chemical materials	11
Food	33
Electrical machinery	39
Textile	41
Chemical products	61
Wearing apparel	76
Metal products	78

23   Small and Medium Business Assistance Center (1985).
24   *Taiwan Statistical Data Book,* various years.
25   For a broader discussion of this, see Metraux (1991, p. 126).

The shift toward export orientation marked the second major widening of the circle of economic and political elites. In an effort to promote export-oriented industrialization, the government embarked on a large-scale effort to entice the private sector into shifting resources into this area. The majority of business leaders able to take advantage of these inducements were Taiwanese entrepreneurs. As these entrepreneurs gained economic stature, they were eager to exercise political clout and to assist in the formulation of economic policy.[26]

In 1969, the KMT permitted the reinstatement of national parliamentary elections. Although the KMT solidified its hold on the political structure, the elections did bring in a number of native Taiwanese and foreign-educated (and presumably more open-minded) parliamentarians. The economic and party reforms of the 1950s and 1960s culminated in an election that began the transformation of the KMT.

LIMITED STEPS TOWARD LIBERALIZATION: THE 1970s

Taiwan, because of its limited natural resources and its high population density, has needed to rely on foreign trade to promote economic development. The country accomplished this feat through a three-stage process: development of labor-intensive industries, the active promotion of its exports and other policies of free trade, and, finally, a concerted effort to join the West politically.

The last step, Taiwan's hesitant dance in and out of the world party, has gone through distinct phases over the last four decades. When the United States eliminated aid in 1968, the overseas Chinese community picked up much of the slack. These foreign-born Chinese investors were some of the strongest supporters of Taiwan's transition to an export-based economy and backed President Chiang Ching-kuo's U.S.-trained technocrats, James Soong, Ma Ying-chiu, and Lee Teng-hui, on much of their economic policy.[27] Soong, Ma, and Lee advised the Taiwanese government that foreign investment would not only help correct the balance-of-payment deficiencies but would bring much needed new technology and technological skills into the country. Such market-opening measures, coupled with Taiwan's already existing cheap labor pool and political stability, would make Taiwan a desirable

26   Yu (1985, p. 10).
27   Lu (1991, p. 42).

place for investment.[28] The upshot of the export-oriented strategy during the 1960s and 1970s was the creation of new ties with foreigners, foreign markets, and foreign direct investment.

In addition to the influx of investment capital (and the money managers, executives, and lawyers who followed it) into Taiwan during the 1960s through 1980s, came hundreds of thousands of tourists. The increasing economic viability and the relaxation of the authoritarian regime made Taiwan a destination for many overseas travelers. Figure 6.6 shows the rapid rise of tourism in the mid 1970s.[29] These visits from overseas relations, friends, and adventurers brought more than currency into the country. They brought in the ideas of the West, the ideas of democracy, and the knowledge of process that would allow the Taiwanese people to self-govern.

The Chiang dynasty continued into the 1970s with Chiang Ching-kuo becoming premier in 1972, party chairman in 1975, and president in 1978. Well before he claimed these titles, Chiang Ching-kuo had already solidified his base within the party. He relied on the following

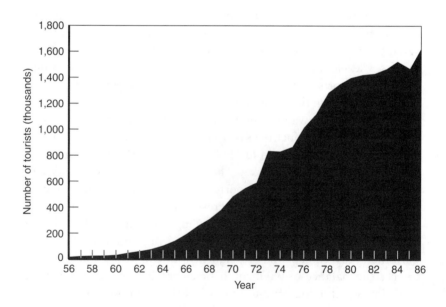

Figure 6.6. Increase in Taiwanese Tourism: 1956–1986

28   Cheng and Haggard (1991).
29   Cheng and Hsiung (1994, p. 335).

strategies to entrench his power base: He cultivated loyal aides and promoted them whenever possible; he co-opted his father's inner circle by promising to maintain their spheres of influence, thereby reducing the likelihood that older hardliners would resent his rising prestige; and he actively excluded other leaders with separate bases of support.[30] Recognizing his own lack of business connections and his weak ties within the economic community, beginning in the late 1960s, Chiang Ching-kuo began to personally chair the Financial and Economic Committee and sought to expand his close circle of advisers by the inclusion of young economists. Under pressure from these well-educated technocrats who pushed for a number of economic and political reforms, he increased the frequency and authority of local elections and took certain actions (albeit most were cosmetic) to reduce governmental corruption.

Perhaps the appearance of liberalization was enough to convince a number of opposition candidates to join together to form the Tangwai.[31] This groundbreaking social experiment of a concerted opposition would not last long, decommissioned through overt and covert KMT actions, but its legacy served as an inspiration for the opposition parties of the early 1980s. Ting Tin-yu, writing about the Tangwai, observed that "the factional character of the Taiwanese opposition is mainly the result of KMT policies, including localized elections, strict media control, and restrictions under martial law on such citizens' rights as free assembly. These policies successfully prevented the emergence of strong and unified opposition parties and island-wide opposition leaders."[32] The Tangwai, comprising many independent factions all representing diversified interests, broke apart from infighting. To ensure its demise, the KMT invoked the power of the official ban on political parties in effect since 1949 and harassed Tangwai leadership into submission.

Balancing the stick with the carrot, the KMT ended the 1960s by expanding the free market in numerous ways. Private property rights and a codified system of laws protecting these rights became the lynchpins for future market reforms. There is little doubt that a prime motive behind these gradual movements toward economic liberalization was the belief that a prosperous nation would be less likely to challenge the

---

30   Winckler (1988, p. 157).
31   Literal translation: outside the ruling party.
32   Ting Tin-yu (1991, p. 81).

status quo. However, the legal institutions created to protect private property became the foundation for the rule of law that would support democracy.

Taiwan began the 1970s well positioned as an export-oriented nation with a growing standard of living. In 1970, the government created the China External Trade Development Council (Taiwan's answer to Japan's Ministry of International Trade and Industry, MITI) with the mission of providing trade information, publishing trade data, and continuing the rapid expansion of Taiwan's export sector. During the decade before the first oil crisis, 1965–1972, the ROC's economic growth rate rose as high as 10.8 percent, yet the economy never lost its stable footing, with wholesale and consumer prices remaining below 3 percent.[33] Two events changed this rosy picture: the severing of relations with the outside world and the Arab oil embargo.

The two decades of international political seesawing between the two Chinas ended in October 1971 when the United Nations General Assembly adopted Resolution 2758 designating the People's Republic of China as the sole legitimate government over the whole of China and awarded it the China seat in the United Nations. The expulsion of Taiwan from the world order forced Taiwan to take stock of itself. Despite Taiwan's growing political isolation, the island nation refused to develop a siege mentality. Rather, Taiwan nurtured a healthy self-confidence from overcoming its international challenges. This was aided by the staunch support from certain members of the U.S. Congress. Taiwan received a steady flow of U.S. overt and covert assistance (including defense equipment and technology), support of Taiwan's membership bids into international organizations, and open access to the U.S. market.

The Arab oil embargo sent the Taiwanese economy into a rapid decline (Table 6.2) and put the new premier, Chiang Ching-kuo, under substantial pressure to take political action to support domestic exporters.[34] In particular, certain economic quarters were calling for government intervention in the interest rate, the monetary growth rate, and the foreign exchange rate. Chiang Ching-kuo, perhaps remembering the inflation that plagued the mainland during the KMT's brief rule, refused to interfere with Taiwan's monetary system. Although losing the support of the small, but extremely powerful, community of ex-

33   Li (1988, p. 90).
34   *Taiwan Statistical Data Book*, various years.

Table 6.2. *Economic effects of the 1973 oil crisis on the ROC*
(in percent)

	1973	1974	1975	1976
Real GNP growth	12.8	1.1	4.3	13.9
Real industrial growth	16.2	-4.5	9.5	23.3
Real savings growth	21.7	-7.5	-11.4	37.2
Consumer price growth	8.2	47.5	5.2	2.5
Real export growth	24.3	-5.3	-7.8	45.7

porters, the premier gradually earned the respect of the wider population, which recognized that the burden of price inflation would have fallen on its shoulders.[35]

What Table 6.2 shows, besides disastrous economic results in 1974 and 1975, is a substantial recovery by 1976. The ROC mitigated the damage from the oil crisis and de-recognition through two main tools—reining in inflation through conservative fiscal policies and actively promoting its export sector through an enhancement of international competitiveness. In 1975, the government organized the First Nation-Wide Economic Conference to bring together the private and public sectors to discuss how to overcome the recession produced by the oil crisis. Business leaders were given an expanded role in fashioning economic policy and, for the third time, the circle of elites widened. This rapid socioeconomic change and restructuring of the traditional elites served as a catalyst for further political reform. The growing entrepreneurial class began to exert its influence and saw in the opposition a force that could effect compromise from the KMT.

One of the first policies recommended by the business-government coalition was a reassessment and reduction of the government's role in the economy. The criticisms of the government sector focused on four areas:[36]

1. Public sector enterprises are inefficient;

2. Individual decisionmaking in the government, without the monitoring device of personal loss, leads to disastrous consequences for the country;

35   A good discussion of this is contained in Fei (1993).
36   Yu (1985, p. 5).

3. Public sector concerns produce inferior commodities and services in relation to those produced by the private market;

4. There is no appropriate decision matrix to justify "competition between public and private enterprises over profits."

Taiwan's movement from a developmental state, in which the regime plays an active and intrusive role in the economy, to a regulatory state, in which the government merely facilitates the process, came about, in large part, from the constant pressure of the rapidly increasing business class. One outcome from the conference was the clear consensus of the business community that financial liberalization was necessary if Taiwan was to win back the international investors and consumers lost to an appreciating Taiwanese dollar and political alienation. Through a concerted effort to rein in inflation and continue the privatization of the SOEs, the ROC advanced from the 24th largest trading nation in 1979 to the 12th largest by 1992[37] (Figure 6.7).

By the end of the decade, it appeared that Taiwan had overcome its oil crisis recession. Real GNP averaged 12 percent growth between

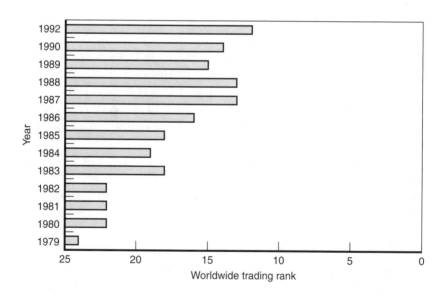

Figure 6.7. Taiwan's Worldwide Trading Rank: 1979–1992

37   United Nations, *Monthly Bulletin of Statistics,* various years.

1976 and 1979, per capita income rose from US$956 to over US$1,600, and the trade surplus grew to US$1.7 billion in 1978, an indicator of Taiwan's successful export strategies. The second oil embargo, of 1979–1980, temporarily halted this economic expansion, but it did not derail Taiwan's long-term vision of economic success. Taiwan still had one major obstacle to overcome to become a modern market economy—legal and structural barriers preventing international competition within Taiwan's home market. The 1980s would see the elimination of many of these barriers through the strengthening of the independent business class and the simultaneous weakening of the regime.

Although Taiwan survived the 1970s in a relatively strong position economically, politically it was still suffering under the blow of de-recognition. Relations between Taiwan and the United States became extremely tenuous in 1979 when the United States officially recognized the PRC and simultaneously passed into law the Taiwan Relations Act. The act eliminated any official relationship between the United States and Taiwan, substituting instead the American Institute in Taiwan and Taiwan's Coordination Council for North American Affairs. The increasing power and authority granted to the mainland forced a reevaluation of the KMT both inside and outside the party. It had been over 25 years since the exodus to Taiwan. Was it time to reassess the mission of the ROC? Would the KMT reconquer the mainland or was it staffed with old Mainlanders who dreamed dreams of glory from the safety of their rocking chairs? First in hushed tones, but then in louder voices as the decade drew to a close, Taiwanese began to ask these questions. Urban-based politicians with roots in the regional opposition parties found common ground in their vision for the future of the ROC. These early discussions would evolve, over the next decade, into Taiwan's first successful opposition party—the Democratic Progressive Party (DPP). However, back in the late 1970s, these discussions led President Chiang, suffering from diabetes and quite removed from his younger colleagues, to begin grooming the much younger prime minister, Sun Yun-hsuan, as his successor.

THE TRANSITION TO DEMOCRACY: THE 1980s

As the 1980s began, Taiwan continued on its path toward privatization. The ruling elites recognized, albeit reluctantly, that a vibrant economic sphere, separate and distinct from excessive government control or influence, would further Taiwan's development. Taking steps to promote such growth, the government enlarged the sphere of personal property rights and continued to encourage free enterprise.

Figure 6.8 depicts the gradual, yet continuous, shift in ownership of Taiwan's industrial base from the public sector to the private sphere.[38]

Much of the growth in nongovernmental business took place in the small and medium-sized firm sector. Having gathered clout in the 1970s, by 1982 small and medium-sized firms represented 95 percent of all firms and provided 70 percent of employment, 65 percent of total business revenue, and 65 percent of export earnings. The continued viability of the entrepreneur is crucial to marketization efforts in Taiwan. Marketization not only encompasses the transfer of ownership from the government to the private sector but includes the rise of an entrepreneurial class that can lead the country's drive toward economic growth and prosperity. In Taiwan this has meant keeping the economy competitive with low barriers to entry so that small entrepreneurs can gain a foothold.

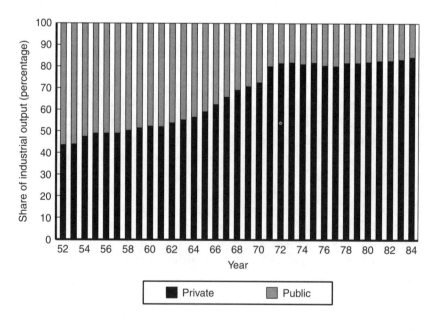

Figure 6.8. Public versus Private Industrial Output in Taiwan: 1952–1984

38   *Taiwan Statistical Data Book,* various years.

After recovering from the second oil crisis, Taiwan embarked on a concerted effort to open its markets. Import and payment liberalization were accelerated by reducing tariffs and quotas and allowing the market to determine exchange rates. Still, foreign investments were subject to restrictions under the 1961 Statute for the Encouragement of Investment, which limited foreign investment into key sectors. Coupled with the difficulty in repatriating its profits abroad was the risk of losing its foreign direct investment base. As a result, Taiwan allowed the Taiwanese dollar to float within a given range in 1979 as part of a broader liberalization package, a change from the adjustable peg to the U.S. dollar Taiwan had relied on for most of the 1970s.

To further international integration and maintain a steady flow of foreign direct investment, a central rate trading system was established in the foreign exchange market in 1982. Direct foreign investment into Taiwan was extremely important in building Taiwan's export markets, advancing its technological base, and solidifying the trend toward economic and political liberalization. In 1977–1979, foreign investment in Taiwan accounted for 29 percent of Taiwan's exports. By 1982 certain sectors, such as electronics and chemicals, had a foreign investment rate of over 60 percent.[39] Figure 6.9 traces the increase of DFI into Taiwan from 1952 through 1990.[40]

As the 1980s continued, Taiwan was faced with a series of economic problems that stemmed from its rapid expansion over the previous two decades. Taiwan's 1986 merchandise trade surplus as a share of GNP was 19.3 percent, the highest of any non–oil-producing country. This massive surplus put upward pressure on the Taiwanese dollar, eroding Taiwan's international competitiveness. Aside from the natural market mechanism in place to appreciate its currency, Taiwan bowed to U.S. pressure to cut Taiwan's trade surplus and allowed the Taiwanese dollar to appreciate 32 percent against the U.S. dollar in the 1985–1988 period. In 1986, foreign banks were allowed to set up branches in Taiwan, and, in 1989, capital inflow limitations were increased to US$1 million from US$200,000.[41] In addition to the currency appreciation, Taiwan removed all foreign exchange controls in June 1987; substantially lowered import tariffs; relaxed import restrictions, such as the issuance of import documents; and opened the domestic market to foreign

39   Cheng (1992).
40   Investment Commission, various years.
41   Moreno (n.d.).

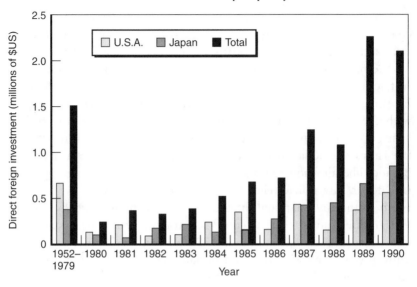

Figure 6.9. Increase of Direct Foreign Investment in Taiwan: 1952–1990

competition in fast food services, banks, insurance, and leasing agencies.[42] The limited float on its currency exchange remained in effect until 1989 when the Taiwanese dollar was allowed to float freely.

Taiwan had to deal not only with the rapid appreciation of the currency, but also with its massive foreign exchange holdings, the rapid growth of its money supply, and its escalating excess savings. Fiscal policymakers began to heed the advice of economists that, in part, Taiwan's unusually high savings rate was due to market distortions and highly regulated equity markets.[43] Although Taiwan supported a number of different types of financial institutions, from its central bank to full service domestic commercial banks, foreign bank branches, and investment and trust companies, the size of the curb market remained extremely high throughout the 1960s and 1970s, reflecting the shallowness of the financial market. From 1964 to 1970, curb market financing accounted for 27.22 percent of all business financing, totaling over NT$14 million. Because of the gradual market opening mechanism imposed in the mid 1970s, the curb market fell to 25.72 percent between

42   For an expanded discussion, see Schive (1995, p. 13).
43   Woo and Liu (1994, p. 92).

1981 and 1987.[44] Taiwan continued to marketize its banking system (Figure 6.10), yet it was a difficult task to break banks of the habit of allocating funds solely on the basis of favoritism and of pricing small and medium-sized firms out of the market by demanding high levels of collateral.[45] In 1983, firms with assets under NT$1 million relied on the curb market for 89 percent of their funding, whereas firms valued at above NT$1 billion counted on the curb market for about 10 percent.[46]

Taiwan was able to overcome the economic setbacks of the late 1970s and early 1980s by relying on the mechanisms that had originally created its stunning growth—successfully shifting from low-tech, low-skilled agriculture and manufacturing to higher-value-added, higher-skilled production (thereby increasing the level of productivity) and by opening its financial sector to more competition. The first policy con-

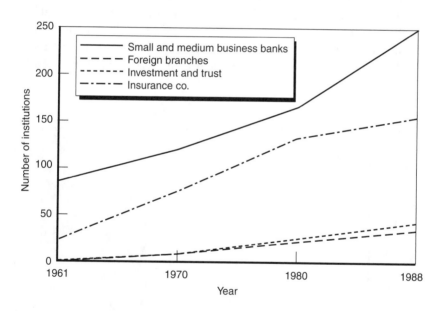

Figure 6.10. Number of Financial Institutions in Taiwan: 1961–1988

44   Ministry of Finance, SEC Statistics, 1988; Woo and Liu (1994, p. 203).
45   *Yearbook of Financial Statistics of the ROC* (1988); *Taiwan Statistical Data Book,* various years.
46   Shen and Yang (1994, p. 214).

tinued the expansion of GDP per capita. The second policy kept the market functioning and permitted the broad distribution of economic power. Both policies served to strengthen the voice of citizens in demanding responsiveness from their government. Figure 6.11 shows the remarkable change in productivity from 1952 to 1986.[47]

These rapid changes in the structure of the Taiwanese economy in the late 1970s led to modifications in the political landscape during the next decade. In particular, three events in the early 1980s led to the appointment of Lee Teng-hui, the man who would oversee Taiwan's transition to democracy. In the 1980 elections of the Supplementary Legislative Yuan, opposition candidates won a significant number of seats, thereby setting the stage for the beginning of political discord and the first serious breaches of authoritarianism. Second, President Chiang, to break with the regime's history of martial law, demoted the head of the military's political warfare department, Wang Sheng, effectively denying the military a strong position in Chiang's succession. Finally, Chiang's handpicked heir apparent, Sun Yun-hsuan, suffered a cerebral hemorrhage, opening the field to more nontraditional candidates.

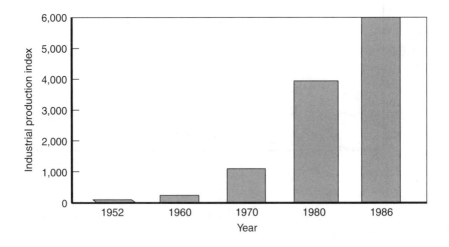

Figure 6.11. Taiwan's Industrial Production Index: 1952–1986

47   *Yearbook of Financial Statistics of the ROC* (1988); *Taiwan Statistical Data Book,* various years.

In February 1984, Chiang picked Lee Teng-hui, a Taiwanese, as his vice-presidential running mate. The old guard within the KMT recognized the shift in the political winds. Lee, a political outsider and Taiwanese, was not trusted. Only Chiang Ching-kuo's absolute authority within the KMT allowed him to embark on a cautious path toward native Taiwanese rule and a more independent stance from the mainland. There is strong evidence that Chiang Ching-kuo recognized the uncertainty of the KMT's political future and sought to forestall its demise by agreeing to a devolution of power in the short term in exchange for a longer tenure of control. The selection of Lee was part of the bargain; so was the eventual legalization of the DPP. A third aspect may have been Chiang Ching-kuo's announcement, near the end of his career, that he considered himself Taiwanese.[48]

The powerful Mainlanders in the KMT were correct in their suspicions that change was on the horizon, for on March 22, 1984, when Lee Teng-hui became the seventh Vice President of the Republic of China, the authoritarian regime of Taiwan entered its final phase of existence. The next three years established the base for the democratic transition within Taiwan with the formal establishment of the first opposition party, the lifting of martial law, the removal of restrictions on the press, and parliamentary and constitutional reforms.

On March 29–31, 1986, in a series of speeches to the KMT elite and rank and file, President Chiang Ching-kuo announced that the time had come for political reform and that he was establishing a committee to investigate policy options. The major reforms included:

1. *Lifting of martial law.* This was favored by academics, intellectuals, activists, and even some supporters of the old line, since, by 1986, the costs of martial law clearly outweighed its benefits. Despite this analysis, a substantial core of the KMT favored keeping the law in place, as it provided political stability amid threats from the mainland that had yet to dissipate. Nonetheless, the newly formed DPP convinced the majority of the KMT leadership to adopt a weakened national security strategy and lift martial law. After nearly four decades, martial law was abolished on July 15, 1987. The KMT's decision to promote democracy came after strong pressure from the opposition DPP, as well as from a broad-based coalition of citizens.[49] Part of the DPP's rhetoric revolved around the need for Taiwan to reevaluate its

---

48 Winckler (1993, p. 117).
49 Ting (1991, p. 75).

relationship with the mainland. The DPP pointed to the hypocrisy of the official policy of "no contact, no negotiation, no compromise" on the one hand and the ever-increasing economic ties between the two nations on the other. In the early 1980s, as Taiwan's economic environment began to erode, financiers broadened their investment horizon. Market returns outweighed political ideology, and Taiwanese capital began to flood onto the mainland.

2. An *end to the ban on political parties*. Imposed in 1949, the provision was first used in 1960 to jail Lei Chen, editor of *Free China*. Into the 1980s, Lei Chen remained a hero to many. Robert Dahl argues that a democratic transition occurs when political opposition is institutionalized and competition for control exists in both national and local elections.[50] Institutionalization of the opposition, brewing for the last decade, became formalized in September 1986, when 112 Tangwai leaders formed the Democratic Progressive Party, the first true opposition party in Taiwan since 1949. In its first race for power, the DPP won 12 seats of the 95 contested in the Legislative Yuan election in November 1986.

Although the DPP became the strongest opposition voice within Taiwan's political structure, it did not remain the only one. During the 40 years of martial law, there were only three registered political parties, but by 1992, the number was up to 69.[51] In November 1987, the influential Labor Party was formed. The strength of the opposition was a direct outgrowth of the expanding circle of elites who were not satisfied with the KMT government and were ready to field their own candidates.

3. *Reform of the national legislature and local government system.* The National Legislature comprises three bodies: the Legislative Yuan, the Control Yuan, and the National Assembly.

The legislature has two categories of members—those chosen in Mainland China in 1947 and those elected since 1947 from the Taiwanese and overseas Chinese communities. Although the first category held a majority throughout the 1980s, most of these officials were elderly and supported views contrary to those of both the younger representatives and citizens in general. The younger delegates realized that a reform of Taiwanese politics would be possible only after the retirement of the elderly KMT members. During 1988, a plan was developed

50   Dahl (1971, pp. 4–14).
51   Soong (1992).

for providing retirement incentives. To ensure the transition, any member who failed to attend two consecutive legislative functions was to be retired with or without his consent. The plan was implemented in January 1989.

Reformation of the central and local governments, as well as the increased distribution of economic power derived from marketization, encouraged citizens, previously apathetic in their involvement in governmental affairs, to run for office and otherwise become involved in the political arena. The growth of the private sector created an elite separate from the government and free of the KMT's control. These young entrepreneurs, and the intellectuals who were mostly educated in the West and who found this rising business class a perfect vehicle for pursuing their own political agendas, began to expand their influence out from their traditional realm (the marketplace) and into the political sphere. The halls of political power, once closed to native Taiwanese, were opening in the wake of a reality where party politics no longer outweighed economic power, in terms of importance to the state. Included in this group of the new elite, willing to take advantage of the openness provided by increased economic liberalization, were various social segments that mobilized themselves into political action groups. Intent on opening the doors of power and providing for themselves a measure of political autonomy, these groups included organized consumer movements led by urban intellectuals and professionals, conservation groups, and women's movements. Probably the best organized and the most determined of these groups was the farmers' movement.

The farmers' movement had been in existence since the 1960s, but during the 1980s it changed from a small, loosely based grass roots association to a well-organized national establishment. In 1986, the farmers of Yunlin and Chiayi counties refused to pay their irrigation water tax, setting off a round of protests that would lead to a drastic change in the government of Taiwan. On December 13, 1987, representatives of the movement agreed to present the protesting farmers' demands to the Legislative Yuan. The farmers called for the establishment of a Ministry of Agriculture (which would allow farmers to participate in farm policy decisionmaking), a restriction on imported fruit, improvements in farm product marketing, the establishment of an equity fund for agricultural products, and the enactment of a farmers' health insurance system.[52] The Legislative Yuan paid little more than

52   Hsin-Huang (1994, p. 214).

lip service to the farmers' representatives, leading to an escalation of street protests in 1988. At one point, the protests became so frequent and the disruption so great that 75 KMT legislators requested the reimposition of martial law. Their request was denied and the farmers' movement became, along with a number of growing social organizations, instrumental in ushering in democracy. By the late 1980s, the circle of elites had widened to such an extent that a broad segment of Taiwan's society was now actively involved in the functioning of the government. The schism between the Mainlanders, who once controlled the party and the state, and the Taiwanese was closing in upon itself. The time had come for democratic reforms.

In 1988, for the first time in the history of the ROC, a majority of the KMT Central Standing Committee's members were Taiwanese natives (16 out of 31). Increased participation by the populace not only increased membership in the KMT but swelled the ranks of opposition parties. In late 1989, the KMT suffered its first serious setback when the DPP captured six county seats, putting them in a good position for the 1990 elections.

July 4, 1990, was a high-water mark in the path toward Taiwan's democratic future. The DPP and the KMT agreed to work together to find a way to hold direct presidential elections in the near future, to revise the Constitution, and to eliminate the provisional articles added in 1948 to the 1947 Constitution, in which the president retained absolute authority. The rationale at the time was that Taiwan was in a state of war with the Communists. In 1990, with a booming economy and a politically liberalizing system, citizens (voicing their criticism through the DPP) found the state-of-war rationale less compelling. An illegal political party just four years previously, the DPP was changing the face of the ROC both in the halls of government and out on the street where demonstrations organized by the DPP and its allies—laborers, farmers, and ordinary citizens resentful of the regime's intrusions into their lives—erupted every few weeks.[53]

Despite its base of support, in the Second National Assembly elections of 1991, the DPP was handed a stunning defeat, winning only 23 percent of the vote. Political analysts believed that although the general public supported the DPP's reform measures, they shunned the party's more strident talk of independence.[54] Nonetheless, the DPP moved fur-

53   Myers (1994, pp. 53–54).
54   Soong (1992).

ther in the direction of independence when it announced, in October 1992, that its party platform included the following three planks: (1) Taiwan does not belong to the PRC, it has an independent sovereignty; (2) Taiwan should adopt a "one China, one Taiwan policy"; and (3) the PRC is a sovereign government governing Mainland China.[55]

CONSOLIDATION AND TRANSFORMATION

The effect of the 1987 reforms was the consolidation of democracy and a normalization of politics. Normalization included the 1991 repeal of the Temporary Provisions Effective During the Period of Mobilization for the Suppression of the Communist Rebellion, the establishment of a constitutional government, the formation of the Chinese New Party in 1993, and the rise of interest group politics.

In the early 1990s, Taiwan embarked on a transformation of its electoral system—the hallmark of democracy. The elections of December 3, 1994, highlighted a shift in voter attitudes from concern over parochial issues to an awareness of more general issues and platforms. In the election for the mayor and city council of Taipei, the DPP won with 43.76 percent of the vote, with the KMT coming in a distant third. The KMT was shocked by the stunning defeat. Table 6.3 shows the steady erosion of KMT authority.[56]

The question remains whether the KMT can survive the political transition that is clearly under way. Wang Jin-pyng, a KMT lawmaker, remarked in a *Far Eastern Economic Review* article that he believes the

Table 6.3. *KMT seats in the Taipei Municipal Council*

Year	% of Seats
1977	85
1981	75
1985	73
1989	71
1994	38

55   Auw (1994, p. 9).
56   Wu (1995, p. 97) writes that "the fact that three-quarters of the Taipei electorate chose not to support the KMT incumbent sent a shock wave through the ruling party which had become accustomed to dominating the capital city."

problem of Taiwanese reform lies in the fact that for "many years, the KMT made decisions in total disregard of party and public opinion. This practice has to change and has already changed a great deal. But the changes have not yet gone far enough."[57] The public obviously agreed when they voted down the KMT in the 1994 elections. The KMT lost 10.7 percent of its seats in the Provincial Assembly, 34.1 percent in the Taipei City Council, and 16.8 percent in the Kaoshiung City Council. The KMT losses shifted the KMT from being the "ruling party" to the "majority party."[58]

There was one bright spot for the KMT however. In the race for governor of Taiwan Province, the KMT candidate, James Soong, won 56.2 percent of the vote. Soong's landslide victory shocked the DPP, but the opposition accepted the result without incident, proving that a peaceful transition of power was possible. Representative government and a peaceful transition of power were achieved through the widening of the circle of economic elites brought about through marketization (Figure 6.12). These new elites—the farmers' movement, the small and medium-sized firm owner, and the foreign-trained technocrats—recognized that they must take an active role in government if they were to maintain their economic independence. Their increasing economic power served as a counterbalance to the vested interests of the KMT and a shift in regime became inevitable.

The inevitable moved one step closer when the results of the mayoral and municipal elections held on November 29, 1997, were announced. The DPP had won 12 of the 29 contested local government posts. Even more astonishing, for the first time, the DPP won a higher percentage of the popular vote: 43 percent to the KMT's 42 percent. As a consequence, more than 70 percent of all Taiwanese now reside in DPP-controlled districts. The unthinkable, that the KMT could lose the presidency in the 2000 elections, had become a distinct possibility.

STUMBLING BLOCKS TO FURTHER DEMOCRACY

Although Taiwan has become, for all intents and purposes, a fledgling democratic nation, the country still faces a number of hurdles to assure the long-term viability of its democratic institutions, including

57   Baum (1993, p. 11).
58   Taiwan Communiqué (1995).

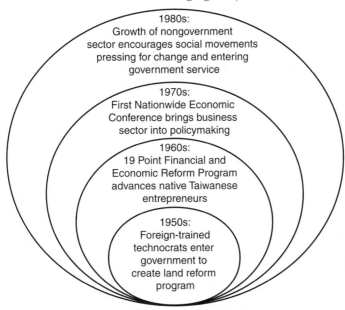

Figure 6.12. The Widening of the Circle of Taiwan's Elites

a crackdown on political corruption and the strengthening of the rule of law. In 1993, Premier Lien Chan wrote that Taiwan's

> greatest cause for concern is lack of respect for the rule of law. Democratic government means government by the law; this is basic common sense, but is also a truth that is easy to disregard. Our people speak out their support for democracy and fight for rights; but at the same time they are unwilling to accept the controls of law and justice, and their burden of responsibilities to society. There is an increasing tendency to make any and every issue into a political issue, leading to widespread skirting of the law, playing with the law, and violation of the law.[59]

In particular, the polarization of extremists is cause for concern—that opposition forces will refuse to join the process and will thereby delegitimize the outcome. Constitutional reform hinges on whether the country's political parties can engage in a free and open exchange and accept citizens' determination of who won the debate. All participants

59   From a speech delivered at the opening of the 14th National Congress of the Kuomintang on August 16, 1993, reported in Hu (1994, p. 12).

must agree to accept the rules that govern the competition and to live by the outcomes dictated by the citizenry. For Taiwan to strengthen its democracy, the "processes" of self-government must be imbedded into the Taiwanese culture. This can come through increased political competition and as an outgrowth of further marketization, which vests the people in the workings of the state.

The power of the KMT resides in its entrenched governmental position and its control over the media and society. The DPP opposition party has learned to rely on elections and the run-up to elections to elicit promises from the KMT and in this manner push through its agenda of reforms. But as the DPP and other opposition parties gain a stronger voice, all must be willing to accept consensus and compromise. This means living with the vagaries of democracy. In a country with a history of an authoritarian regime imposing stability at all costs, this uncertainty is not easy to take. The specter of instability not only frightens the average citizen, it has the tendency to spook the market. An August 23, 1993, *Business Week* article stated that "executives . . . are waking up to a revolution in Taiwanese politics. Big deals clinched with handshakes between political power brokers are falling apart."[60] The reason is that opposition politicians are scuttling favored (and, until recently, politically protected) projects of the KMT. Despite the short-term instability stemming from the change in "business as usual," Taiwan is committed to lessening government corruption. Ma Ying-chiu, Minister of Justice since 1993, has made it his mission to fight corruption. In the last two years, Ma has indicted 341 officials, or 39 percent of Taiwan's 883 city and county councilmen, on vote-buying charges. The courts have convicted 282 of them.[61]

Aside from the "democracy pains" Taiwan may suffer as it moves from a centrally controlled economy and political system to a more liberalized one, the prognosis is positive for continued reform. As long as marketization advances, citizens prosper, and active hostilities with the mainland do not resume, democracy should continue to strengthen on the island of Taiwan.

The United States can take an active role in ensuring Taiwan's continued reformation. Martial law in Taiwan never sat well with the United States, and the murder of Henry Liu in California in 1984 by Taiwan's military intelligence authorities served to increase the pressure

60   Engardio and Wehrfritz (1993, p. 40).
61   Wong (1995).

to reform politically.[62] Strong allies in Congress did battle with those who wondered why the United States should support an authoritarian regime. During this period, trading ties between the countries continued to strengthen while the political association remained stalled. This netherworld of a relationship remains suboptimal to both sides and becomes less viable as the U.S. trade imbalance with Taiwan grows. In 1988, the U.S. Department of Commerce recognized that "the burgeoning U.S.-Taiwan trade balance is a matter of serious concern to both Taiwan and the United States. In the absence of diplomatic ties, harmonious commercial relations, particularly with a former ally and important trading partner, are of considerable importance not only to Taiwan's domestic economy but also to its international status."[63]

In a 1994 conference sponsored by the Carnegie Council on Ethics and International Affairs entitled *Policy Development in Democracy: U.S.-ROC Relations Toward the Twenty-First Century*, the dominant opinion expressed by the panelists was that the U.S.-ROC relationship should be strengthened. There was no clear consensus, however, on the way to accomplish these stronger ties and the proper pace of improving the relationship. Robert Sutter, senior specialist in international policy for the Congressional Research Service, summed up the two main positions as follows. First, there are those U.S. policymakers who believe that the entire U.S.-Taiwan relationship should be predicated on the cross-strait relationship between the PRC and Taiwan. For the time being, this means slow going for any type of relationship between the United States and Taiwan. The second camp argues that the PRC should not be the determining factor upon which the Taiwan relationship is based. Taiwan is an economic power, an emerging democracy, and a legitimate counterbalance to the PRC (the "Taiwan card"). Whereas Sutter concluded his remarks by saying that he thinks the "pendulum is swinging toward those who favor moving forward on Taiwan," his comments came before Lee Teng-hui's visit to his alma mater, Cornell, and the resulting backlash from the PRC. The PRC viewed the U.S. visa for Lee as a validation of their fears that Taiwan was indeed actively seeking independence. Expressing its anger at the United States for granting Lee recognition, as well as for being duped into assisting Taipei in baiting Beijing, the PRC imprisoned American

---

62 Nathan and Ho (1993, p. 48).
63 U.S. Department of Commerce (1988, p. 4).

Harry Wu and rejected a bid by the Big Three automakers in favor of Mercedes-Benz for a lucrative van and engine contract.

Reinforcing their policy that Taiwan will never become independent, the mainland began a series of cross-strait military exercises, building up to a significant show of strength in the weeks before the Legislative Yuan elections in December 1995.[64] When the intimidation failed to work, the Chinese stepped up their vitriol against the man who would be Taiwan's first democratically elected president, Lee Teng-hui. Backing up their hostile words, the PRC undertook a battery of missile tests across the strait and a highly profiled amphibious training session on the eve of the March 1996 elections. The United States was forced to dispatch two aircraft carrier battle groups to the strait to impress upon the Chinese that their actions were not taken lightly. Whether intending to or not, Taiwan had sent the U.S.-PRC relationship to its lowest level in decades. Taiwan is not blind to the dilemma of the United States. The United States remains committed to peaceful reunification and the One China Policy, as well as an opening of the Chinese market, but is unwilling to let its democratic ally Taiwan go it alone. However, it is unclear whether, in the event that Taiwan declares independence, the United States will sanction the spilling of American blood to protect Taiwan's movement from a de facto to a de jure independent country. So for now, the U.S. policy toward Taiwan remains ambiguous, the Taiwanese policy toward the PRC remains one of antagonize and pacify, and the PRC refuses to denounce the use of force in maintaining one China.

Many on the island nation realize that their best chance of rejoining the international community lies not in outright confrontation with the mainland, but through a steady transformation of the PRC into a marketized economy. Casper Shih, General Manager of the China Productivity Center, writes that for the good of Taiwan and the Chinese people the world over, Taiwan should embark on a three-point economic plan in its dealings with Mainland China. First, Taiwan should undertake a training and education program of high-ranking mainland

64   The 1995 follow-up talks to the 1993 talks between Wan Daohan, of Mainland China's Association for Relations Across the Taiwan Straits, and Koo Chen-Foo, of Taiwan's Straits Exchange Foundation, were also canceled. Many viewed the Wan-Koo talks as the best hope for resolving the ongoing civil war, and their cancellation in 1995 was seen as a symbol of how fraught with danger the situation had become.

businessmen. Second, since "thought is the foundation of all actions," Mainlanders should become familiar with the concepts of the free market through extended visits to Taiwan, which will hasten economic and political liberalization on the mainland. And third, the transfer of experience to small and medium-sized enterprises on the mainland should be encouraged through a broad organization composed of the Taiwanese currently investing in the mainland.[65] In 1992, the *Asian Wall Street Journal* interviewed a Taiwanese financier doing business on the mainland who believed that the Taiwanese were the catalyst behind the democratic reforms occurring in the PRC. His plan for promoting democracy in the PRC entailed "encouraging Chinese to make lots of money, then proselytizing democratic virtues. It worked that way on Taiwan. Businessmen like me are the revolutionaries."[66] The increased economic ties between the two Chinas are clearly visible in Figure 6.13.[67]

The growing economic and social linkages between Taiwan and the mainland, coupled with the ROC's political liberalization, bode well for

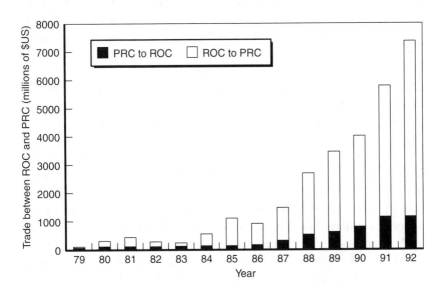

Figure 6.13. Increase in Trade Between Taiwan and the PRC: 1979–1992

65   Shih (1994, p. 141).
66   Brick (1992).
67   *Taiwan Statistical Data Book*, various years.

Taiwan's future. Nonetheless, both Taiwan's internal evolution and the cross-strait relationship are fraught with potential hazards that could, under certain scenarios, reverse the economic and political modernizations that Taiwan has achieved. In Taipei, partisan politics may strangle the country's fragile attempts to systematically embark on the constitutional reforms that have been evolving in a piecemeal fashion over the last decade. The KMT, not completely free of its Leninist roots and willing to mobilize its vast political and economic resources to pursue its agenda, still struggles with the pace of political liberalization.[68] President Lee, against the counsel of many of his advisers, has begun advocating a "chieh-chi yung-jen (preventing eagerness and exercising patience)" policy toward investment on the mainland.

Direct contact between the PRC and Taiwan, which had been suspended since 1995, was resumed in 1998. However, the two sides remain deadlocked over the same set of issues that has bedeviled them for decades. The PRC demands that Taiwan accept the principle of One China and halt its maneuvering to gain further international recognition. Taipei refuses to engage in negotiations on anything other than "technical" issues, brushing aside China's calls for "political" discussions, and demands that Beijing renounce the use of force. Aside from these lingering issues, there is reason to believe that the situation across the strait is becoming unstable. China continues to modernize and professionalize its military, and it is increasing the size of its conventionally armed ballistic missile force. The best estimates of the U.S. Department of Defense are that despite "anticipated improvements to Taiwan's missile and air defense systems, by 2005, the PLA will possess the capability to attack Taiwan with air and missile strikes which would degrade key military facilities and damage the island's economic infrastructure."[69] Meanwhile, the generation of Mainlanders in Taiwan continues to fade from the scene, and the younger population increasingly identifies itself as Taiwanese rather than Chinese, which tends to suggest that the voices for independence will become louder in the future. Ultimately, the status across the Taiwan Strait will be a matter for PRC and Taiwan to decide between themselves. The best the world can do is to assist Taiwan in its transformation toward a fuller democracy and hope that China follows suit.

68   For an excellent discussion of the future of Taiwan, see Goldstein (1997).
69   U.S. Department of Defense (1999).

7

Indonesia: Unrealized potential

Indonesia, a country of 210 million citizens and over 13,000 islands, is little understood outside East Asia, and many would argue that it is misunderstood even within its own part of the world. For the past three decades, following the 1965 coup and the ouster of the flamboyant Sukarno regime, Indonesia has been relegated to the backburner of international geopolitics as a politically stable country that promotes Western interests in the region and poses little threat to the status quo.

In the fall of 1997, Indonesia crashed onto the world stage as a victim and, many would argue, a perpetrator of the Asian financial crisis. The rupiah and Jakarta stock market crumbled nearly beyond repair, numerous large companies went bankrupt, the country's GDP per capita fell from US$1,700 to US$300, and the International Monetary Fund had to step in with a $43 billion bailout package to salvage what remained of the economy. This type of notoriety was not what the Indonesian leadership had in mind in the early 1980s as it went about fashioning a higher profile for itself upon the world stage. But the humiliation of having to go, hat in hand, to the lender of last resort, would not wind up being the world's lasting image of Indonesia. Those images were replaced, in the spring of 1998, by images of university students storming the gates of Parliament, demonstrating on college campuses across the country, and, most strikingly, embracing soldiers that were sent to contain them. The images of Indonesia as a beggar nation were also replaced by images of Asia's longest-ruling autocrat, Suharto, peacefully stepping aside to watch the inauguration of his Vice President, BJ Habibie, as the nation's third president since independence.

Despite the economic setbacks and political turmoil that it has suffered, Indonesia remains a de facto major subregional power. Over the last two decades, it has used its growing economic might, large population (fourth largest in the world), and vast territory to become head of the Non-Aligned Movement, champion of the Third World, and vocal spokesperson within the Association of South East Asian Nations (ASEAN), the ASEAN Regional Forum (ARF), and the Asian Pacific Economic Cooperation (APEC). Indonesia possesses a well-financed and technologically sophisticated military and a significant amount of natural resources. If the country heeds the advice of the IMF and marketizes its economy, and listens to the Indonesian people and reforms its political structure, Indonesia may yet be able to transform itself into an economic success, regional leader, and functioning democracy.

Nonetheless, it would be naïve at best and dangerous at worst to ignore the number of serious hurdles that remain to dash any hope of these scenarios unfolding. Although the IMF plan will help push the economy toward fuller liberalization, it does not go far enough in removing the many government monopolies that still exist and does not even attempt to help create a bureaucratic culture of deregulation to ensure the long-term implementation of market-opening measures. In addition, Indonesia, one of OPEC's founding members, is scheduled to become an oil importer by the turn of the century, ending one of the government's most lucrative sources of revenue. Internationally, Indonesia's efforts to gain worldwide recognition may be doomed by future conflicts with its ASEAN neighbors, as well as potential discord with China. Finally, despite Suharto's resignation and Habibie's calls for new elections, Indonesia's political landscape will remain rocky for some time. In the aftermath of Suharto's political demise, the dam that held many political aspirations in check broke. Within days of Suharto's ouster, dozens of political parties formed and the political stage became a free-for-all on which numerous competing actors all read from different scripts.

This chapter analyzes the likely economic and political future of Indonesia by addressing whether the nation will become more politically open as its economy liberalizes or whether destabilizing factors will prevent such a transformation despite growing marketization and prosperity. Four key interest groups are discussed in light of their potential roles in this transition: the entrenched bureaucracy, the

Angkatan Bersenjata Republik Indonesia (the military, or ABRI), the business elite, and the general citizenry.

THE PERIOD OF GUIDED DEMOCRACY: 1959–1965

The modern history of Indonesia began with Suharto's rise to power in 1965, but understanding a number of the key elements that drive many of the policy decisions in the New Order regime necessitates a basic understanding of the Sukarno era.

After 350 years of colonial rule by the Dutch, with a brief but brutal repression by the Japanese during World War II, Indonesia declared its independence in 1945. A short Constitution was drawn and the colony declared war on the Netherlands. Formal recognition of independence was granted in 1949. A new Constitution was ratified in 1950, organizing the nation as a parliamentary democracy with an independent judiciary, government accountability, and guarantees for individual freedom. This period of "liberal democracy" lasted from 1950 to 1957. The final free multi-party election was held in 1955, when 90 percent of the populace voted but no clear majority emerged. Sukarno's Indonesian Nationalist Party garnered top honors with 22.3 percent of the vote. Despite its attempt at instituting liberal democracy, the young nation failed in its efforts of consensus building. Sukarno seized power in 1959, disbanded the National Assembly, reinstituted the 1945 Constitution, and declared the beginning of his "Guided Democracy" regime.

Sukarno advocated an Indonesian-style democracy based on consensus (his) and communal order. Western democracy, he advised, could not work in a country as diverse as Indonesia. Although liberal democracy was premised on competition between parties, Indonesia sought and desired unity. According to Sukarno, unity could be achieved only through the strong leadership of the President and an obedient citizenry. The new President legitimized his actions by reinstating the 1945 Constitution, under which "all power and responsibility [for the State] resides in the hands of the president." Under Sukarno's Guided Democracy, Indonesian statehood would rest on five principles (panca sila): belief in one Supreme God, justice and civility among peoples, the unity of Indonesia, democracy through deliberation and consensus among representatives, and social justice for all. In theory, panca sila differed little from the ideology of the West. In practice, panca sila became the underlying structure for an intolerance of regionalism and a Javanese-dominated political culture. In Sukarno's own words, Guided Democracy's main ingredient is "leadership. The Guider . . . incorporates a spoonful of so and so's opinions with a dash of such-and-such, always taking care to incorporate a soupçon of the opposition. Then he cooks it and serves his final summation with 'OK, now my dear brothers, it is is like this and I hope you agree. . . . It's still democratic because everybody has given his comment.'"[1]

By the late 1950s, Sukarno had extended his reach as "Guider" into the economy, believing that economic resources were at his disposal to allocate as he saw fit. Sukarno turned away from a Western-style free market, which was attempted during the early 1950s (as evidenced by the opening of a securities exchange in 1952), and toward a state-controlled economy. In 1958, all Dutch firms on Indonesian soil were nationalized, and trading in shares of Dutch firms was prohibited. Over the next five years, Sukarno nationalized another 800 enterprises. Foreign direct investment trickled to a halt and government debt and inflation skyrocketed. Inflation rose to over 600 percent in both 1965 and 1966, and net foreign exchange reserves fell to *minus* US$75 million.

Sukarno marshaled the resources of the economy to strengthen and arm Indonesia's Communist Party (PKI). Many in the West saw this move as an outgrowth of the hatred Sukarno felt for the West, and a desperate bid to gain a loyal following, rather than as a shared ideology with the Communist regimes of East and Southeast Asia. Nonetheless, in the mid 1960s, Indonesia's Communist Party counted nearly 3 million members. The specter of Indonesia falling into the hands of the Communists not only frightened the West but alienated Indonesia's own military, who were staunchly anti-Communist.

In 1963, Malaysia gained independence from Britain, but Sukarno refused to recognize its neighbor, stating that the new country was a stooge for the colonialists. As part of his aggressive and ill-thought-out foreign policy, Sukarno launched the Konfrontasi (the Crush Malaysia campaign), hoping it would distract both the army and the people from the desperate condition of the economy and the President's unpopular relationship with the Left. Konfrontasi was a failure. Not only did the nation incur the wrath of the West and Indonesia's Asian neighbors, but

1   Sukarno (1965).

it further depleted the country's resources and split an already divided military. Infighting among the regime and the military exacerbated the problems of a degenerating economy and led to a general dissatisfaction with Sukarno and his policies of Guided Democracy.

Into this turmoil stepped a very unlikely leader—General Suharto. Raised in rural Java with little formal education, Suharto rose through the military ranks with an undistinguished career. He was described by a 1945 generation army general as "an unsophisticated regional commander with little time for Western ideas and even less for those around him who espoused them."[2] Suharto saw himself as a man of the people and a protector of the status quo—although he favored progress if it was accomplished in slow and measured steps. His personal style, created while serving in the army but solidified once in power, was to meet people one by one rather than en masse. This business style coined an Indonesian phrase, KISS—Ke istana sendiri-sendiri (to the palace one by one). Both during his military career and in his three decades as President, Suharto used this style to engender staff loyalty by sowing seeds of distrust among his advisers. This modus operandi also succeeded in keeping alliances and organizations, of which he was not a part, from solidifying. Although luck, timing, and bravado played a substantial part in Suharto's initial rise to power, his political acumen was the key to his successful tenure for three decades.

A COUP, ANOTHER COUP, AND A NEW ORDER: THE 1960s

On September 30, 1965, six ABRI generals were murdered and a palace coup attempted. In the three decades since the event, the masterminds of the coup have remained unknown and their motives unclear. The now-official version is that a PKI-backed faction of the army committed the murders in an attempt to overtake the government and install a Revolutionary Council. The army renegades, known as the Thirtieth of September Movement, addressed the nation on the morning of October 1, 1965. They claimed that they were loyal to the regime and their actions had thwarted a CIA-backed coup against Sukarno. At 9 PM on October 1, General Suharto, commander of the Army Strategic Reserve Command, made a radio address in which he announced that the Revolutionary Council were not heroes at all but the ringleaders of a coup against the President. General Suharto then announced that he

---

2   Vatikiotis (1992, p. 31).

had taken control of ABRI, crushed the Thirtieth of September Movement, and restored order to the palace.[3] Whether the initial coup was orchestrated by the PKI (with or without backing from Sukarno), was simply an internal army affair, or was a manipulation by anti-Sukarno ABRI officers (including Suharto) to provide an excuse to crush the PKI may never be known. The event, however, would leave its mark on Indonesia.

In the days that followed the coup attempt, General Suharto consolidated his power within both the army and the regime and laid the groundwork for the ouster of Sukarno by the end of 1966. The public's desire for retribution against the PKI for the killing of the six generals was exploited by ABRI. Citizens were encouraged to alert authorities to the existence of neighborhood PKI members. Muslim leaders were exhorted to "mobilize students from their religious schools to drag Communists, members of pro-PKI organizations, and suspects [including atheists] from their homes and take them to riverbanks where their throats were cut and their bodies thrown into the river."[4]

The public's rage against the PKI, as well as its frustration about the state of the economy (real GDP per capita had fallen to a negative growth rate), quickly escalated into mass rioting and islandwide massacres of PKI members and supporters. Ethnic Chinese enclaves on Java and Sumatra also became targets of the Muslims and Nationalists. The civil strife of late 1965 continued into the early months of 1966. By the time the nation was quieted, hundreds of thousands of Indonesians had died.

On March 11, 1966, Sukarno, under pressure from a newly revitalized ABRI, publicized a letter in which he ordered General Suharto to "take all measures considered necessary to guarantee security, calm, and stability of the government and the revolution." The letter, which became known as the Supersemar (in reference to a Javanese mythological character vested with magical powers), marked the official beginning of Suharto's rule. Within a week, General Suharto had banned the PKI and its affiliated organizations and had arrested key members of Sukarno's cabinet who refused to support the new regime.

Suharto was confirmed as President in March 1968. While Suharto slowly transfigured the old regime into the New Order under the banner "economics first, politics later," a number of aspects of the Guided

---

3   For a more detailed discussion, see Crouch (1988).
4   Crouch (1988, p. 152).

Democracy period remained and more than a few were strengthened. Panca sila became a state ideology, and Javanese hegemony extended to the outer islands. The important role of the military in directing developmental policy and preserving national security was formalized in the Constitution as dwi fungsi, or dual function, permitting the military a reserved number of seats in the parliament as well as the directorship of the regime's political party, Golkar. Golkar was formed in 1964 as an anti-communist movement within ABRI and institutionalized early in the New Order as the government's parliamentary vehicle.

Although the PKI was eradicated and the streets of Java and Sumatra quieted under Suharto's New Order, the underlying societal fissures remained. Schwarz recounts that "a divided Muslim community; a resented ethnic Chinese business class; a weak legal system and, closely related, a rich tradition of corruption, nepotism, smuggling and patronage" continued to plague Indonesia.[5] Intermittently over the next three decades, these sources of instability would return and threaten the unity of the state. Dealt with in various ways during those times, these societal ills persist until today and are the leading factors preventing Indonesia from becoming a liberal democracy.

The years of economic deprivation, as well as unprecedented violence, left the people of Indonesia longing for order and stability. The New Order's promise of economic expansion was widely supported by the majority of Indonesians: students, intellectuals, Muslims (who feared the encroachment of atheistic communists under Sukarno), and the business class (who feared an economic crisis and hoped that Suharto's vision of economic success would come to fruition). In exchange for peace and stability, Indonesians agreed to accept Suharto as a father figure and follow his lead in acknowledging that Western democracy had no place in Indonesia. At the time it seemed a small price to pay for stability.

Suharto's New Order became the foundation for the creation and expansion of industrialization and capitalism. By extension, these policies led to the rise of a capitalist class.[6] To effect this economic restructuring, Suharto relied on a cadre of U.S.-trained neoclassical economists led by Drs. Widjoyo Nitisastro and Ali Wardhana. These men, along with the well-trained crew they enlisted into the New Order, shaped the society in ways that are only beginning to come to light. The tech-

5   Schwarz (1994, p. 3).
6   Robison (1994, p. 41).

nocrats, as they came to be called—both in admiration and in derision—transformed the Indonesian economy. Throughout the 1970s and 1980s, the technocrats implemented policies that would radically restructure the monetary system, the securities exchange, the government budgetary process, and, in general, the fundamental nature of the Indonesian market. The technocrats are largely responsible both for the strength of the Indonesian economy and its prospects for continued viability, and for laying the foundation of greater political liberalization. Their work is even more remarkable given that it was accomplished despite the often clear opposition by the regime (including Suharto) and the ruling elites.

In the first years of the New Order, Suharto gave the technocrats free reign to implement an economic restructuring package and to solicit assistance from the outside world. The technocrats achieved a good deal of success on numerous fronts. Recognizing the need to garner foreign investment and international technical assistance, the technocrats placed a premium on restoring relations, damaged during the Sukarno years, with the world trade system. In their efforts to pursue outside money, the technocrats introduced a dual foreign exchange market and disbanded a number of the control mechanisms over how, and when, foreign exchange could take place.[7]

To restore peaceful ties with its Asian neighbors, Indonesia became a key architect in the formation of the Association of South East Asian Nations (ASEAN), created in 1967. Indonesia's then foreign minister, Adam Malik, believed that ASEAN would ease Indonesia back into the good graces of its neighbors after its confrontation with Malaysia and would show that the nation could exist peacefully without hegemonic designs.

In tandem with the progress being made on the international and economic fronts, Suharto was formulating his plan for the role of the government within society. The new President was convinced that for the economy and the society to recover from Guided Democracy, order must be established. Suharto planned for the state to control the process, both in the political sphere and in the marketplace, but allowed for the average citizen to receive enough freedom to remain passive. Like Sukarno before him, Suharto believed that Western democracy was not appropriate for Indonesia.

---

7   For a more detailed discussion, see Cole and Slade (1996).

"ECONOMICS FIRST, POLITICS SECOND": THE 1970s

After three years of serving as the nation's President, Suharto was officially elected to the office in 1971. The early years of the 1970s were a continuation of the late 1960s with the technocrats steady in their course of economic reform. Their watchwords became stabilization, rehabilitation, and growth. For inspiration, they relied on their Berkeley training and on the examples set by their East Asian neighbors, Taiwan and Korea.[8] Investment was the linchpin of their strategies of growth and, through an amalgam of investment incentives and deregulation, total gross investment as a percentage of GDP rose from 8 percent in 1967 to almost 18 percent in 1973. As seen in Figure 7.1, the emphasis on investment has continued into the 1990s.[9] Meanwhile, the technocrats pushed for a stronger involvement of the general public in the workings of the economy, understanding that the more people

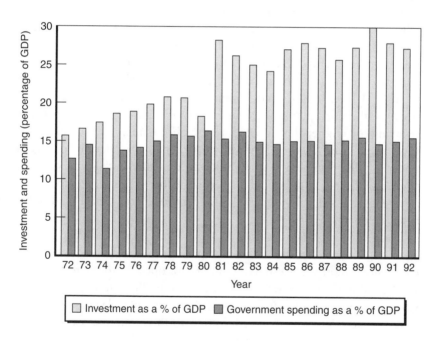

Figure 7.1. Indonesian Investment and Government Spending: 1972–1992

8 See Gillis (1984) for an expanded discussion of these linkages.
9 Summers and Heston (1991).

they could enlist in their struggle for deregulation, the better their chances for successful implementation of their programs. As the Indonesian economist Hadi Soesastro wrote, "Deregulation implies both a reduced role for government intervention and wider and more creative participation by the public."[10] For these sentiments, the technocrats were often branded as reactionaries by more conservative members of the regime.

The first measures enacted by the technocrats were aimed at reining in the inflation that had devastated the economy during the period of Guided Democracy. Tight austerity measures, including a complete ban on construction of government buildings and sharp increases in prices charged by state-owned entities (SOEs), were established. To stabilize the rupiah and help get foreign debt under control, the currency was devalued by 10 percent in 1971. It was hoped that devaluation would increase the amount of reserves held by the treasury. Reserves had fallen to negative levels under Sukarno, had risen sharply in the late 1960s, but had begun to decline after 1970 because of an expanded economy that desired more imports and the weak world prices for primary exports. The devaluation of the rupiah, in conjunction with the austerity measures, increased reserves in 1972 by US$528 million over their 1971 level.[11] After controlling inflation and bulking up foreign reserves, the third plank in the platform for economic growth was the securing of higher levels of foreign aid, loans, and investment. Investment missions were sent abroad to repair the relations damaged under Guided Democracy when Sukarno told the United States to "go to hell with your aid."[12] The overseas effort was mildly successful, raising over US$1.3 billion in U.S. government grants and credits between 1966 and 1975.

Despite the best intentions of the technocrats, not all of their policies were implemented in the manner or pace that they advised. Political concessions granted to vested interest groups opposed to the technocrats resulted in many of the reforms being executed in a piecemeal fashion. Consequently, in numerous sectors of the economy little change was effected. The main sources of opposition to the economic restructuring came from economic nationalists who, having gathered strength in the early 1970s, by the mid 1970s were proclaiming that unless the state

10   Soesastro (1989, p. 853).
11   Gillis (1984, p. 250).
12   As recounted in Schwarz (1994, p. 18).

sponsored research in key areas, Indonesia would forever lag behind its neighbors, Malaysia and Singapore. Joining forces with the economic nationalists were the entrenched monopolists, who understood that deregulation would deprive them of their protected position, and the landholders, who saw the reforms as biased against agriculture. Suharto, in keeping with his style of playing both sides against the middle, continued to encourage his technocrats while at the same time publicly decrying "free-fight capitalism and liberalism," which could break the fragile unity achieved in the wake of Sukarno.

The technocrats had to confront their own concerns as well. They were changing an entire economic system, and although Taiwan and Korea seemed to have made a successful transition, the mid 1970s experience of a number of Latin American countries gave pause. One particular concern of the technocrats was that if deregulation was not enacted evenly across industries or exports, de facto government strategic targeting would replace market driven resource allocation, defeating the basic premise of neoclassical economics. In addition, although economic reform acts were passed into law, the statistical evidence showed that at the sectoral, industry, and local levels, little was implemented. A faction of the technocrats began to push for broader, deeper, and more timely reforms, but the leadership, understanding the political risks inherent in alienating the elites, scaled back the more ambitious proposals. In response to criticism regarding the "muddling-through" nature of deregulation, Ali Wardhana, former Minister of Economic Affairs, has said that the gradual approach "has enabled policy makers and implementors to work within their capacities to plan and execute reforms. Moreover, gradualism has the advantage of progressively winning over a new constituency for further reform."[13] The question remains as to whether any new constituencies were actually converted.

As the economy began to recuperate, Suharto took on the mantle of Bapak Pembangunan (Father of Development). He increased his decisionmaking role by liberally interpreting the 1945 Constitution. Indonesia was formed as a republic, with a separation of powers between the executive, legislative, and judiciary branches, but the President could carry out legislative functions through his position as head of the ruling party of the House of People's Representatives (DPR). Suharto kept a close watch over the DPR by his active involvement in Golkar and by his proclivity to handpick Golkar members of the DPR.

13   Wardhana (1989).

Opposition to the New Order was severely curtailed in 1973 when the regime dissolved nine out of ten of the nation's political parties. Suharto reasoned that "with one and only one road already mapped out, why should we then have nine different cars?"[14] More likely, the restriction on political parties was a result of the 1971 elections in which Golkar received only 61 percent of the vote. To quiet the outcry from the ban, Suharto permitted the formation of two new parties: the PDI (Partai Demokrasi Indonesia, Indonesian Democratic Party—a loose affiliation of Christian and Nationalist groups) and the PPP (Partai Persatuan Pembangunan, United Development Party—composed of an amalgam of Muslim groups). To avoid recreating the opposition once found in the nine banned parties inside the PDI and PPP, Sukarno created the concept of the "Floating Mass." Under this strategy, citizens were allowed to participate in elections every five years but were restricted from political participation in the interim—unless it took the form of political participation within the state-sanctioned activities of Golkar. The reach of Golkar into the business, political, and social life of the ordinary citizen was, and is, overwhelming. Golkar controls youth group activities, religious centers, and business, law, labor, and other professional organizations. The Floating Mass policy not only diminished the organizational capabilities of PPP and PDI, it co-opted a large segment of the population into agreeing that political action taken through Golkar upheld the injunction of panca sila for government democracy through deliberation and consensus among representatives.

Working at odds with the technocrats who persevered in their campaign for less government involvement, Suharto persisted in doling out political and economic favors to key groups of elites. The President's system of favoritism rejuvenated the corruption of the Sukarno years. Despite this, and because of the economic restructuring, foreign investors continued to funnel investment dollars into Indonesia. These foreign dollars were important to the general economy, but they ended up almost exclusively in the hands of the chosen elite—who were primarily of ethnic Chinese origin. Serious dislocations in the economy began to arise. Pribumi, or native Indonesians (as opposed to the ethnic Chinese minority), protested against the influx of Japanese investment and the wealth of the ethnic Chinese, who represented only 3 percent of the population but controlled nearly 75 percent of the capital.

14   Schwarz (1994, p. 32).

In a frightening replay of events from the 1960s, pribumi activists rioted in the streets to protest the Indonesian visit of Japanese Prime Minister Kakuei Tanaka. Both Japanese and ethnic Chinese holdings were destroyed in what became known as the Malari Incident (Malapetaka Januari, or January Incident). The incident would have been important enough if it symbolized only the pribumi's frustration with economic reform and the deep-rooted suspicion of outsiders (ethnic Chinese included). However, the causes and implications of the incident clearly indicated that key leaders within the military were as frustrated with their role in the New Order as was the ordinary citizen.

The dissatisfaction of many key military officers stemmed from the changing role of the armed forces. Established in 1945 to fight for freedom, the older generation of officers believed that the military stood above politics and the political process and embodied the Indonesian national character. Brigadier General Nugroho Notosusanto writes that the Indonesian military

> was born by the Indonesian People in the midst of our struggle for Independence. Members of the [military] are first of all fighters for independence, defenders of justice and truth and shields of the People against all kinds of threats of oppression, exploitation and tyranny. And it is only the second place that members of the [military] have the aspiration to become a professional military.[15]

Because of this self-image, the military lobbied for the enshrinement of dwi fungsi. The generation of 1945, those who had won the country's independence, believed not only that they were entitled to a constitutionally sanctioned role in political affairs but that it was incumbent upon them, as protectors of the country, to ensure order in society through their active participation in policymaking.[16] As the generation of 1945 aged and younger officers, trained in the military academies, were promoted, the concept of dwi fungsi became less appealing. The younger officers wanted a professional military and resented the lack of professionalism among the armed forces as exemplified by Suharto's appointment of "financial" and "political" generals. The military reformers feared that ABRI would lose its position within society as the protector of both national security and development if the populace understood the breadth of corruption in the armed forces that occurred

15 Notosusanto (n.d., p. 128).
16 For a discussion of ABRI's mission, see Singh (1995).

because of the close ties between the military establishment and the business sphere.

In late 1973, the schism between the factions widened when the deputy head of the armed forces and leader of the reformers, Lt. General Sumitro, openly criticized recent statements by the regime. Early in January, Sumitro was called to the presidential palace and ordered to retract his statements. Not only did Sumitro refrain from doing so, there are clear indications that as a message to Suharto, he ordered his forces to refrain from quelling the riots that wracked the country during the Malari Incident. When the riots got out of control and threatened many of the major business concerns in Jakarta, Sumitro was forced to direct his military to restore order.[17] Sumitro's advocates within ABRI retreated to the background when it became obvious that the citizens supported Suharto in a choice between a continuation of the New Order and a replay of the "Year of Living Dangerously" (as the 1965–1966 period was known). The play for power by the reform-minded military officers did not succeed in 1974, and the tensions that led to the breakdown in order remained.

In response to the civil unrest, the regime clamped down on the media and forbade student demonstrations. Later in 1975, the government announced a reform of the foreign investment laws to better protect pribumi interests. To reduce the encroachment of foreign economic influence, 100 percent foreign ownership of Indonesian businesses would be prohibited. Suharto believed his actions to be in keeping with his doctrine of "economics first, politics second."

Continuing this dual path of promoting economic prosperity while restricting civil liberties, the mid 1970s saw both the opening of the Jakarta stock exchange and further restrictions in freedom of the press, speech, and association. To prevent the spread of institutionalized corruption that could threaten the newly opened Jakarta exchange, a capital market supervisory agency was established in 1976 to institute discipline and oversee trading. Despite these precautions, the formalized market opened to an extremely slow start. On the sell side, private firms were fearful of dilution that comes with public ownership and resented the public disclosure requirements—most large firms enjoyed the privileges of negotiating their tax liabilities. Additionally, it was often easier for firms to rely on less-expensive state financing or to raise money through personal contacts rather than to resort to the imperson-

17   Crouch (1988, p. 316).

ality of the market.[18] The slow pace of initial listings is highlighted in Table 7.1.[19] As shown, the volume increased dramatically in the early 1980s.

Despite efforts to quiet civil unrest by expanding the protection of pribumi interests and liberalizing the market, campus demonstrations against authoritarianism continued to plague the regime. As a response to the outbreak of protests in 1977, Suharto instituted the Campus Normalization Law in 1978, which severely restricted speech and the rights to assemble. ABRI reformers, quiet since the Malari Incident, hoped that the new restrictions would mobilize the country to support their goals of changing the regime. This perceived support led a number of retired ABRI officers to publicize their complaints against Suharto in a petition that circulated throughout the press. But once again the reformers had overestimated the strength of their base and underestimated the power of the Suharto regime. Signatories to the Petition of 50 (as the document became known) saw their coalition crumble as Suharto retaliated in force, hounding his critics into submission and forbidding the media, under threat of arrest, from publishing any article in which the petition was mentioned.[20]

Table 7.1. *Highlights of the Jakarta Securities Exchange*

Year	No. of Companies Listed	Year End Stock Price Index
1977	1	98
1978	1	115
1979	4	110
1980	6	103.5
1981	9	100.3
1982	14	95
1983	19	80.4
1984	24	63.5
1985	24	66.5
1986	24	69.7
1987	24	82.6
1988	24	305.1
1989	56	359.4
1990	122	417.8
1991	138	247.4
1992	155	274.34
1993	174	588.77

18   McLeod (1984, p. 97).
19   *Fact Book of the Indonesian Capital Market.*
20   Neher and Marlay (1995, p. 85).

Suharto's ability to break the organizations that continued to rise up to threaten his regime stemmed from more than just his power to coerce and punish. Indeed, much of Suharto's strength was predicated on the belief by the Indonesian people that continued economic growth required a strong disciplined populace. Citizens, still reeling from the excesses of the Sukarno regime, were unwilling to question the basis for their newfound wealth and wished to continue enjoying the benefits of government social programs instituted as a result of an expanded economy and increased oil revenues. If individual freedom was the price for this stability—so be it.

Meanwhile, the technocrats argued that the oil windfalls were not going to last forever and that plans must be made for the eventuality of their decline. They pointed to the steady increase in inflation (which averaged 16.1 percent per annum during the 1974–1981 period) and the unhealthy reliance of the Indonesian GDP on oil exports. Oil prices had risen from US$3 a barrel in 1972 to over $30 by 1980, and oil revenues accounted for 49 percent of total government revenues in 1985–1986 and up to 56 percent over the entire 1979–1983 period.[21] The sectoral shares of GDP for agriculture and mining (oil and gas) shifted from 52 percent and 4 percent, respectively, in 1965 to 39 percent and 12 percent in 1974.[22] As the technocrats argued for continued reform and long-term economic planning, their opponents belittled their schemes as too conservative and unnecessary in times of government surpluses. Consequently, many of the proposed economic restructuring packages failed to win government approval. However, the technocrats were able to push through a devaluation of the rupiah by 33 percent in 1978, which curtailed imports and expanded exports of manufactured goods in 1979 to triple their 1978 level.[23]

The 1970s ended with a veneer of economic expansion covering a foundation of serious instability. The technocrats watched as their economic reform packages were perverted to protect the bureaucratic elites and the regime-sanctioned monopolies of Suharto's cronies. ABRI was battling to maintain order among its ranks as historical divisions once again erupted following the military's invasion and annexation of East Timor. The Muslim Party was gaining sympathizers in response to the regime's continuation down a path toward further corruption and

21 Vatikiotis (1992, p. 34).
22 Gillis (1984, p. 234).
23 Gillis (1984, p. 250).

greater secularization of the state. And citizens in general were slowly becoming aware that the great increases in wealth experienced by the country during the oil boom years had not trickled down to affect their lives.

DYNAMISM WITH STABILITY: THE 1980s

The Indonesian economy began to falter early in 1980 when oil prices started their steep descent. It is a telling example of the entrenched power of Golkar and the New Order that although citizens were fearful over the declining economic situation, the nation's students were actively protesting for increased political liberalization, and key members of the military were harshly critical of their function in society, no coherent opposition was formed to challenge Suharto. The Father of Development remained entrenched in power.

To safeguard his authority, Suharto elevated panca sila to a national ideology to which all social-political groups were forced to adhere. The aim of this, as well as the 1985 passage of the Law on Mass Organization, was to prevent the type of citizen protest that led to the Petition of 50 and the challenge to the regime in the late 1970s. In conjunction with the limits on civil liberties, Suharto also set about co-opting his opposition. He reorganized his government to include 11 military officers among his 24 cabinet positions and amended the Constitution to include dwi fungsi.

Suharto placated the peasants by expanding on his promises of land reform and by making self-sufficiency in rice a top priority of his administration. In this endeavor, the New Order was particularly successful. Between 1968 and 1985, rice production increased from 11.7 million tons per year to over 26 million tons, despite the extended drought in the 1982–1983 season. By the middle of the decade, rice surpluses outpaced the country's storage facilities.[24] In addition, basic health and education services started to appear in more rural villages. Secondary school enrollment is presented in Figure 7.2.[25] The slight downturn in the late 1980s and early 1990s reflects the reduction in demand for adult education, which was mostly satisified in the mid 1980s, and the continued migration to the cities where the public services were becoming overtaxed.

24   Thorbecke and van der Pluijm (1993).
25   Consortium for International Earth Science Information Network (n.d.).

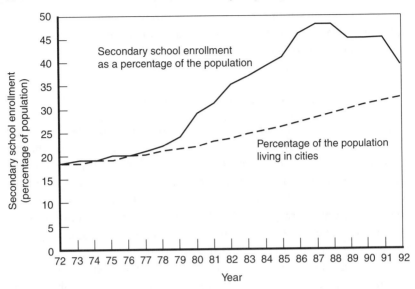

Figure 7.2.   Secondary School Enrollment in Indonesia: 1972–1992

The immense reduction in oil revenues continued to plague the country, however. The technocrats, out of favor during the oil boom years, were once again called by Suharto to restructure the economy and dampen the recession. The technocrats faced an uphill battle in their effort to institute new reforms. Strong interest groups opposed to liberalization and in favor of economic nationalism had increased their political standing during the mid to late 1970s. One of the first pitched battles between the technocrats and the technologists (as the economic nationalists were called) in the new decade revolved around proposed solutions to Indonesia's deteriorating balance of payments. The technologists defeated the technocrats (who had proposed greater liberalization) and, in 1982, passed into law further restrictions on import licensing. By the mid 1980s, 35 percent of the value of imports was controlled by a quota system. Figure 7.3 details the importance of tariffs as a percentage of GDP during the late 1970s and early 1980s.[26] In another testament to the political clout of the technologists, between 1974 and 1983 the state grew at double the population growth rate, from

26   International Monetary Fund, *Government Statistics*, various years.

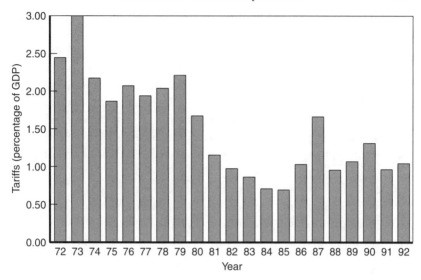

Figure 7.3. Importance of Tariffs to Indonesia: 1972–1992

1.67 million to 2.63 million civil servants. By 1983, state-owned enterprises accounted for 25 percent of the GDP.[27]

Despite these sweeping reforms across many sectors within the economy, the benefits of these changes accrued to only a small minority. Popular resentment against the rising disparities in income, and the policy measures that spawned this difference, began to rise.

When oil prices continued to drop throughout 1983, the technocrats initiated a public relations campaign to garner support for their reforms. Their main targets were the community of foreign-trained economists and the business elite who had not yet joined a faction.[28] They also put their message out to the growing segment of the middle class who believed that although their standard of living had risen, they were not yet fully vested in the structural reforms of the Indonesian economy. Instilling fear over the economic collapse that was sure to follow further decreases in oil revenue if the government's intrusive industrialization strategy was not reassessed and the market allowed to liberalize, the technocrats won support for sweeping reforms of the financial

27   Vatikiotis (1992, p. 37).
28   Soesastro (1989, p. 859).

sector to allow competition in the credit, exchange, and capital markets. Senior economic minister Radius Prawiro said in a 1990 speech, reflecting on the changes in the mid 1980s, that "without foreign exchange from oil, it would be necessary to expand dramatically the range of non-oil export products which would be competitive internationally. To do this would require an efficient, low-cost, and productive economy—this meant creating the conditions for a competitive market."[29] Highlighting the growing strength of the private sector resulting from these reforms, Figure 7.4 shows private sector credit as a percentage of GDP.[30]

Credit quotas were lifted and state banks were allowed to offer market-driven interest rates on deposits. But even after five years, state banks accounted for 70 percent of total bank credit.[31] The same problem that faced the technocrats in the mid 1970s continued to plague

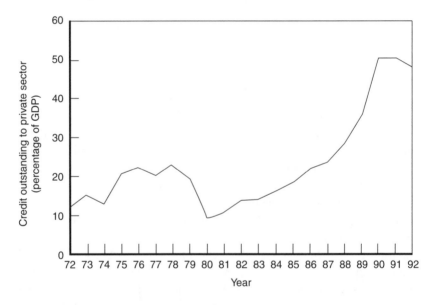

Figure 7.4. Credit Outstanding to the Private Sector in Indonesia:
1972–1992

29 Vatikiotis (1992, p. 38).
30 International Monetary Fund, *International Financial Statistics*, various years.
31 *Indonesia Handbook* (see Cole and Slade (1996)).

them in the 1980s: the weak implementation of the reforms on the regional and local levels, the fact that many of the reforms were implemented as presidential decrees but never enacted as laws (making their reversal much easier), and the pervasive system of exemptions for firms designated as "vital" by Suharto. The elites skirted the toughest of the reform measures by consulting with the appropriate state ministries before the reforms were announced publicly, thereby staking themselves a prime position in the new market-driven environment. Such procedures may have been necessary to get the cooperation of the entrenched money interests, as well as Suharto's family, but they minimized the market-opening effects of the technocrats' programs. Consequently, despite the best efforts of the technocrats, much of the country's industrialization strategy remained in place and natural resources continued to form the core of the nation's exports. One positive outcome of the technocrats' public relations campaign was that small businesses began to organize in an effort to eradicate the system of privileges and limit the encroachment of the state. The Chamber of Commerce and Industry in Indonesia (Kadin) was created in 1987 and became the official liaison between government and business.

By the late 1980s, the New Order's agenda, which included strengthening the economy, liberalizing the market, and bettering the life of the average Indonesian, seemed to be succeeding. Real gross domestic product per capita had rebounded to US$1,847 by 1988. Monetary institutions were undergoing a period of stability, with *mtwo* as a percentage of GDP rising to 29 percent, up from 16 percent earlier in the decade (Figure 7.5).[32]

In a late 1980s census report, 12,000 firms out of the nearly 13,000 surveyed were privately owned. Unfortunately, because of data restrictions stemming from government censorship, language barriers, and the limited availability of business statistics, it is nearly impossible to quantify the level of privatization of the "private" firms. The remainder of the firms surveyed were split almost equally between private-foreign joint ventures and government-private-foreign joint ventures.[33] On another dimension of success, a study from the World Bank estimated that the Gini coefficient for urban dwellers in Indonesia fell from 0.33 in 1969 to 0.32 in 1987, and the rural coefficient dropped from 0.34 to

32 International Monetary Fund, *International Financial Statistics*, various years.
33 *Indonesia Handbook.*

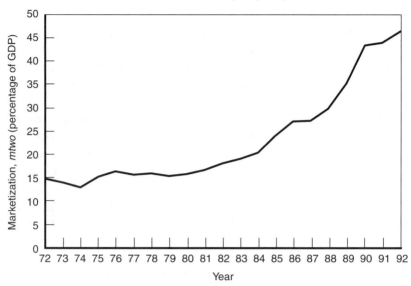

Figure 7.5. Marketization *(mtwo)* in Indonesia as a Percentage of GDP:
1972–1992

0.26 in the same time period, measuring a more equitable distribution of wealth in the population.[34] It seemed that "dynamism with stability" was once again within the reach of Indonesia. Popular support for the regime was manifested in the election results of 1987 when Golkar won 73 percent of the vote.

By 1988, the general public, pleased with the economic restructuring over the last two years, was anxiously awaiting the next reform. In October of that year, the public was rewarded with a comprehensive restructuring of the financial sector. The financial reform package, known as PAKTO, included a stock exchange reform, removal of restrictions on banks, deregulation of interisland shipping, broad based trade reforms, and reform of foreign direct investment laws—which encompassed raising the maximum equity holding for foreign investors from 49 to 85 percent.[35] As seen in Figure 7.6, stock market capitalization rose significantly as a result of PAKTO.[36] The largest changes

34   World Bank (1990).
35   *Far Eastern Economic Review* (1989, p. 85).
36   Merrill Lynch & Co., Inc. (1995).

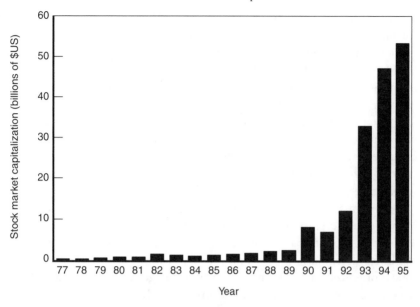

Figure 7.6. Indonesia's Stock Market Capitalization: 1977–1995

were adopted in the financial sector. This occurred not only because the technocrats were mostly neoclassical economists who were comfortable liberalizing the capital markets but also because the financial markets were under their direct control and so shielded from criticisms from other ministers who balked at losing their state-sanctioned monopolies.

In his continuing game of playing both sides against the middle, Suharto pacified these riled ministers and their allies among the economic nationalists by creating the new and improved DPIS (the Council for Strategic Industries) in 1989. The DPIS would serve as a counterbalance to the economic liberalization taking place elsewhere in the economy. Suharto installed himself as Chairman of DPIS and posted BJ Habibie (Minister of Research and Technology and an avowed economic nationalist) as DPIS's Vice Chairman. The board of advisers included the Minister for Industrial Affairs, the Minister of Defense and Security, the Minister of Transportation, the Minister for Tourism, and the Chief of Staff of the Indonesian army. Working through its managerial arm, the Agency for Strategic Industries (also headed by Habibie), DPIS was charged with providing technical support, organizing policy implementation, and generally supervising the management of the 10 state-owned strategic enterprises. The targeted firms included producers of heavy machinery, industrial equipment, explosives, telecommunications equipment, aircraft, electronics, and weaponry.

Reacting in part to the creation of yet another state mechanism to protect Suharto's cronies and in part to the movement of democratic reform sweeping Eastern Europe, student protests increased in frequency and intensity in the final months of 1989. The demonstrations were mostly nonviolent and were rumored to be supported by ABRI members who, despite their representation on DPIS, felt increasingly marginalized by the promotion of "financial" and "political" generals over professional military officers and their increasingly unpopular occupation of East Timor. In response to the demonstrations for democracy, State Secretary Murdiono stated that "deregulation in economics calls for its counterpart in politics. However, I will not invent the term 'political deregulation.' I would prefer to call it the self-reliance of political organizations. On many occasions the government has urged sociopolitical organizations to build up their self-reliance, and there are indications of this development."[37] The press hailed Murdiono's statements as reflecting Suharto's desire to slowly liberalize the political system, but few citizens believed change was imminent. Although the economic reform continued to progress, no policy was suggested to strengthen the country's rule of law. Indonesia's justice system continued to permit arrest without warrant, detention without the filing of formal charges, and trial without representation.

TIME FOR A CHANGE? 1990–1997

For decades, Suharto's methods of allocating political and economic freedom co-opted the large majority of the population. Gross domestic product per capita steadily increased (Figure 7.7), the streets remained free of violence, and the country was at peace with its neighbors.[38] During the previous 10 years, however, certain segments of the population had become discontented. Young Indonesians wanted to be part of the world democratizing movement. Muslims were concerned over the increased secularization of the government. The army feared a loss of prestige; the business elite a loss of their monopolies as economic liberalization continued. The growing middle class wanted a general re-

37   Vatikiotis (1992, p. 116).
38   Summers and Heston (1991).

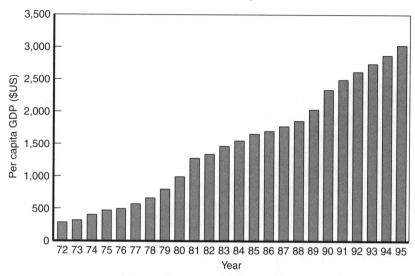

Figure 7.7. Per Capita GDP in Indonesia: 1972–1995

structuring of the political and economic system, which would give them the ability to earn a greater share of the wealth and the political voice to enshrine the rights necessary to accomplish this task.

Despite increased political awareness, the beginning of the 1990s saw an entrenchment of vested interest groups in preparation for what many believed would be Suharto's final three years in office. One of the prime contenders, BJ Habibie, had used his position on DPIS as a bully pulpit for greater government intervention into the market. Significant as a show of support for Habibie's ideas, Suharto proclaimed in his National Day address in August 1990 that "deregulation and de-bureaucratization are precisely aimed at re-awakening public initiative, creativity and participation in development. They are certainly not measures to abolish the role of the state. It is definitely not a step toward liberalism."[39]

In contrast to the clear course set by Habibie and the technologists, by early 1991, ABRI was seen as morally corrupt and intellectually bankrupt. The ranks were split on the issue of ABRI's mission, as it related to dwi fungsi, resulting in a decline in troop morale. The number

39   Vatikiotis (1992, p. 173).

of active-duty personnel showed small increases throughout the 1980s, as shown in Table 7.2, but ABRI's budget remained modest in comparison with those of other Southeast Asian nations, and the lack of any serious external threat in the previous 25 years had eroded military capabilities.[40] Frustration on the part of younger officers, unsure of their mission or role in society, was again leading to a call for a large-scale restructuring of the armed forces.

Recognizing its dwindling power base, ABRI agreed to co-sponsor, along with an amalgamation of Muslim groups, the Forum for Democracy in 1991. The forum issued a statement in which it announced that since the Communist threat had been wiped out and the economy set on its course of modernization (GDP had risen to 7.4 percent in 1990—placing Indonesia on the verge of becoming the next Newly Industrialized Country), it was time for the liberalization of the political structure. Following on the heels of the forum, the Development Foundation of Indonesian Youth published an open letter to Suharto later that year which read, in part, that "there is a need to further cultivate responsible openness which is the key to political dynamism in society. Legal order based on panca sila must prevail in the effort to create an image of the state based on the rule of law."[41] The slogan keterbukaan (political openness) began to appear in government press releases.

As in many parts of the former Soviet Union, an atmosphere of political openness not only led to increased calls for democracy but reignited ethnic, racial, and religious tensions that had lain dormant for the last 25 years. The catalyst for renewed civil strife came from a very

Table 7.2. *Armed forces of the Republic of Indonesia (ABRI)*

	Number of Active-Duty Personnel	
Service	1983	1992
Army	210,000	215,000
Navy	42,000	44,000
Air Force	29,000	24,000
National Police	92,000	180,000
Total	373,000	463,000

SOURCE: IISS, London, *Military Balance 1983–1984; 1992–1993.*

40   *Indonesia Handbook.*
41   Vatikiotis (1992, p. 6).

unlikely source—the creation of a new corporate giant, the Humpuss Group, by Suharto's son Tommy. The Humpuss Group planned to monopolize the lucrative clove industry by attempting a hostile takeover of the third largest kretek (clove cigarette) maker. To fend off the takeover, the company incurred massive amounts of debt and finally defaulted on its overseas loans, raising concern among foreign investors about the state of the economy in general. The ensuing financial panic resulted in a contraction of the stock exchange price-to-earnings (P/E) valuation from its high of 31 times earnings in April 1990 to only 11 times earnings by the early part of 1991.[42] Pribumi business interests blamed the crisis on the government's close ties to the ethnic Chinese community. In response to these charges, Suharto directed 31 of Indonesia's most successful businessmen (all ethnic Chinese) to sell up to 25 percent of their firms to the public through cooperatives. This obvious pandering to anti-Chinese groups prepared the ground for an increase in ethnic tension throughout the country.

On November 12, 1991, ethnic violence erupted in Dili, the capital of East Timor. A full press blackout has made it difficult for experts to assess what actually occurred during the Dili Incident, but it is believed that ABRI forces, in cahoots with local Muslim leaders, opened fire on Timorese protesters, killing or wounding over 100 people. Although this was only a small massacre compared with the 50,000 to 75,000 who have died in the last 20 years from combat, mistreatment, privation, and disease, the Dili Incident brought to the forefront the ethnic and racial tension that threatens the unity of the country.[43] The world spotlight that focused on Indonesia after the Dili Incident could not have occurred at a worse time for the President. Suharto was actively petitioning to become chairman of the Non-Aligned Movement (which he succeeded in doing for the 1992–1995 term) and wished to increase his visibility as a leader of the second-tier powers. After two decades of focusing exclusively on domestic development, with the only foreign policy drive being one to obtain foreign aid, loans, and investment, Indonesia was clamoring for worldwide recognition as an Asian leader. The Dili Incident was a setback for Suharto's public relations campaign. As a defensive tactic, when the Netherlands issued a formal criticism of Indonesia for the Timor killings, Suharto disbanded the IGGI (Inter-Governmental Group on Indonesia, created earlier in the century to

42   Fleming (1993).
43   Haseman (1995, p. 758).

help assist Indonesia after the Dutch withdrawal in 1949) and created the Consultative Group on Indonesia (CGI) in its stead. As a pointed insult to the Netherlands, Suharto excluded them from the new organization. The move was a clear reflection of Indonesia's often-schizophrenic relationship with the outside world. On one hand, the nation felt vulnerable and inferior to the West because of its economic backwardness and the insecurity resulting from the knowledge that the apparent unity of its vast number of cultures could implode at any time. On the other hand, Indonesia demonstrated a sense of entitlement based upon its strong natural resource base, its large population, and its dominant geographic position with Southeast Asia.[44]

The Dili Incident and the weakening economy served as a backdrop to the 1992 general elections. On first examination, it would appear that the 68 percent garnered by Golkar in the elections was a resounding approval of the New Order. On closer inspection, however, this was not the case. Golkar lost nearly 5 percent of the support it gained in the 1987 elections. Most of that 5 percent swung to the PDI, which saw its share of votes increase from 10.9 percent in 1987 to 14.9 percent in 1992.[45] The Muslim-backed PPP also saw an expansion in its rolls. The increase in votes for the opposition was astounding given that the PPP and the PDI were not allowed to campaign or advertise for their parties. Golkar, in contrast, was permitted to use the full force of the sitting bureaucracy to push its platform. The increase in support for the opposition was not accepted kindly by the regime. The top leadership of PDI, including Sukarno's daughter Megawati Sukarnoputri, was harassed for not having special permits to host gatherings of more than five people. The overblown response by the regime betrayed the underlying insecurity of the New Order and its fear that it might be losing its absolute authority within the nation.

As was expected after his announcement that he would not step down as President, Suharto was elected to his fifth term in 1993. Following his reelection, Suharto called for a final economic deregulation package focusing on investment procedures in the provinces. Despite the reforms in the late 1980s and early 1990s, provincial investment was still overly complicated and inefficient. The government understood that to meet its targeted economic growth rates, efficiency in allocating resources must be improved. The reform package focused

44   For a broader discussion, see Leifer (1983).
45   *Indonesia Handbook.*

on simplifying general investment procedures, foreign direct investment, exports and imports licensing, import duties, pharmaceutical industry regulations, and environmental laws.[46] The new regulations allowed for 100 percent foreign ownership of Indonesian firms, with a minimum investment and exclusively in export-oriented businesses, but with the caveat that these investments were subject to divestment regulations under which 51 percent of shares must be transferred to Indonesian partners beginning in the 10th year of operations and fully completed by the 20th year.

True to form, immediately after the announcement of the new reforms, Suharto reshuffled his cabinet and ousted the main architects of the restructuring. The purge of the technocrats attested to both the increased power of the technologists and the regime's suspicion that the technocrats were behind the rising chorus of middle-class voices demanding democratic reforms. By approving the reforms but firing the reformers, Suharto was able to take credit for the economic package without being beholden to its developers.

Where once Suharto's cynical strategy may have succeeded, by the mid 1990s the business sphere was savvy enough to discount smoke and mirrors. This new middle class consisted mainly of the Indonesian baby boomers—the students who had taken to the streets in the 1960s to battle for Suharto and the New Order had acquired wealth and stability in the 1970s and 1980s. By 1995, they wanted fuller political participation. Ironically, much of this new demand for openness was fueled by Suharto himself. To deflect criticism of his handling of Timor and the lack of implementation of his economic policies, Suharto opened up a number of pathways to political liberalization in the early 1990s. These included more press freedom and permission for the formation of the Muslim Intellectuals Association. Suharto also played up his role in forcing the Chinese elite to sell 25 percent of their firms to the public as a move made to increase citizens' ability to enjoy the benefits of the marketplace. Suharto did not calculate that his actions, by allowing the people a higher standard of living and an outlet for their grievances, would open a Pandora's box.

Not only was there rising discontent among the citizens, Suharto's critics within the government had not been silenced with the ouster of the technocrats. The armed forces, at odds with Suharto and Habibie for the last decade, were covertly instigating the middle classes. In retal-

46   "Keeping the Wheels Turning" (1993).

iation to what Suharto viewed as disloyalty in ABRI, the government revoked the press permits for the country's three leading weeklies (*Tempo, Detik,* and *Editor*) after they reported on alleged differences in the Cabinet over military procurement.[47] The regime alleged that the papers, in both their articles and editorial columns, were instigating civil unrest by creating doubts about the stability of the government. On November 16, 1995, the New Order announced that 300 extremists were to be tried for using "communist tactics to lure weak-minded Muslims to establish an Indonesian Islamic State."[48] It is difficult to assess whether the crackdown by the regime on "extremists" was a sincere attempt to curb ethnic violence or a cynical attempt to strengthen the power of the state.

Credence was given to the latter theory in the summer of 1996 when rioting shook Jakarta. The cause of the civil unrest was the ouster of Megawati Sukarnoputri, daughter of Sukarno, as leader of the PDI. The removal of Megawati was accomplished through a special party Congress but manipulated by the government. In the immediate aftermath of the announcement, Megawati's supporters gathered at PDI's headquarters in Jakarta to protest the decision. Megawati, backed by a strong following, refused to deal with the state's puppet, Surjadi, installed as her replacement. The depth and breadth of Megawati's support astonished the regime; nearly 30 different organizations rallied around her.[49] The rapidity with which these organizations mobilized their rank and file underlies the sophistication of their internal communication systems and the inability of the government to successfully infiltrate and disrupt the groups.

For over a month, the demonstrations continued. As the ASEAN Conference on July 25, 1996, drew closer, Suharto grew more nervous and impatient with the protesters. He bided his time until the last of the foreign ministers left and, on July 27, engineered a takeover of PDI headquarters. Cynically dressed as PDI supporters, but most likely armed force members and police, a phalanx of troops moved in to repossess PDI headquarters from Megawati supporters. The move, interpreted as a government attempt at intimidation, catalyzed 5,000 protesters to take to the street. A dozen or more buildings were set ablaze, at least three died by the time the protest was quelled, and 250

47   U.S. Department of State (1995).
48   As reported in "Red Scare" (1995, p. 35).
49   Baker (1996).

people were arrested by the riot police. The riots of 1996, in retrospect, seemed eerily prescient of the upheaval that would beset the country the following year. Unfortunately, no one read the signs correctly. And the signs were there.

As foreign investment continued to escalate throughout the early 1990s, reaching a cumulative total of US$5.775 billion in the balance of payments for 1973–1990, Indonesia's debt situation continued to worsen, as seen in Figure 7.8.[50]

As became apparent in the aftermath of the 1997 crash, the huge sums of money that poured into the country during the earlier years of the decade did not find their way into market-tested investments. Rather, the money was often funneled into highly speculative pet projects of Suharto's family and friends, with little oversight as to the credit worthiness of the ventures. Over the years, the monopolies of the country's wealthiest grew to absurd proportions. Table 7.3 categorizes the vast holdings of this small circle of elites.[51]

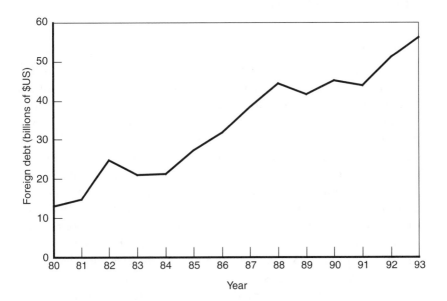

Figure 7.8. Increase in Indonesia's Foreign Debt: 1980–1993

50   *Indonesia Financial Statistics,* various years.
51   Reprinted from *The Christian Science Monitor,* January 21, 1998.
      Source: *Warta Ekonomi Magazine,* 1996. 10,350 rupiah = US$1.

Table 7.3. *Assets of the elites*

	Conglomerate	Number of Companies	Total Assets (US$)
Children			
Siti Hardijanti Rukmana (d)	Citra Lamtoro Gung Group	55	451 million
Bambang Trihatmodjo (s)	Bimantara Group	50	390 million
Hutomo Mandala Putra (s)	Humpuss Group	40	202 million
Sigit Haryoyudanto (s)	Hanurata Group	39	63 million
Siti Hediati H Prabowo (d)	Datam/maharani	23	38 million
Relatives			
Hashim Djojohadikusumo	Tirtamas/era Persada	40	150 million
Probosutedjo	Mercu Buana Group	38	37 million
Friends			
Liem Sieo Liong	Salim Group	600	4,068 million
Bob Hassan	Nusamba Group	90	648 million

SOURCE: *Warta Ekonomi Magazine* (1996).
NOTE: 10,350 rupiah = US$1; (d) = daughter; (s) = son.

When the cracks first appeared in the Thai economy in the summer of 1997, the Indonesian elites thought themselves impervious. But as the year drew to a close, it became obvious that not only would the Indonesian economy not be spared, it would take the hardest hit of all the East Asian economies. Although the fundamentals of the crisis were the same for both Thailand and Indonesia (poor financial regulation, rampant corruption, and excessive borrowing), Indonesia's recklessness and greed far exceeded that of Thailand. By the time the International Monetary Fund was asked to bail out the beleaguered economy to the tune of $40 billion, Indonesia lay in shambles. Its currency had plunged more than 50 percent against the U.S. dollar since August 1997, 80 percent of corporate Indonesia was technically bankrupt, the private sector debt exceeded $65 billion, stock market capitalization had fallen from $118 billion to $17 billion, and only 22 of 286 publicly traded companies were considered solvent.[52]

In typical Suharto fashion, the President agreed to a draft IMF bailout package in October 1997, only to contradict his pledges in his address to the nation on his 1998 budget package two months later. The new budget reflected wildly unrealistic budget assumptions: an ex-

52   McBeth (1998a).

change rate of 4,000 rupiah to the U.S. dollar (at the time of the speech the rupiah had already fallen to 7,500), a 4 percent GDP growth rate, and only a 9 percent inflation rate. The fantasy presented by Suharto and his ministers proved that the regime had no intention of implementing the tight austerity measures agreed to in principle with the IMF. The international market responded in kind. It gave a resounding vote of no confidence to Suharto when it plunged the currency to 10,000 rupiah to the dollar on the day following the budget speech and let the stock market freefall. Suharto quickly engaged in damage control by meeting with the IMF and expanding its purview over his crippled economy. On January 15, 1998, Suharto signed a 50 point Memorandum of Understanding with the IMF agreeing to adopt a policy of fiscal transparency, reform the national banking system, and remove numerous monopolistic practices.[53] Suharto also agreed to prepare a realistic budget for 1998–1999. On January 23, 1998, Finance Minister Mar'ie Muhammad delivered the new state budget. The revised numbers were based on an exchange rate of 5,000 rupiah to the dollar, a zero percent economic growth rate, and an inflation rate of 20 percent. The entry of net capital (the total of government and private capital) was revised downward from US$6.472 billion to US$1.531 million. This phenomenal decrease was explained as being caused by payments for unpaid basic foreign debts. Finally, the balance of payments, which was originally estimated to have a surplus of $1.76 billion, was estimated as a $1.96 billion deficit.[54] The momentous month of January 1998 ended with Suharto's Cabinet members rolling up their collective sleeves to begin the work of reforming their economy, equipped with the IMF bankroll and an extension on debt payments from the world's banks.

Unlike previous crises that Suharto had bullied his way through, this one had the makings of a swan song. The Father of Development had broken his promise. His charges began calling for a drastic overhaul of both the economy and the political structure. Significant reforms passed into law during the last two decades liberalized the market to a certain extent, but corruption, monopolies, and insurmountable barriers to entry remained in place. Robison describes Indonesia's state-market mechanism as both mercantilist and patrimonial:

53   "Indonesia: Camdessus Views Indonesia's Economic Reform" (1998).
54   "Indonesia: Minister Unveils Revised State Budget" (1998).

On the one hand the state intervenes in mercantilist fashion to protect national enterprise and national economic agendas, including the development of such upstream manufacturing industries as steel and petrochemicals, through tariffs, monopolies and state-funded industrial projects. In another dimension, its officials appropriate state resources and authority on behalf of specific political and corporate interest.[55]

Nonetheless, broader economic liberalization spilled over into the political realm by creating an access to the government from the marketplace for Indonesia's growing middle class. Taking advantage of a more liberalized press during the fall of 1997, those in the middle class began to vent their frustrations. Business leaders began to criticize the government for moving too slowly in implementing promised economic reforms, entrepreneurs complained that they were forbidden market access because of licensing restrictions, and countryside peasants demanded better distribution for their products.

In the early part of the decade, the middle class, while pleased with economic reform, became increasingly uneasy because of the escalating civil violence on the islands of Sumatra, Java, Timor, and Irian Jaya. Unsure of how such unrest would affect their country's international reputation, as well as the repercussions on the economy through foreign investment boycotts or domestic labor protests, the middle class began to resent the government's ham-fisted handling of these domestic crises.[56] Increasing citizens' frustration with the regime was the well-publicized colossal greed of the Suharto family.

As 1997 closed out a year of financial turmoil, the question remained: Would the middle classes, dependent as they were on the pervasive state apparatus, work to dismantle it? As in Korea, when the chaebol finally realized that without political reform their economic growth would be hampered, many in Indonesia began to realize that the chance to preserve, and perhaps raise, their standard of living in the new global business environment would be constrained unless Indonesia opened its markets. As a logical extension of that argument, the director of the Indonesian Business Data Center, in a symposium on political liberalization held before the crash of 1997, remarked that "economic liberalization without first carrying out political and social liberalization is nonsense." Without political liberalization, poor countries become

55   Robison (1994, p. 55).
56   Schwarz (1994).

lackeys for wealthier ones. The head of the Indonesian Workers Union agreed, adding that the government has had success in economic development but needs to embark on "institution building."[57]

The concept that economic and political liberalization are causally related has, throughout the last few years, gained wide acceptance in many quarters of Indonesian society. In 1995, Finance Minister Mar'ie Muhammad spoke about the importance of opening up the avenues for success to mainstream Indonesia. He highlighted the fact that a strong economy cannot depend on a few key monopolies but must allow for the efficient distribution of resources (and economic power) to the citizenry. "If we properly develop our small businessmen and cooperatives," the Finance Minister remarked, "it is not impossible that they can serve as the backbone of the national economy."[58] The implied threats to the state bureaucracy, as well as to the cronies of Suharto, would have been unthinkable a decade earlier.

To increase the likelihood that Indonesia could succeed in the new global environment, the business class began demanding a voice in policy formulation. Aside from the standard economic reforms and deregulation packages, businesses began pushing for more stringent enforcement of the corruption laws recommended by the IMF. Unfortunately, corruption extended past the state-level bureaucracy and big business into communal activities. Siswono Yudohusodo, Minister of Transmigration, remarked that he feared that corruption was becoming part of the nation's "culture." After citing an earlier German study on corruption that listed Indonesia as the worst offender, the Minister remarked, "In other words, corruption exists in almost every sector." As an example, he referred to the use of the influence of the father on behalf of the children—a clear taunt at Suharto. To stop the spread of corruption, the Minister recommended eradicating the "economic autocracy, . . . [the centralization] and control of economic assets . . . [and state-sponsored] monopolies."[59] Later that same year, Indonesian economist Dr. Sritua Arief stressed that structural change in the economic management of the country must be addressed if democracy is to succeed. In a well-publicized speech, he remarked that "it was useless to give a fishing

---

57   "Official on Need for Political Liberalization" (1995, p. 86).
58   "Minister Stresses Importance of Small Businesses" (1995, p. 59).
59   "Minister Cites Prevalence of Corruption" (1995, p. 60).

rod to a weak economy as long as monopoly, connections, nepotism are dominant features in national economic development."[60]

In the spring of 1998, the Indonesian people, led by student demonstrators, decided to take matters into their own hands and speed the process of both economic and political reform. The protests began in February 1998, with the students calling for a lowering of prices and an end to the systemic corruption of the Suharto regime. Although many in the country cheered from the sidelines, the students seemed to be on their own at first. This changed in May 1998. The catalyst seems to have been the government's May 5 announcement that they would raise premium petrol prices by 70 percent and electricity rates by 60 percent. The protest movement gathered momentum as it spread throughout Java, Bali, and Sumatra and onto the outer islands of Kalimantan, Lombok, and Sulawesi. A broader swath of the population joined in the protests. First came the labor activists and workers, then academics and college administrators, then finally the peasants. A solid groundswell of support formed around the students, and a fractured disparate group of youths mobilized into a solidified movement.[61]

In those early days of May, the regime held its own and scoffed at the idea of convening a special session of the People's Consultative Assembly (MPR) to choose a new president. President Suharto released a statement that reforms would be sanctioned only after 2003, the end of his term. The pronouncement galvanized the forces of the opposition. As the political turmoil deepened, the rupiah lost more and more of its value. The Indonesian currency fell from a disastrous 10,000 to the dollar to an unheard-of level of 14,000. On May 6, the organization most closely associated with Vice President BJ Habibie, the Association of Muslim Intellectuals (ICMI), called Suharto's reform agenda "vague, too little and too late."[62]

On May 14, the protests turned deadly. The army killed 6 and wounded 15 in protests outside of Trisakti University in Jakarta, one of the country's most elite colleges. The deaths raised the stakes for all concerned. Suharto was now seen as an enemy of the people, the students realized there was no turning back in the game they had begun, and the army was caught in the middle of these opposing sides.

60   "Observers Comment on National Economic Situation" (1995, p. 79).
61   Cohen (1998).
62   McBeth (1998b).

Although the students considered ABRI a friend of the people, the shootings made them question this assessment. A similar assessment was occurring inside the army as well. General Wiranto, the head of the armed forces, was regarded as a reasonable man trying to steer through uncharted waters without letting either his country or his President be injured. He resisted openly declaring his loyalties, yet at the same time tried to control the rogue elements inside the army. Further complicating matters, these elements were led by Lt. General Prabowo Subianto, Suharto's son-in-law and head of the elite combat troops (Kostrad).

In the three days that followed the shootings, Indonesia seemed to implode. Nearly 2,000 people died in rioting and nearly 5,000 buildings burned to the ground. On May 18, Harmoko, Speaker of the Parliament, called for Suharto's resignation. One by one, Suharto's ministers, generals, and friends joined in the chorus calling for him to step aside. On May 21, 1998, with an apology for the "mistakes, failures or shortcomings" of his three decades in office, President Suharto resigned. The man who had overseen the growth of his country from a poor nation with a GDP per capita of US$70 to a regional power with a GDP per capita of US$1,000 was ousted from office.

Suharto stood by while Vice President BJ Habibie was sworn in as Indonesia's new President. Within a week, Habibie had appointed a new Cabinet (albeit 19 of the 35 ministers had been retained from the Suharto regime) and had set a timetable for new elections within the year and a major reformation of the economy within six months.

With hesitant steps and frequent backward movements, Indonesia may be able to move slowly toward economic liberalization. Whether this will lead to political reform is still uncertain. However, the best possibilities for greater political reform lie with increased marketization. Not only are the traditionally entrenched power brokers losing their absolute grip over the process, they are losing it not to another small block of "players" but to a large segment of the Indonesian people—the growing middle class. This rising power, in cahoots with academics and intellectuals, is finding its voice to call for political reform. Nonetheless, a number of factors that will present themselves in the next decade may scuttle any chance for a lasting liberalization of the political regime. The next section discusses some potential scenarios that may hamper a lasting democratic transition.

SCENARIOS FOR THE FUTURE

Aside from further degradation of the economy and the potential of civil unrest that may spring from a lowered standard of living, the most likely source of instability stems from the presidential elections scheduled to occur by mid 1999. In one of his first acts as President, BJ Habibie slackened the restrictions on the formation of political parties, letting loose a torrent of party politicking. Although many individuals are declaring themselves as candidates, and others are looking to form alliances, some remain wary, understanding that if the openness does not last and a crackdown occurs, the first to be rounded up will be those who formed opposition parties.

Of those who have emerged as potential leaders, their full political platforms have not yet been announced. Habibie, having risen to office without a solid base of support, is trying to solidify his power using his new position as a springboard. Many believe this will mean appealing to the country's politically active Muslim community. In a recent interview, Alex Irwan, an editor of Indonesia's largest business daily, predicted that "the more Habibie feels his political position is weak, the more he'll mobilize support [from the Muslim community], the more that will scare the Chinese community and foreign investors, the worse the economy will get."[63] Amien Rais, chairman of the mainstream Muslim organization Muhammadiyah and close friend of Habibie, has used the goodwill he generated as an early supporter of the students to advance his political aspirations. And Megawati Sukarnoputri, ousted chairwoman of the Democratic Party, remains a viable figure although many were disappointed with her noninvolvement in the May protests.

The future role of ABRI further complicates the internal transition within the country. Although ABRI has enjoyed its dwi fungsi for the last three decades, serious breaches are occurring within the military over whether such a peculiar position should be maintained in a rapidly developing country. Younger officers question the wisdom of staffing the military hierarchy with "financial" and "political" generals who are more concerned about profit and loss statements than about arsenals, the rise of domestic terrorist groups, or potential threats from abroad. Many of these young officers want a restructuring of the military to lead to the professionalization of the corps. Some of these reformers have found common ground with members of the Islamic Movement,

63   Gaouette (1998).

who also desire a decreased role for the military in the political establishment.[64] It is unknown how the military will react to a diminution
of its authority. It is possible that ABRI will support a more assertive
foreign policy posture to justify itself, possibly provoking confrontation
with Malaysia or even China. Another possibility is that, rather than
relying on the transition process to reflect the will of the people, ABRI
will become actively involved in the succession and attempt to install a
military government.

A functioning democracy relies on numerous parties advocating diverse positions before the general electorate, but a strong process to ensure that the elections remain free and fair is essential if the system is
not to disintegrate into chaos. Indonesia lacks a strong process of transition, and what does exist within the codified law has remained un-
tested for three decades. Equally problematic is the lack of any real
process for resolving conflicts among political factions. Consensus
building and compromise among various interest groups are novel ideas
in Indonesia. Antagonism toward the vagaries of democratic elections
and the illicit means used to by-pass the uncertainties were commented
upon in a report commissioned by the Army Staff and Command
School to review the election procedures of the country. The comman-
dant of the school reported that "the district system . . . faces numerous
difficulties, which among other things, are vote-buying and the
'rampant murder' of politicians."[65]

Some of the most significant pushes for reform are coming from
those in the growing business class who are frustrated at the extensive
corruption within the government and the intrusive and restrictive busi-

---

64 President Habibie is a founder of the Indonesian Muslim Intellectual
    Association, which advocates a greatly reduced role for ABRI. The stress
    between Habibie and ABRI was barely concealed in a November 30,
    1995, *Far Eastern Economic Review* article about oceanic research in
    Indonesian waters. ABRI has refused to grant Australian and U.S.
    oceanographers access to Indonesian waters for fear that "scientific
    intelligence about sea conditions . . . could be used by foreign submarines
    to dodge . . . sonar equipment." However, the article also states that the
    refusal to issue security clearances came "despite Research and
    Technology Minister BJ Habibie's direct intervention with Indonesia's
    armed forces chief." Such a rebuff is rarely covered publicly unless it is
    leaked to the media, not an unlikely event in light of the battle between
    the armed forces and the economic nationalists.

65 "Army Chief: No Need to Change Election System" (1995, p. 56).

ness laws. The threat to the bureaucracy and the political elite from this rising class of citizens is not taken lightly. A rise in such societal tension could lead to the breakdown of the nation as it prepares for the presidential election, and it could also lead to the formation, by an alliance of the business elite and intelligentsia, of highly organized parties able to participate, and indeed stabilize, a democratic system.

Suharto concentrated power in a small military and bureaucratic elite and a highly centralized governmental administration. He claimed that such an organization was essential in a country as geographically and ethnically fragmented as Indonesia. As the country moves toward its first presidential election, Suharto's proposition will be tested. However, although there are factions demanding independence and threatening the unity of the Republic of Indonesia, it is unclear whether they have the power to dismantle the country. The three largest independence groups operating currently are Fretlan (the Timorese Independence Movement) with 100 to 200 armed members, the GPK (the Security Disturbance Movement of Irian Jaya) with 100 armed members, and the Free Aceh Movement, which demands the establishment of an independent Islamic state in westernmost Sumatra. Although Islamic fundamentalists remain a small minority in Indonesia, there is concern that the strengthening of Christianity and the unequal wealth held by the Chinese could lead to a broader instability. Incidents like those that occurred in the early 1980s could be repeated if instability on other fronts—such as economic degradation—arises. The most effective way to thwart the outbreak of such civil unrest is a continued broadening of economic opportunity through the liberalization of the market.

As occurred in Taiwan and Korea, marketization will slowly liberalize the government of Indonesia. Citizens who have a vested interest in pushing for broader and deeper economic reforms will find the voice to challenge the status quo of the political elite. Whether their voices will be found before they can be drowned out by the fractious noises of regionalism, religious intolerance, and ethnic strife remains to be seen.

8

———————————————————————————————————————

China: A transformation of the societal contract

Over the last two decades, China's political and economic structure has been undergoing a radical transfiguration in the form of a restructuring of the societal contract. Until recently, the state has been the acknowledged repository of power within China. In exchange for this fealty, citizens were guaranteed protection from the forces of chaos and an iron rice bowl. During the last 20 years, however, this social contract has been slowly transforming. The state has been less able to provide for the needs and wants of the nation, and, as a consequence, the populace has been less willing to support the absolute authority of the state.

This chapter explores the gradual restructuring of this contract—a restructuring that has led to a diminution in the state's authority and legitimacy and has resulted in a de facto movement toward political openness. The economic factors that catalyzed this movement are analyzed and provide the basis for determining whether further marketization will increase the prospects for political liberalization within China.

In particular, three aspects of China's economic reform (the demise of the rural cooperative and its replacement by a freer market, the expansion of financial markets, and the opening of China's economy to foreign investment) are discussed within four time periods: 1979–1982, the mid 1980s, the late 1980s, and the 1990s. These three aspects of reform have been selected not only to limit an immense field of research but because each represents a step in the transformation of Chinese culture—away from the collective and toward individualism; away from a government-determined fate and toward economic autonomy; away from an isolationist China and toward an open society.

The implementation of agricultural reform and the creation of a functioning financial market have inspired China's citizens to become actively involved in their economic livelihood and, to ensure the continuation of such, their political well-being. In addition, China's strengthened ties to the outside world brought into the country the ideas of liberty and democracy and a road map for achieving these goals. All have led to a reduction in the power of the state. The redefinition of the state and the growth of the private sphere serve as necessary conditions for China's movement toward political liberalization. As the economic reforms loosen the ties of citizens to the state, their fealty declines and the challenges to the state's legitimacy increase.

Nathan cites four reasons why democracy cannot take hold in China: China's ideology and political culture; the country's national security problems; the underdevelopment of institutions, education, and civil society in general; and the peasant mass.[1] What Nathan fails to understand is that as the Chinese economy liberalizes, these four *supposedly* insurmountable obstacles begin to erode. Marketization is gradually replacing the Marxist-Leninist-Maoist ideology of the past with a more individualistic, incentive-driven society. The peasant mass is becoming increasingly urbanized, and the institutions that form the core of a civil society are slowly being erected. Naysayers such as Nathan should take a closer look at the recent histories of Taiwan and Korea where political liberalization has made incredible strides. In the aftermath of Taiwan's first democratic presidential election, what seemed impossible just a decade ago has become a reality. Institutions can be built, civil society can be created, and cultures can adapt. Similar to their cousins on the island of Taiwan, the people of the PRC are finding that their own economic boom is beginning and is allowing a level of personal autonomy unthinkable 20 years ago but quickly becoming a fact of life to be taken for granted. But significant changes to a nation do not usually occur overnight. This chapter discusses the possibility for a more democratic future for China and the foundations that are being laid for such a time by focusing on the changes within Chinese culture from increased marketization and the resulting alteration of the societal contract.

1   Nathan (1993a, p. 3).

AGRICULTURAL REFORM AND THE BEGINNING OF A CULTURAL
TRANSFORMATION: 1979–1982

An often-heard phrase in China is that the revolution was made in the countryside but will be unmade in the city. Although the urban centers are certainly the foci for many of the changes occurring in China, the initial market-opening reforms and the first hesitant steps in the restructuring of the societal contract began in the rural provinces. Harding writes that the effects of these early agricultural reforms were felt on many levels of society:

> For the peasant, the reforms have transformed agricultural production from a collective undertaking into a family enterprise. For the state, the reforms have greatly reduced, although not eliminated, the government's role in the establishment of production targets and the determination of prices. For the enterprise, the moderate reforms have given managers more autonomy in making decisions, more control over the allocation of profits, and more responsibility for the outcomes of their decisions. For the industrial worker, the reforms are slowly changing the systems of education, employment, discipline, and remuneration.[2]

The impetus for the agricultural reforms of the late 1970s and early 1980s was an escalating crisis in the farming sector. Because of years of inefficient resource allocation stemming from the state's complete domination of the productive and commercial roles of agriculture, by the late 1970s much of the rural population was mired in chronic poverty and many rural enterprises were running at huge losses. In 1976, the average per capita income of peasant households was lower than that of 1956 at constant prices.[3] Rural enterprises needed substantial subsidies to remain operating, yet their products were expensive and often inferior. In the mid 1970s, the poor quality of fertilizer and the shoddy construction of farm equipment did much toward reducing the level of agricultural product to near its lowest point in decades.[4] By 1978, China was forced to import grain to feed nearly 40 percent of its urban population.[5] Watching their standard of living continue to erode, the peasant mass began to demand reform. As Zhu Ling writes, the "beginning of economic reform arose from farmers' spontaneous at-

2 Harding (1987, p. 101).
3 World Bank (1986).
4 Wong (1991, p. 25).
5 World Bank (1986).

tempts to break away from the restrictions involved in the egalitarian distribution of rewards."[6] The state was failing to provide for the peasants, and consequently, citizens were reclaiming some of the authority over their lives that they had ceded to the government.

On March 5, 1978, a new Constitution of the PRC was adopted by the Fifth National People's Congress. Deng Xiaoping, who opposed the Marxist dictum of "to each according to his need" and hoped to relink the concepts of work and reward, used the Congress as a stepping stone for his own political rehabilitation. Understanding the wish of the peasant mass to improve its standard of living, Deng supported the decollectivization of the country's communes and the promotion of private land plots.

The system of communes that effectively dominated the lives of the vast majority of Chinese began during the 1950s under Mao's plan for "self-reliance." Before that time, the Chinese peasant economy was fairly diversified with 90 percent of Chinese living in towns or villages.[7] Formation of the People's Communes (PCs) began in earnest in 1958 during the Great Leap Forward. Most of China's unincorporated territory merged into the PCs. The communes operated on both an economic and political level. The communes' economic functions consisted of operating and maintaining everything from schools to hospitals to the local militia.[8] On a day-to-day basis, the communes controlled the life of the peasant from the cradle to the grave.

During the 1960s and 1970s, 80 percent of the Chinese population belonged to a PC. To take advantage of perceived economies of scale, during the first decade of the communes, the state reorganized individual collectives into massive organizations. By the late 1960s, it became apparent that because of the low level of technology, little efficiency was gained by increasing the size of the communes. Consequently, the PCs shrunk in size but tripled in number. Still, levels of efficiency improved only slightly. As the 1970s drew to a close, there were increasing calls from the countryside to improve the living standards of the masses. Deng and other reformers recognized that the commune system, having deprived its workers of incentives, was paying the price by an atrophied productive force.[9] The consequent economic reforms di-

6   Ling (1991).
7   Schran (1993, p. 133).
8   Khan (1984, p. 77).
9   Ghose (1984, p. 253).

rected at the countryside resulted because the political elite recognized that a serious crisis was festering in the interior provinces. Particularly worrisome was the fact that close to 30 million Chinese were either unemployed or underemployed. The drain on the system's resources was tremendous, and the leadership was growing fearful of peasant unrest.

To alleviate the problems in their districts, enterprising local officials had begun acting like entrepreneurs, soliciting bids for their purchases, aggressively seeking customers, and even developing local industries to ensure an adequate supply of materials.[10] Such behavior exacerbated competition among the provinces and between the central ministries and the local party cadres.

A reform of the communes was desperately needed to prevent the escalation of tensions among provinces and to defuse the mounting frustration of the peasant mass. To coordinate the patchwork of local measures, while at the same time solidifying his new base of power, Deng proposed a sweeping agricultural reform beginning with the promotion of private land plots. By the end of 1979, the share of private plots had increased to 15 percent from 12 percent in 1978.[11] The movement toward private ownership was rapidly gaining acceptance among the peasant population that had worked for the last three decades without realizing the benefit of its toil. In the mid 1980s, the system of privatizing land plots was again restructured. As a result of this restructuring, two types of plots now exist in each village. The first is allocated equally to the village households and kept for private use. The second type is allocated through contracts, secured through an open bidding process.[12]

The economic openness fostered by the reforms resulted in the transformation of the collectives' leadership into something more akin to a corporate management team.[13] Many rural governments (Guanghan municipality in Sichuan Province, for instance), in cooperation with the local collectives, created astute systems of labor management to handle the rural labor surplus—finding out where shortages existed and creating incentives for the workers to migrate to those areas. Workers and

---

10   Goldstein (1988, p. 226) recounts that "central ministries and planning organs already weakened by the turmoil of the Cultural Revolution lost major sinews of financial and material allocative powers."
11   Khan (1984).
12   Bell, Hoe, and Kochhar (1993, p. 15).
13   For a broader discussion, see Hsieh (1993).

commune leaders with natural business abilities were able to benefit themselves and their communities under the reforms. The biggest boon to these fledgling entrepreneurs was the incentives available through the production responsibility system. The new system linked the income of individuals directly to their work output. The concept of personal profit incentives had a profound effect on the peasant culture. No longer bound so tightly to the state, citizens began to experience a small measure of personal autonomy.

The other major event of the late 1970s took place in December 1978 during the Third Plenary Session of the 11th Central Committee of the Chinese Communist Party. If the March Constitution laid the groundwork for a more liberalized economy, the December meeting provided the building blocks to realize this goal. Private markets were legitimized in the rural areas, and the private sale of agricultural goods was sanctioned in the cities. To increase the effects of the incentive systems, the state significantly reduced the tax burden in rural communities, allowing new industrial enterprises to operate tax free for a number of years.[14] The extent to which the agricultural sector was freed from government control can be seen in Table 8.1, which shows the percentage of agricultural produce bought by cash as opposed to a government bank transfer.[15]

These cash transactions opened up both the rural market and the urban centers as the peasants traveled into the cities to sell their produce. The nascent market was given an additional boost by the political rehabilitation of millions of wealthy peasants, rural landowners, and urban businessmen scapegoated during the Cultural Revolution. Their expertise and business acumen proved vital to the burgeoning market.

Table 8.1. *Percentage of agricultural produce bought by cash (PRC)*

Year	Percentage Paid by Cash
1978	27.9
1979	33.7
1980	40.2
1981	46.6
1982	52.3
1983	60.0

14   Ghose (1984).
15   People's Bank of China (1988).

The reforms of the late 1970s and early 1980s began to slowly change the Chinese culture. The strongly held belief that all official power must reside in the center began to give way to a more nonauthoritarian view. The increase in personal economic freedom, allowed by Deng in exchange for the people's support of his reform policies, corresponded to a dispersion of official authority and a loss of a good deal of the state's intrusive powers.

Despite the apparent enthusiasm for the reforms in many sectors of society, a large portion of the population was still extremely wary of the change in policy away from the Marxist-Leninist line. Joining forces with those skeptical for ideological reasons were those who were suffering from the increase in primary product prices. Although the state expended nearly eight and a half billion yuan in 1979 in subsidies to counter these ill effects, the overall purchase price index rose by 22.1 percent during the same year. The schism between the conservatives and reformers grew wider as the reform policies expanded in scope and breadth.

To strengthen support for his reform plan, Deng enlisted an unlikely ally—the political activists willing to speak out against the remaining Maoists within the party. Deng particularly promoted those in opposition to his own arch rival, Hua Guofeng. Taking a very large gamble, one which many say he lost, Deng permitted the anti-Hua faction to voice its concerns through the large character posters attached to the walls of Beijing. Deng succeeded in ousting Hua, but he was surprised to find that the multitude of government critics cultivated to purge Hua next turned their sights on him. The posters on the walls of Beijing criticized Deng for not taking his reforms further and for failing to liberalize the political system as well as the economy. These protests became known as the Democracy Wall Movement and served as the forerunner of the Tiananmen protests a decade later.

To express the concerns of the people, Wei Jingsheng, editor of an opposition journal, wrote the following in 1979:

> Everyone in China is well aware that the Chinese social system is not democratic and that this lack of democracy has severely stunted every aspect of the country's social development over the past 30 years. . . . Does Deng Xiaoping want democracy? No, he does not. . . . He describes the struggle for democratic rights—a movement launched spontaneously by the people—as the actions of troublemakers and of people who want to destroy normal public order which must therefore be repressed. . . . So the

crux of the matter is not who becomes master of the nation, but rather that . . . the people must maintain a firm control over their own nation, for this is the very essence of democracy.[16]

In the subsequent political crackdown against the Democracy Wall activists, Wei was convicted and jailed for "counterrevolutionary crimes." Still in jail a decade later, his plight became a rallying cry during the 1989 protests. Wei's bravery and his eloquent description of a more democratic Chinese society raised the hopes of millions of Chinese. Although the actions in 1979 did not lead to any short-term results, they set the stage for a gradual increase of personal liberties throughout the next decade. The 1979 crackdown temporarily silenced the voices of reform, but it did nothing to contain the broader societal movements that were pushing the country toward liberalization, namely, the provincial support for continued opening-up.[17]

By the beginning of the 1980s, the face of the countryside had altered dramatically. Although 1981 saw the official recognition of the Household Responsibility System, the system had already been adopted by 45 percent of production teams.[18] Government involvement was continuing to decline, and the rural population was growing accustomed to its first experiences with individualism. Decentralization not only occurred on a national level but within the communes as well. The reforms of the previous few years had greatly reduced the power and scope of authority of the central government over the provinces. In addition to the removal of a number of restrictive and intrusive regulations in the lives of the peasantry, the government was curtailed from a number of activities by a lack of funds. State revenues were declining as taxes were reduced and private enterprises, further from the oversight of government officials, flourished. As a consequence, state investment projects were undertaken at lower levels or were shelved completely.[19] As the central government's financial involvement in the provinces declined, so did its authority.

The rural reforms of the late 1970s taught the peasants that they had a strong hand in determining their economic future. In particular, they learned the power of creating and implementing policy at the local level

16   Wei (1984, p. 107).
17   Lin (1993, p. 75).
18   Gelb, Jefferson, and Singh (1993).
19   Ghose (1984).

and undertaking these policies in a private, as opposed to collective, venue. Such activity would have been swiftly curtailed by the central ministries had not farm yield increased significantly.[20] The average per capita income from the collective sector had dropped from 66 percent to 52 percent, whereas income from private occupations had increased from 27 percent to 38 percent.[21] The provinces, encouraged to experiment with individual reforms, were continuously pushing the boundaries of liberalization. Indeed, a 1994 OECD study stated that "China's economic reform began without any comprehensive blueprint or timetable. This strategy allowed Chinese reformers to experiment on a limited scale, and when policies proved successful, the government endorsed them."[22] In many respects, the provinces were leading the center further down the road of modernization, a remarkable occurrence in a culture that stressed the discipline of systems of authority.

Not wishing to antagonize the allies cultivated among the farmers and growing middle class, Deng continued to push through economic reforms. In the 1982 Constitution (adopted in December 1982), certain restrictions on township governments were abolished, creating a separation of power between the managerial and economic functions of the PC. Deng recognized the advantages of allowing business leaders to control the business of the communes and of retaining the administrative duties for the appointed party officials. A commingling of financial and administrative duties had allowed for negligible oversight of the commune system and had created an environment rife with graft and corruption. This separation of the financial and administrative functions, first tested in Sichuan, would limit such opportunities for fraud and embezzlement while at the same time streamlining the operation into a more efficient form.

The policy was promoted in the interest of increasing commune efficiency, but in actuality it had its most far-reaching effects on reducing the stature of the party and the party officials within the rural communities. No longer did the party designee dictate all aspects of commune life. With the 1982 Constitution, the value of work and productivity was rewarded through the promotion of successful business leaders. These rural reforms culminated in the dissolution of the communes by

20   Kelliher (1992, p. 242).
21   State Statistical Bureau (1981).
22   Fukasaku and Wall (1994, p.12).

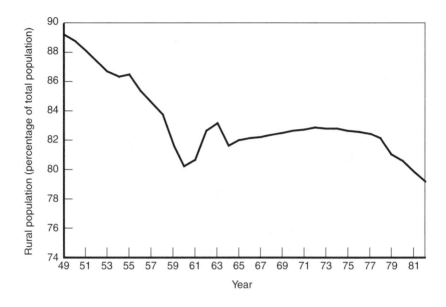

Figure 8.1. Decline of Rural Population in the PRC: 1949–1982

1984 and expanded the development of rural population centers. The decline of the rural population can be seen in Figure 8.1.[23]

As in Korea during the 1950s and Taiwan during the 1960s, China was experiencing the first generational phenomenon of land reform—the breakdown of rural life. Coming on the heels of this transformation was the gradual influx of displaced workers into the urban centers. Nearly 200 million surplus workers were thrown out of work after de-collectivization, and many migrated to the cities to find employment. To curb the growing discontent of these displaced workers, Deng created four Special Economic Zones (SEZ) in Shenzhen, Zhuhai, Shantou, and Xiamen between 1979 and 1980 in an attempt to stimulate the urban markets and thwart the coalescing of a mass movement bent on matching political reforms with those seen in the economic sphere. The four original zones (Hainan was established in 1988) were on China's coast, a natural gateway to the outside world, permitting the state to limit the portals to the outside world while at the same time taking advantage of the synergies created by the influx of capital and technology

23   State Statistical Bureau, various years.

Table 8.2. *Exports and foreign direct investment of China's SEZ*

	Exports (US$ millions)		FDI (US$ millions)	
SEZ	1981	1991	1981	1991
Shenzhen	17	5,990	589	510
Zhuhai	222	1,110	220	108
Shantou	272	820	9	84
Xiamen	141	1,270	48	73
SEZ % of national	3	12.9	69	23

to a confined area.[24] As seen in Table 8.2, the four SEZ became, over the next decade, major contributors to the national economy. [25]

Despite Deng's economic reforms and the promises of an improved standard of living, the lessons of the Democracy Wall Movement were not forgotten by the people. Distrust of the CCP was deepening, and sentiment was growing that economic freedoms could not be maintained without an accompanying political voice. Meanwhile, the government continued to balance a seesaw between economic liberalization, which had the effect of marginalizing central control, and political repression, which strengthened the regime (at least in the short term).

The hardliners in the government embarked on an anti-pollution campaign in 1983 to halt the spread of economic reform and reassert control over the independence-minded provinces. In these efforts, the elites were supported by a sizable portion of the population who feared that a weakening of the state could result in civil chaos.[26] Because of the sheer magnitude of the population and the disasters that would result from civil strife, generations of Chinese have been willing to relinquish individual autonomy to a strong state that can preserve harmony. The hardliners played upon this fear in the prosecution of their campaign.

But the reforms of the previous five years resulted in a citizenry less willing to support the absolute authority of the state. In response to both domestic and foreign fears that the anti-reformists were taking the

24   For a broader discussion, see Kleinberg (1990, p. 47).
25   Jia (1994).
26   Pye (1985) writes of the Chinese's "near-pathological fear of factionalism and social confusion or disorder [that result] if brothers fight, if villages have feuds, or if there are factions in their elite politics."

campaign to an extreme that would have a lasting effect on China's modernization efforts, the reformers were able to curtail the excesses of the conservatives. On November 20, 1983, Hu Yaobang attacked the campaigners for allowing the purges to negatively affect economic work. The following month, a central party directive dictated that the countryside would be off-limits in the prosecution of the campaign.[27] By the time economic theorists, scientists, and religious leaders were placed off-limits, the campaign was on the verge of collapse. The short-lived anti-reform campaign, in conjunction with the "open door" policies, led many in China into the mid 1980s with a feeling of guarded optimism that political liberalization might yet come to the Middle Kingdom.

CULTURAL CHANGE AND ITS EFFECT ON THE STATE: MID 1980s

Once the anti-pollution campaign was discredited, reformers began to take stock of the marketizing measures enacted in the late 1970s and recognized that the reforms were not moving fast enough and were often contradictory. The economic development plan of 1978 was long on promises and short on specifics. It failed miserably. The 1984 urban reforms were intended to correct these deficiencies. In the official "Decision of the Central Committee of the Chinese Communist Party on Reform of the Economic Structure" adopted in October 1984, a number of major policy decisions were announced.

The most important reforms created incentives for the private market to flourish. Firms were encouraged to increase productivity and efficiency through responsibility contracts in which planned state targets were drastically reduced and firms were allowed to retain surpluses after fulfilling their contracts. To stimulate the productive investment sector, enterprises were encouraged to borrow from banks rather than the state, thereby diminishing the amount of politically motivated loans that often caused substantial drains on the economy when the investments failed.

Many of the reforms announced in 1984 were more broad brushstrokes than a master plan. Deng and his aides hoped to cultivate an environment where economic experiments could be tried locally and, if successful, exported to other regions. Encouraged by party reformers including Zhao Ziyang and Vice Premier Yao Yilin, Hainan Island was

27   Hamrin (1990, p. 73).

allowed to experiment with many of the foreign trade and investment rights granted to the SEZ. Likewise, Chongqing lobbied for, and became, the first large city allowed to plan its economic development apart from the overly bureaucratic provincial authorities. Enterprising localities, and the firms within their borders, were pushing the envelope of marketization. Three such "private experiments" occurred over the next two years. In May 1983, an investment company in Baoan County, Shenzhen, tried the experiment of instituting a shareholding system by publicly issuing shareholding cards; in mid 1984, the Tianqiao Department Store Shareholding Company in Beijing emerged as the first of its kind; and in late 1984, the Shanghai Feirue Acoustic Company became the first to issue shares to the public in a professional, standardized way.[28] These would serve as the initial blueprint for the stock markets established later in the decade.

In the environment created by the announcements of 1984, citizens felt more comfortable voicing their demands for further reforms. Some of the loudest calls were for a complete revamping of the financial system. One major criticism of the existing system was that firms could use bank transfers only in business dealings. Firms hoping to export or form joint ventures with foreign partners were stymied not only by the restriction on cash withdrawals on bank accounts without official approval, but also by an overly bureaucratic, extremely inefficient banking system. Advocates argued that without changes to the financial sector, the efficacy of the recent spate of economic reforms (the contract responsibility system, the market pricing allowances, and the tax rate changes) was minimized. Considering these comments appropriate, the party reformers instituted widespread changes to the entire monetary system.

By the end of 1984, the single bank, the People's Bank, had been replaced by a central bank, a reserve system, and four specialized banks charged with providing loans to various sectors of the economy. The extent of this decentralization of control was considerable. Before the reforms of the early 1980s, the People's Bank controlled 91 percent of the total assets of the Chinese financial sector.[29] By 1986 this had dropped to 25 percent. The four specialized banks—Industrial and Commercial Bank of China, Agricultural Bank of China, People's Construction Bank of China, and the Bank of China (which manages

28   Wang Hui (1994).
29   Yi (1992).

foreign exchange and international transactions)—took over most of the commercial functions from the People's Bank.

Another consequence of the financial reform was that the income velocity of money (also known as the transaction velocity) decreased. Cash in circulation in 1988 was 10 times greater than it had been a decade earlier. The increase in MO (cash in circulation) has been greater than the sum of the GDP growth rate and inflation. Since the quantity theory of money holds that the velocity of money plus the nominal money supply must equal the price level plus real GNP, then the velocity must be negative. This can result if the actual price level is higher than the official price level or there has been a monetization process in China. Such a process implies that the proportion of economic activities conducted with money, as opposed to barter or self-sufficiency (a farmer consuming his own product), has increased. As a result, the money supply is increasing not only in relation to the expanded economy but also as the economy monetizes. From the advent of agricultural reform, citizens had been entering the market in greater numbers and learning to conduct commerce without the state as middleman. The financial reforms had the effect of commingling the currency in circulation and bank transfer money. The result was that the central monetary authority had less control over the money supply.[30] The state was losing an important tool of supervision and control over everyday business transactions.

China in the mid 1980s was quite different from its totalitarian predecessor. Not unlike those in Taiwan, the political elites were recognizing the need to bring into government a breed of economic technocrat able to competently guide the emergence of a modern economy. These technocrats were willing to give a freer hand to specific sectors of the populace if the people would assist in the modernization effort. Despite this move toward more openness on the one hand, the political elite kept a firm grasp over the regime, silencing dissent in whatever quarter it arose. Nonetheless, economic modernization had the effect of decreasing the scope of political interference in daily life, increasing the outlets for expression in political affairs, and expanding the purview of provincial and local governmental agencies at the expense of the central government.[31]

30   Yi (1992).
31   Harding (1986).

Just as the economic reforms of the late 1970s set in motion the protests of the Democracy Wall Movement, the administrative reforms announced by Deng Xiaoping in the spring of 1986 led to widescale protests later that year. Deng, in the hopes of increasing the efficacy of his new policies, announced a large-scale bureaucratic downsizing intended to trim government waste. The implied opprobrium of party officials opened the flood gates for censure of the government as a whole. This, in turn, served as a catalyst for political reformers to move forward from simply "revising ideology" to restructuring institutions and laws.[32] To broaden their base of support, these political activists, or "democratic elite," recognized the need for an association with a number of special interest organizations that had begun to form as advocacy groups of reform. Known as "small parties," organizations of this type were banned during the Cultural Revolution but revived in 1980 under the auspices of the United Front Work Department.

In 1985, a reform-minded bureaucrat, Yan Mingfu, was appointed head of the department and worked to broaden the economic clout of these small parties by bringing them together under an umbrella organization, by building on their contacts within the government and within the overseas Chinese communities, and by convincing the groups that they must work together to create a viable plan of further economic modernization and present this plan to the government. Exploiting the increased visibility and strengthening ties to the West, the small parties felt confident enough to demand an institutionalized role to help formulate policy. Such a desire immediately raised fears among some party elders who suspected that the small parties were beginning to coalesce into a formal opposition. In sharp contrast, party reformer Hu Yaobang actively encouraged the small parties, as well as more vocal critics of the government, to continue their calls for further reform. The tensions between Hu and Deng Xiaoping, escalating for some time, reached a crisis point when Hu refused to condemn the physicist and dissident Fang Lizhi for statements made regarding the pace of political reforms. Fang's statements, as well as the Hu-Deng split, created the right environment for students to take to the streets protesting that the societal contract must be renegotiated to adequately reflect a more equitable distribution of power between the state and the populace.

The overt demands of the protesters were for more independence for the student unions and increased democracy. It should be noted, how-

32 Goldman (1994).

ever, that democracy was often just a catchall phrase for a better life—encompassing everything from a freer press to better student facilities. Whether the impetus for the protests was a desire for the lofty goals of political liberalization or the more mundane material needs of everyday life, the mere fact that the protesters were willing to take to the streets in defiance of the party elders was quite significant. At the outset of the protests, there was little active support from workers and urban residents. Soon, however, the small parties formally endorsed the calls of the students for greater economic and political freedom.

Employing the protests as the excuse, the party elites embarked on a purge of political reformers. Lei Jieqiong, legal expert and vice chair of the CPPCC (Chinese People's Political Consultative Conference) National Committee responded to this new rounds of purges by counseling moderation on both sides. The CPPCC was created in the 1940s to explore the possibility of the Communists and Nationalists forming a coalition government. Outlawed during the Cultural Revolution, the CPPCC was resurrected in the 1980s to give voice to noncommunist individuals, parties, and professional groups. In an editorial, Lei wrote:

> For young students who are concerned about state politics to voice their views through demonstrations is in line with the Constitution. . . . If it is just a demonstration, then it cannot be considered illegal . . . [however] as long as our people are still suffering from poverty and ignorance, democracy can hardly be realized. Since it has taken Western countries a long time to establish democracy, we cannot on our part accomplish a high degree of socialist democracy in one move, nor can we reach our goal by simply shouting slogans and demonstrating.[33]

Despite his words of caution to the protesters, the CPPCC worked closely with the small parties and added their voice to the rising chorus calling for greater political and economic reforms.

Laying the blame for the protests squarely on the shoulders of Hu Yaobang, party elders began maneuvering for his ouster. On January 16, 1987, Hu was forced to resign as party general secretary for the crimes of opposition to the campaigns against spiritual pollution and bourgeoisie liberalization, tolerance of intellectual dissenters, and failure to crack down on the protesters. Just as Deng had exploited the Democracy Wall protesters to purge Hua Guofeng, so did he strengthen the hand of the elders to effect the removal of Hu Yaobang. And, just

33   *Zhongguo Xinwenshe* (1987).

as the 1979 protesters moved past the mandate charged to them by Deng, so did the party elders widen their campaign against liberalization from the political to the economic sphere—Deng's protected reforms. Deng had wanted the purges to end with Hu and his loyalists, to keep the crackdown on political reformers, but party leadership stepped up their attacks on Western lifestyles and Western-style capitalism.

Deng, having been compromised in his dismissal of Hu, turned to Zhao Ziyang, the party premier promoted in 1980, to contain the elders' campaign. Zhao moved quickly to protect the intellectuals behind the 1987 protests while at the same time greatly expanding marketization reforms and China's outward orientation. Of special concern to Deng, Zhao, and their supporters was the way China was perceived by the West in comparison to Taiwan. Taiwan was slowly moving to end martial law, and its leaders were embracing political reform. This political liberalization, in combination with Taiwan's growing economic might, raised fears among the Chinese leadership that the West would become favorably disposed to the ROC at the expense of the PRC. Recognizing that economic liberalization was the key not only to a prosperous future but also to an international position of leadership, Zhao, through sheer force of personality, ended the repression and returned China to a path of reform. Although the actual reforms instituted were weak and only questionably moved the country toward political liberalization, the fact that the political conservatives had been beaten back by the reformers was treated as a great success by the democratic elite. For support within the regime would be needed if the societal contract was to be rewritten stipulating a fairer distribution of power between the state and the people.

Following on the heels of Zhao's new economic reforms, the democratic elite began building bridges to the growing middle class, pointing out to the new entrepreneurs and urban professionals that they needed a voice in government to protect their interests. The new middle class understood that its interests revolved around formalizing property rights and expanding economic freedoms, yet the democratic elite were hoping to strengthen both the rule of law and the institutions that would form the basis for a democratic restructuring of society. Despite differing on the particulars, all sides agreed that the movement needed an expanded role in government.

Throughout the summer and fall of 1987, public opinion polls showed that the majority of Chinese wanted political reforms to keep

pace with economic ones.[34] Zhao presented his report on political reforms at the Thirteenth Party Congress in October 1987. He expressed
concern over the concentration of power and supported a meritocracy.
Although no separation of powers was considered, language was included that implied that the CCP should remove itself from absolute
control over the process. This led the way toward the rural democracy
project in which villages were allowed to elect local leaders to replace
the village chiefs appointed by the communes. Although often the only
candidates running were CCP members, the project was nonetheless a
grass roots experiment with democracy. Unverified by outside researchers, Beijing officials maintain that the experiment has reached 90
percent of the countryside.[35]

Zhao consistently advocated the need for the small parties to have a
political voice, stating that "there should be channels through which the
voices and demands of the people can be easily and frequently transmit-
ted to the leading bodies, and there should be places where the people
can offer suggestions or pour out any grievances. . . . Different groups
of people may have different interests and views, and they too need opportunities and channels for the exchange of ideas."[36] The concept of a
people's voice, a hallmark of Communism, was shunned during the
Mao years. For a party premier to sanction such involvement, although
the actuality of such an occurrence was unlikely, was viewed as an institutional paradigmatic shift.

The ability for the small parties to organize was aided by the rapidly
ebbing role the central government CCP played in the life of the citizen. As
shown in Figure 8.2, the contribution of state-owned industries to industrial output was declining and, as a result, so was the coercive power
of the state.[37] Those employed in private sector endeavors reduced
their reliance on state agencies for health, food, and housing benefits.
As a result, they were less inclined to follow the directives of the state
regarding other matters of personal autonomy. The societal contract
stipulating the responsibilities and obligations of the state and its citizens was being restructured. Each party held fewer claims over the
other.

34   Goldman (1994).
35   Tempest (1996).
36   *Beijing Review* (1987).
37   *Statistical Yearbook of China*, various years.

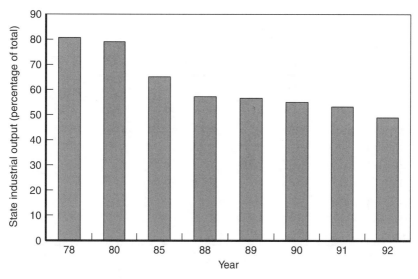

Figure 8.2. Contribution of State-Owned Industries to Industrial Output
in the PRC: 1978–1992

As shown in Figure 8.3, private industrial firms and domestic-foreign joint ventures were quickly becoming the modus operandi for operating outside of the state sector.[38] Joint ventures served an important role at the individual, firm, and state levels. Individuals involved in foreign joint ventures were learning more than economics from their new partners. Customs, mores, and the culture of freedom were also being brought to the mainland. Slowly at first, but gradually in larger numbers, Chinese executives were traveling to the West for business meetings and experiencing freedom first hand.

At the firm level, the Chinese were learning the importance of a more equitable position in state-business relations. Western partners were demanding tax incentives and property protections, and the Chinese partners were having to convey these desires to their party officials. Buoyed by the confidence of their Western affiliates, the Chinese were adding their own set of demands to the list. At the state level, the economic reformers led by Zhao Ziyang, but backed in large part by the small parties and the CCPPC, were pushing to expand these new rela-

38   *Statistical Yearbook of China,* various years.

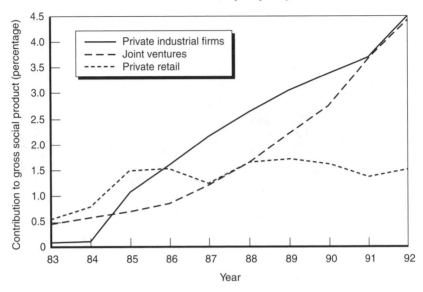

Figure 8.3. Contribution of Private Sector Firms and Joint Ventures to Gross
Social Product in the PRC: 1983–1992

tionships. China was losing ground to its East Asian neighbors and was in desperate need of infusions of high technology and efficient management practices. To rectify this situation, the state allowed 2,100 foreign technological items to be imported during the 1981–1986 period at a cost in excess of US$9 billion—a far cry from the days of Mao's "self-sufficiency."[39] The open door policy forced existing institutions to adapt to a wide-ranging series of changes. Foreign capital and foreign investors demanded greater transparency in accounting and management practices from their Chinese partners. As a consequence, the SOEs, the CCP, the army, the central bank, and the growing private sphere were finding themselves compelled to undertake varying levels of modification.[40]

Marketization can also be gauged by assessing the percentage of investment by the private, as opposed to the public, domain. Individual firm investment in fixed assets increased sharply during the mid 1980s as shown in Figure 8.4.[41] Individual businesses are those owned by a

39   Zheng (1994).
40   For a broader discussion, see Howell (1991).
41   *Statistical Yearbook of China*, various years.

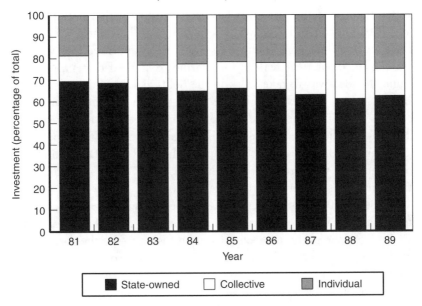

Figure 8.4. Increase in Total Investment in Fixed Assets in the PRC:
1981–1989

household or individual and employing no more than seven people. Such a rapid development of the non-state sector occurred not only because of institutional reform but also because of the pent-up demand of Chinese consumers. Taking advantage of the financial reforms discussed above, non-state enterprises quickly adapted to the more open environment, whereas the highly bureaucratized and overly bloated state-owned entities could not.

Not everyone has reaped the benefits of these new reforms, however. The majority of workers remain on the state's payroll, and a sizable number of citizens are unemployed or underemployed. Many have lost their jobs from the restructuring or collapse of state firms forced to compete with more efficient private and foreign firms. Official numbers suggest an unemployment rate of 2 percent, but other reports suggest a rate as high as 30 percent, or 200 million citizens.[42] Even citizens who have retained their jobs have seen their real wages decrease, their subsidies slashed, and the prices for food and services rise dramatically.

42   Overholt (1993).

Resentment over these changes has been building within both the rural and urban centers. These were the people who had remained loyal to the state and the state's enterprise system, yet it appeared they were being punished for their fealty. One farmer remarked that "we used to think the idea was to take work in the fields as the fundamental thing. But as soon as we saw the attitude of the people at the top, our hearts sank. . . . When they hold model worker meetings they invite the 10,000-yuan households over and over again. It's only the people who grow grain who are always left out in the cold."[43] Disappointment over the state's failure to provide has left many questioning the traditional relationship between the state and society.

As the 1980s drew to a close, it was becoming apparent that a professionally run economy was undermining the central control of the CCP. Even the party intellectuals were refusing to toe the party line in all instances and were becoming more vocal in promoting their own agendas. The underlying premise of the reforms, that the individual must take on a certain amount of personal responsibility, was more successful than the planners of the reforms could have imagined—more successful than perhaps they wanted. The Maoist tenet that the state's interest, in all aspects of life, takes precedence over the desires of the individual was faltering.

BREACH OF CONTRACT: LATE 1980s

Another round of reforms in 1988 led to another round of changes to the Chinese economy and culture and, as a result, to the societal contract between the state and its citizens. In the economic realm, private firms were legitimized and price decontrols were extended to the broad market. Members of various sectors of society, from peasant to local cadre elites, began pushing for further reforms and less state dominance. State-controlled enterprises continued to lose market share. As an example, in 1979 the state's share of retail output was 54 percent, whereas collectives contributed 43 percent and self-employed individuals 2.9 percent. In 1988, those figures became, respectively, 39.5 percent, 34.4 percent, and 26.1 percent.[44]

Financial market reforms continued as well. Although the government of China had been issuing bonds since 1981, a secondary market

43   Kelliher (1991, p. 336).
44   *Almanac of China's Economy* (1988).

for these bonds was created in 1988, greatly expanding the ability of the government to raise money and giving many sectors of the population their first lesson in capital markets. China's economic growth and expanded entrepreneurial freedoms promoted a high demand for money. In a monetizing economy, a vigorous circulation of currency outside the banking system represents the strengthening of the private sector. Such was the case in China, where *mtwo* as a percentage of GDP increased from 37 percent in 1980 to 83 percent in 1990.[45]

A major foreign exchange reform, signaling China's commitment to the open door policy of the previous decade, occurred when the Ministry of Foreign Economic Relations and Trade (MOFERT), later renamed the Ministry of Foreign Trade and Economic Cooperation (MOFTEC), was granted the authority to enter into contracts with provincial authorities. The amount of foreign exchange earnings, the amount of foreign currency exchange to be remitted to the central government, and the fixed amount of domestic currency that the Foreign Trade Corporations (FTCs)[46] could provide to subsidize losses on export sales were now managed by MOFERT.[47] The effect of this strategy was to reform the historical centrally controlled import system, decentralizing some of the decisionmaking to the provinces, while still allowing MOFERT to supervise the general system. Of equal importance, more Foreign Exchange Adjustment Centers, first opened in 1986 and referred to as swap centers, were opened, and authorized users were enlarged to include SOEs and Collectively Owned Entities (COEs) as well as the traditional Foreign Investment Enterprise (FIE) clients. Liberalization of the swap centers helped raise volume in the secondary markets from US$4.2 billion in 1987 to US$6.3 billion in 1988 to US$25 billion in 1992.[48]

Following the new round of reforms in 1988, "cultural fever" broke out in China. Zhao Ziyang and the rest of the party reformers promoted the street-level discussions of the "New China" and its place in the world. Journals and scholarly books were allowed to explore the issue. Not too surprisingly, such open discussion gave a platform to

45 International Monetary Fund, *International Financial Statistics,* various years.
46 These were the government-authorized centers allowed to carry out external trade.
47 World Bank, *Social Indicators of Development* (1994, p. 26).
48 World Bank, *Social Indicators of Development* (1994, p. 32).

party critics. When a TV series known as the River Elegy (He Shang), produced by former Red Guards, began taking issue with the pace of reforms and questioning the authority of the CCP, the party elders were quick to call the series, and the cultural fever that underlay it, a "betrayal of the nation" and used it to reassert their authority and press for discontinuation of the reforms.[49]

By the fall of 1988, a retreat from both economic and political reforms was under way. The price reforms of June 1988 (in which price controls declined from 100 percent in 1978 to 44 percent by 1990) led to sharply increased prices, rampant inflation, and a run on the banks. Figure 8.5 displays the rapid rise of inflation in the late 1980s.[50] The blame for such a rapid escalation in inflation lay mostly with corrupt government financial officials who exploited the price differences between the economically depressed SOE sector and the booming private economy. The misuse of privileged information, as well as the escalating bankrolls of government officials, only served to increase resentment of the CCP by both the business elite and the general population.[51]

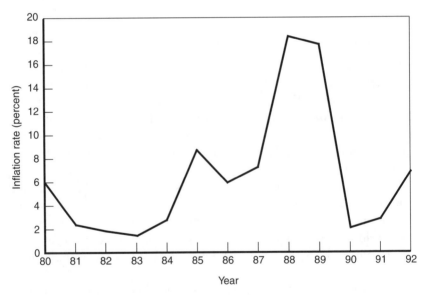

Figure 8.5. Inflation Rate in the PRC: 1980–1992

49	Goldman (1994, p. 259).
50	State Statistical Bureau (1981).
51	For a discussion of this, see Johnson (1990).

The combination of a sliding standard of living and a mounting disgust with a central authority that had lost its moral legitimacy left citizens vulnerable to the appeals of the hardliners that the reforms of the last decade were at the heart of the country's woes. Zhao Ziyang was made to accept the blame for the rampant inflation and was forced to "self-criticize" for overheating the economy. The hardliners took such an admission as a victory in their fight to limit economic liberalization and consolidate power back in the center.

Despite such actions by the hardliners, political reforms continued to make headway in the early months of 1989, propelled in part by the discussions in the cultural fever exchanges. The moral bankruptcy of corrupt party officials and rampant inflation were viewed by many as a breach in the societal contract that obligated the state to provide for the livelihood of the people and prevent civil chaos. As it became apparent that the central authorities were having difficulty upholding their end of the bargain, citizens began to question their own responsibilities to the state. This cultural shift led to a corresponding reevaluation of many of the country's political institutions. In March 1989, the National People's Congress (the Chinese legislature) met to codify for the first time procedures governing elections, the conduct of meetings, impeachment, and investigations of government officials. Another piece of legislation ratified in the March meeting was the Administrative Litigation Law, which stipulated the process by which citizens could sue government officials. The law not only strengthened the rights of individual citizens but increased the legitimacy of the legal process, for it protected the litigants' attorneys from persecution and recrimination.

On March 26, 1989, on the heels of these pronouncements, a number of organizations—including corporations, newspapers, and think tanks—collaborated in calling for constitutional reform. As the political activists began increasing the volume of their demands, their de facto leader, Hu Yaobang, reassessed his political future and decided to reenter public life. Hu unexpectedly died on April 15, 1989. As a catalyst and pretext, Hu's funeral procession and memorial services began a two-month demonstration that ended on June 4 in a bloody crackdown in Tiananmen Square.

In the days following Hu's death, the editor of the *Shanghai World Economic Herald* was prohibited from publishing a eulogy to Hu unless the proofs were approved by the Shanghai Propaganda Department. When he refused to submit the proofs, the editor was fired from his post, publicly criticized by then-mayor of Shanghai, Jiang Zemin, and had his paper taken over by party officials. In the turmoil of the takeover, the newspaper staff managed to print the headline "We need an environment where we can speak freely."[52] The *World Economic Herald* case became a cause célèbre for journalists throughout China. The event became a symbol not only of freedom of the press but of greater political liberalization overall. In formal protest, newspapers throughout the country began to give extensive coverage to the Tiananmen protests. Hoping to defuse a potentially explosive situation before the Sino-Soviet summit, Zhao Ziyang permitted the coverage to continue. He did not anticipate, however, that the increase in reporting would raise awareness of the events and lead to a swelling of the protesters' ranks by nearly one million people.

As the tenor of the protests became more acrimonious, party moderates like Zhao found themselves between a rock and a hard place. On one side were the party elders who, with each passing day, stepped up their calls for a swift and brutal response. On the other side were the students themselves who were disinclined to accept pledges of compromise from a government they perceived as illegitimate. Meanwhile, the protests had expanded from a student demonstration to encompass the rising class of entrepreneurs and urban workers who viewed the protests as a means to express their disgust with the slow pace of reforms, the unfulfilled promises of party leaders, the rapidly escalating inflationary pressures, the lack of legal and property rights, and the appalling amount of corruption within the government bureaucracy. Pye writes that the Chinese "have a long and well-established tradition that government and politics should be thought of only in terms of moralistic ideology."[53] As corruption pervades the government, citizens begin to question the legitimacy of the regime. If the state is unable to perform its duties under the societal contract, citizens become unwilling to surrender autonomy to the central authorities. The 1989 protests were an expression of this perceived breach of contract by the government.

As more of the growing middle class joined the protests, the number and quality of the demonstration's supporters also changed from being exclusively intellectuals and activists to including business leaders and even some forward-thinking government officials. The Shekou Special

52   "The Truth About the Case of Shijie Jingji Daobao," *Xinhua* (1989, p. 23).
53   Pye (1985, p. 186).

Economic Zone donated more than HK$210,000.[54]   Wan Runnan, founder and president of the Stone Group, the producer of a Chinese-English electronic typewriter, contributed 200,000 yuan and encouraged his employees to join the protest movement. With the inclusion of Wan, a successful entrepreneur whose company employed over 900 workers in 600 stores and 27 subsidiaries worldwide, the democracy movement took a giant leap forward. Wan's idea, that economic reforms can be secured only through democratic reform (pursued over the previous few years within the think tank he sponsored), became a rallying cry for the urban elite. Shaken out of their entrepreneurial reverie, which the previous few years of reform and economic bonanza had sunk them into, China's business class joined the protest, aware that their financial interests were at stake and willing to commit their resources to secure their future. Goldman writes that until "the 1989 demonstration, China's private sector was generally thought to be only interested in making money. But the participation of important entrepreneurs in the movement revealed that some of China's new business class also wanted political change and had the financial and personnel resources to support it."[55]

As the protests dragged on throughout May and threatened to interrupt the Gorbachev visit, Deng turned his back on Zhao and sanctioned the martial law decrees of May 19. Without Deng's active support or a coherent student leadership from which to extract a compromise, the moderates lost out to the party elite. On June 3, 1989, the military was called in to suppress the demonstrations. In the weeks following the June 4th crackdown, the state's propaganda machine spun the event to portray the demonstrations as a coup attempt by a small band of counterrevolutionaries. The Central Committee announced on June 5, 1989, that the counterrevolutionaries hoped to "negate the party's leadership and the socialist system by killing all 47 million Communist Party members if necessary. . . . [The plot was masterminded by] an extremely few people who have doggedly persisted in taking the stand of bourgeois liberalization and have colluded with hostile forces overseas, providing party and state vital secrets to illegal organizations."[56]   One government publication printed the statement: "When many people are still pre-occupied by the daily toil for basic survival, it is impossible to

54   *South China Morning Post* (1989, p. 1).
55   Goldman (1994, p. 315).
56   Morrison (1989, p. 196).

expect from them a high degree of democratic participation [and] if so
called democracy is forcibly implemented, interference from various factors will give rise to individualism, factionalism and anarchy, and lead
to de-facto nondemocracy and even chaos."[57] To maintain this party
line, newspapers were restaffed by party loyalists, think tanks were
closed and the researchers arrested, student leaders were jailed, and
scores of workers were executed. Zhao Ziyang was removed from office.

Wang Dan, a Standing Committee member of the student protests
and a member of the Beijing Federation of Students Autonomous
Union, compared the Chinese in 1989 to a starving person eating an
unripe fruit. Knowing that the fruit is unripe, the starving person eats it
anyway and falls sick with a terrible stomachache. Was it correct to eat
the fruit? If one is starving, how can one wait—but a stomachache may
be the result of eating too soon. So too with the Chinese people and
democracy.[58]

Despite the reigning in of political and economic liberalization in the
months following the crackdown, the foundation laid by the reforms of
the 1980s remained in place. Wan Runnan escaped to Paris where he
organized the Front for Democracy and advocated that citizens who
had renounced the party not reregister. Wan's thinking was that if the
newly emerging class of business elite and entrepreneurs held out, the
CCP would be forced into making political concessions, if only to acquire the assistance and brainpower of the professional classes.[59]

DRAFTING A NEW CONTRACT: THE 1990s

The diminution of the state's authority that began in earnest in the
1980s continued into the 1990s. By the early 1990s, the private sector
had 600 billion yuan in registered capital assets and employed 117 million people in rural industries and the formal private sector.[60] The
quasi-private rural industry generated more net profits than the state's
industrial sector, excluding transportation and construction. By 1991,

57   Wang Guofa (1989, pp. 32–33).
58   As paraphrased from a translated interview with Wan Dan (Gordon and
     Hinton, 1995).
59   Goldman (1994).
60   Pei (1994).

China had 73,857 free markets for consumer goods and 3,000 markets for small goods.[61]

The 1988 "enterprise laws," which allowed unit managers to work unhindered by party bosses, drastically reduced the power of the party within the state enterprise system. As an example, during a meeting in the summer of 1994 between American visitors and the president of the Wuxi Electrical Machine Plant, the company's party official was granted a physical seat at the negotiating table, but she never voiced an opinion and was treated with barely concealed contempt.

The great bastion of capitalism, a bourse, was formally established in Shanghai in December 1990 and Shenzhen in July 1991. This new access into the market was heralded throughout China. As an analyst from Yamaichi Securities remembers, "The popularity of stock investments was so high that stocks were also traded in the black market in some areas."[62] Although the issuance of stock had been permitted since 1980, the volume of issuances skyrocketed with the creation of a formal trading system. Whereas a total of RMB1 billion of stock was issued between 1981 and 1987, an additional nearly RMB16 million was issued between 1990 and 1992.[63] The ostensible reason for the opening of the exchanges was to promote the reform of SOEs by allowing the market to perform a watchdog role—rewarding efficient firms and their managers while punishing those who lingered in the Maoist days of guaranteed payroll and featherbedding. Party leaders also recognized that a stock market would help attract foreign capital. An unstated reason for the creation of the exchanges was the growing inability of the government to fund public investment. As the private sector increased in scope and depth during the 1980s, more economic activities were handled outside government control. Bank deposits and cash holdings of urban residents in 1989 exceeded 750 billion yuan.[64] The government desperately needed a new system to recycle funds and direct them toward productive investments. Whether the central authorities recognized that the stock markets would only further the marginalization of the government, or whether they were committed to the concept of economic liberalization to such an extent that the risk was justified,

61   *China Daily* (1991).
62   Yamaichi Securities (1994, p. 247).
63   *China Financial Almanac.*
64   The Fuji Bank Ltd. (1994).

the markets provided an invaluable lesson in democracy by introducing choice, competition, and accountability to the people.

Keeping pace with the push for internal reforms were substantial changes to the foreign investment laws. Obtaining foreign investment and foreign know-how became the linchpin in many of the reforms of the late 1980s and early 1990s. In addition to the laws governing joint ventures, China's antiquated exchange rate system underwent the second stage of transformation. The first occurred in the mid 1980s with the creation of the swap centers and the loosening of restrictions governing exchange. Those reforms centered around increasing the influence of the market in determining trading patterns. From 1981 to 1994, China operated a two-tier exchange rate system. Historically, the official rate was allowed to fluctuate according to central government planning, whereas the internal settlement rate (the secondary rate) was held fixed (usually at a more depreciated rate than the official rate).

On April 9, 1991, the central government expanded on the 1988 reforms when it allowed China's official exchange rate to adjust through a more transparent managed float system. The 1991 development attempted to bring the two rates more in line with one another by allowing the official rate to adjust. The adjustment would be based upon four factors: the balance of payments, the foreign currency markets, the FEACs (swap centers), and changes in the domestic resources cost of earning foreign exchange. Although the official exchange rate remained more expensive than the secondary market, greater convergence was achieved as shown in Figure 8.6. [65]

Although the rules regulating the swap centers eased, many problems remained. In particular, government-imposed ceilings and the unpredictable swap rates made exchanging currency expensive. The official rate was still highly overvalued and resulted in a de facto export tax, the amount of which equaled the difference between the swap and the official rates. The traditional reasoning for this overvaluation was to make government-sanctioned imports cheaper relative to the price of other imports.

Even after reform, the two-tiered system held the cost for foreign investment into China at almost prohibitive levels. Foreign investors were often coerced into converting their currency at the official exchange rate, which effectively reduced their shares in Chinese joint ventures by one-third. Novice foreign investors were often taken advantage of by

65   World Bank, *World Tables*, various years.

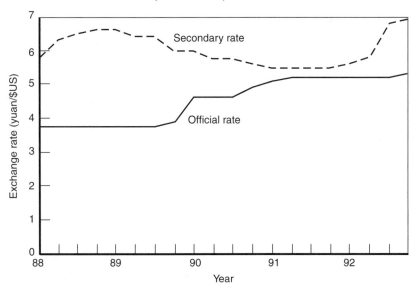

Figure 8.6. China's Two-Tiered Exchange Rate System

aggressive Chinese partners who insisted on project assessment in yuan but payments in dollars. After such an appraisal, the Chinese would convert the dollars to yuan at a higher rate in the swap market.[66] Additionally, in the early 1990s when the Chinese government began exploring different market mechanisms, foreign investors were at the mercy of an ever-fluctuating foreign exchange policy.

To pacify foreign investors, Beijing agreed to revisit its foreign investment laws. Since 1978 when the open door policy began and the first foreign investment laws were enacted, no further reform to the overly bureaucratized rules and regulations had ensued. It took another decade before the Equity Joint Venture Law was implemented in 1990 and the Foreign Investment Enterprise and Foreign Enterprise Income Tax Law were adopted on June 1, 1991. The new laws eased the restrictions on private individuals and firms wishing to enter into joint ventures with foreign parties. Table 8.3 chronicles the tremendous increase in foreign direct investment, pledged and used, before and after the reforms were put into place.[67]

66   "Yuan on Controlled Single-Track" (1994, p. 1).
67   Jia (1994).

Table 8.3. *Pledged and used foreign direct investment in the PRC*

Year	No. of Projects	Value Pledged (US$ billions)	Value Used (US$ billions)	%
1983	470	1.91	0.64	33.2
1984	1,856	2.88	1.26	43.8
1985	3,307	6.33	1.66	26.2
1986	1,498	3.33	1.87	56.3
1987	2,233	4.32	2.31	53.6
1988	5,945	5.30	3.19	60.0
1989	5.784	5.60	3.39	60.5
1990	7,273	6.60	3.40	51.5
1991	12,978	11.10	4.00	36.0
1992	47,000	57.50	11.16	20.0
1993	83,265	110.80	25.80	23.3

As foreign investors flooded to the shores of China, so did their ideas of political liberalization. Although more subdued than the cries for increased democracy in the late 1970s and mid 1980s, once again voices were heard calling for the regime to permit political freedoms tantamount to the economic ones. The deep freeze that overtook China's political activism in the two years that followed the Tiananmen protests began to thaw in 1992 when Deng Xiaoping visited the SEZ of Guangzhou and Shenzhen and officially blessed the way the two areas were conducting business. Particular praise was lavished on China's increased internationalization. Deng's visit to the SEZ, and his promotion of economic reform, thwarted a growing movement among the hardliners who had been promoting an ideological crackdown to rid the country of the moral decay being imported into China by foreign investors.

Deng's Southern China swing in 1992 signified the revival of the moderate-liberal branch of the CCP at the expense of the hardliners. Calling it socialism with Chinese characters, the government conceded to the capitalist movement. State-owned entities, once the pride of the PRC, were being sold off to private interests (even domestic-foreign joint ventures), and highly qualified personnel were allowed to leave their government posts to set up private industries. In a Chinese Academy of Social Science survey from the early 1990s, the most desired form of employment was private entrepreneurship. Many of these new entrepreneurs used their business acumen and private resources to affect government legislation. Many even entered politics. As an example, in the Zhejiang provincial election held in 1991, more than 40 percent of the council chiefs and 70 percent of the council members were local entrepreneurs.[68]

Following Deng's 1992 tour, reform of the private sector gathered momentum. The most far-reaching reform in foreign trade came in 1994 when China decided to end the dual rate system and rely on a daily rate determined by 18 designated Chinese banks and roughly 100 foreign banks operating in China. The benefits of the reform can be seen in Figure 8.7.[69]

Like most reforms in China, both political and economic, more openness often led to a clearer understanding of the tremendous amount of work that still needed to be accomplished to reach the goals of liberalization. Although the mechanics of currency exchange have been simplified by the abolishment of the two-track system, high barriers remain to full convertibility. In particular, the central government maintains a tight hold on the flow of foreign currency by tying up the exchange process in bureaucratic red tape. Another problem that stems

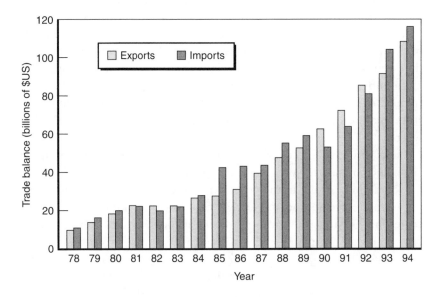

Figure 8.7. PRC Trade Balance: 1978–1994

68   Pei (1994, p. 116).
69   World Bank, *World Tables*, various years.

from China's tight monetary policy is the frequent shortages of foreign currency available in the market. A third barrier to full convertibility remains with the goods and purchases imported by Chinese companies. These goods must be purchased with foreign exchange available only by government application and allocation. Finally, with the dearth of foreign currency available, firms that want foreign exchange privileges have to earn as much hard currency as they borrow from monetary authorities.

The gradual liberalization of foreign trade also serves to highlight the inefficiency and corruption that plagues China's tariff system. Although the average duty is 40 percent, the government collects only 8 percent with the remainder being filtered away by smuggling and graft.[70] The lawlessness that still holds sway over major sectors of the economy limits the ease with which new entrepreneurs can enter the market. And it is this ease of entry that fosters competition and an efficient market, each leading to a further reduction in the state's power.

The slow process of marketization has frustrated many Chinese. Those who hope to enter the market and compete against the inefficient and unproductive SOEs find themselves up against a central government that refuses to eliminate the wasteful subsidies that prop up the near-bankrupt giants. Those who still work for SOEs are paying the price of this welfare system through financial penalties, low or zero bonuses, and removal of their housing or health benefits.[71] These workers are trapped in losing enterprises and, because of the severe restrictions that still remain on private realm, are unable to find productive work elsewhere.

In its effort to speed up the implementation of reform, Beijing is again encouraging the provinces to experiment with individual forms of marketization. Many in the government fear that as Beijing allows the provinces to create and implement their own economic policies, the center moves dangerously close to losing its powers of authority. These critics cite as an example the stubborn resistance from the coastal provinces when Beijing attempted to implement an economic austerity program in 1993. Reluctant to implement the policies by force, Beijing backed away from the measures. In an even more brazen act of defiance, Guangdong responded to restrictions by Beijing on access to natural resources by buying what it needed on the international market and

70   "How and Why to Survive Chinese Tax Torture" (1995).
71   Rawski (1994).

chartering its own tankers to bring it into port.[72] As economic liberalization continues, and the coastal provinces step up their international marketing efforts, Beijing's power erodes even further.[73]

Lured by the promises of wealth that the coastline offers, many Chinese are migrating to the provinces where the private sector flourishes. Table 8.4 shows the provinces in which the non-state sector is larger than the state sector in gross industrial output.[74] Figure 8.8 portrays the rising trend toward privatization in the coastal and northeast regions[75] of the country.[76]

The tidal changes occurring in the broad market are affecting every aspect of life within China. Cash is more readily available; foreign products arrive on grocery shelves; association that is permitted for business reasons often crosses over into political discussion; and the publication of pro-liberalization ideas continues. As demand for publications that had been banned or censored by the government flourished, entrepreneurs were quick to make a market of the shortage. The government's hands were tied on whether to curtail the burgeoning economies of the coast. Recognizing that the PRC still lacks the four essential ingredients of an advanced economy—capital, technology, management skills, and strong linkages to the world's markets—China's leadership is reluctant to constrain the advanced economies of the coastal provinces and, consequently, turns a blind eye to numerous violations of state edicts.

72   For a discussion of this, see Segal (1994).
73   Pollack (1996a) writes that "the economic inefficiencies of the state owned economy have helped sow the seeds of widespread social change. By no longer guaranteeing job security, the established industrial enterprises (as the embodiment of the state) have imparted a powerful signal to vast numbers of Chinese: higher level political or economic authority will not ensure their well being. Under these conditions, Chinese citizens must pursue alternative means and methods to provide for their livelihood, and (at least potentially) to achieve increased prosperity."
74   *Statistical Yearbook of China*, various years.
75   Northeast: Beijing, Tianjin, Hebei, Liaoning, Jilin, Heilongjiang, and Shandong. Central: Shanxi, Inner Mongolia, Anhui, Jiangxi, Henan, Hubei, Hunan, Guizhou, Shaanxi, and Ningxia. Southeast Coast: Shanghai, Jiangsu, Zhejiang, Fujian, Guangdong, and Hainan. Southwest: Guangxi, Sichuan, and Yuannan. West: Tibet, Gansu, Qingai, and Xinjiang.
76   Tien-tung, Hsueh Li Qiang, and Liu Shucheng (1993).

Table 8.4. *Contributions of the non-state sector to gross industrial output in selected provinces (in percent)*

	1985	1987	1989	1991
National	35.1	40.3	43.9	47.2
Fujian	43.7	47.5	50.5	59.4
Guangdong	46.7	50.7	56.6	61.8
Hebei	29.7	46.9	49.6	52.1
Jiangsu	59.6	63.4	65	66.9
Shandong	45.3	49.5	56.6	60.3
Zhejiang	64.6	66.8	68.1	70.6

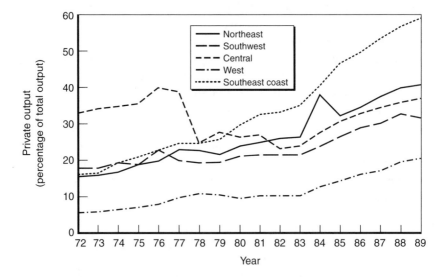

Figure 8.8. Trend Toward Privatization in the Coastal and Northeast Regions of the PRC: 1972–1989

China's great economic strides, however, have not been taken equally within the country. Although the coastal provinces are thriving, many of the interior provinces continue to languish. The income gap between urban and rural residents increased from 1/1.7 in 1985 to 1/2.4 in 1991.[77] As a result, regional tensions are on the rise. Figures 8.9 and

77   Goldstein, Kaye, and Blass (1993).

8.10 show the disparity in output per capita and the percentage of total output that is produced by the five regions of the country.[78]

As the coastal provinces continue to marketize and strengthen their ties with the overseas community, there is reason to believe that the ideas of personal liberty will be imported alongside of international currency. Those in contact with their cousins on Taiwan cannot help but be fascinated by the pace of change occurring in the ROC. Impossible as it may have seemed a decade earlier, on May 20, 1996, Taiwan swore in the first democratically elected president in the Chinese-speaking world. And each year, the number of overseas Chinese visiting the mainland increases—from 20,900 in 1979 to 79,300 in 1988.[79] Each visit, each new business tie, increases the internationalization of the Mainlanders and the likelihood that they too will wish to experience the freedom enjoyed by the outside world.

Although the coastal provinces are leading the country toward further economic liberalization and greater internationalization, the ques-

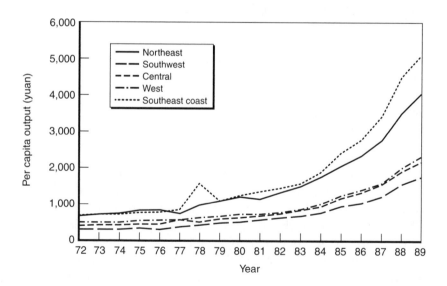

Figure 8.9. Per Capita Output in the Five Regions of the PRC: 1972–1989

78   Tien-tung, Hsueh Li Qiang, and Liu Shucheng (1993).
79   Chen (1991).

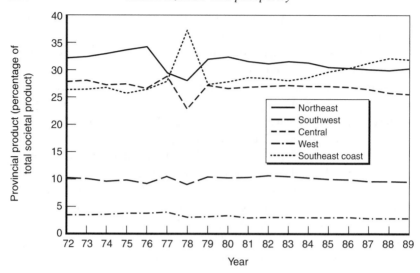

Figure 8.10. Contribution of Provincial Product to Total Societal Product in the
PRC: 1972–1989

tion remains whether the pace of reform and the accompanying political
liberalization will also transform the countryside. This and other potential problems that may lie in China's future are discussed in the next
section.

CONCLUSION

Despite the obvious foundation for increased political liberty laid by
China's burgeoning private sector, it would be dangerous to underesti-
mate the hurdles still faced by the PRC in its transition toward political
liberalization. First is the constant threat that party hardliners will re-
tard the pace of economic development by raising trade barriers or by
continuing to prop up the crippled SOE sector—a sector in which two-
thirds of the enterprises were unprofitable during 1993 and where tri-
angular debt amounted to US$71 billion (one-third of total output) in
1995.[80]

Although China seems to have circumvented the worst of the
Southeast Asian financial crisis of 1997, it was not due to having a fun-
damentally more sound economy. The same structural weaknesses that

80   *Statistical Yearbook of China* (1995).

led to the downfall of Indonesia also exist in China: overdevelopment of real estate, poor investment oversight, and rampant corruption. China, however, was never at the mercy of currency speculators, since the RMB is neither convertible nor overvalued. Despite such a narrow escape, China must still navigate through troubled waters. Three out of four state banks are technically insolvent, with the value of their bad debts exceeding their assets. Nearly half of all SOEs incurred losses in the first nine months of 1997.[81] Consequently, major reforms are still needed in the commodity markets, labor markets (where between 10 and 30 million workers are tenured into redundant and inefficient postings), commercial law, and the banking industry (in which non-performing loans are estimated at 11 to 15 percent of all borrowed amounts).[82] A drastic overhaul is also needed in both the civil and criminal justice systems.[83] Without a more judicious rule of law, the modernization of civil society is hampered, economic liberalization will falter, and the prospect of continued movement toward democracy becomes unlikely. Since the removal of Zhao Ziyang, no dynamic, reform-minded leader has arisen to take his place, leaving many to wonder who will negotiate on behalf of the government if the societal contract is to be restructured.

The next decade in China may prove to be a most difficult time. Continued reforms are necessary to ensure the expansion of economic growth, but rapid changes to society may cause an initial upheaval. As Tocqueville once remarked:

> It is not always when things are going from bad to worse that revolutions break out . . . the most perilous moment for a bad government is one when it seeks to mend its ways. . . . The mere fact that certain abuses have been remedied draws attention to the others and they now appear more galling; people may suffer less, but their sensibility is exacerbated.[84]

81 Yatsko (1997).
82 Rawski (1995).
83 In "China's Arbitrary State" (1996), it is remarked that in China "the point of the law is to act as an instrument of communist power. Guilt is determined, pre-trial, in the light of political circumstances, such as a campaign for which China's leaders have demanded a quota of convictions. A trial is usually designed not to determine guilt, but to be used as a showcase for some didactic point."
84 Tocqueville (1955, pp. 176–177).

This may hold especially true in regard to China's huge peasant mass. Able to access news of the coast more easily, the people of China's interior are becoming increasingly aware of the unequal position they hold in relation to other, more prosperous, regions. The specter of 900 million peasants voicing their displeasure is quite frightening.

To defuse the potential of a peasant revolt, the central government is slowly recognizing and rectifying the disparities between the provinces. In China's Eighth Five Year Plan (1991–1995), technology industries are being promoted in the interior. Figure 8.11 illustrates that the interior regions lag far behind the coastal sectors in terms of the value of increase in fixed assets (a measure of technology).[85]

In another move to pacify the peasants, the price of farm produce was allowed to rise. This, however, has contributed to China's escalating inflation and has upset the urban residents. To control the rise in inflation, Beijing must stop printing money and lending it to the state enterprise system (which uses the funds to pay its workers). However, that would create another potentially explosive situation. In March 1997, unpaid silk factory workers in Sichuan Province held their man-

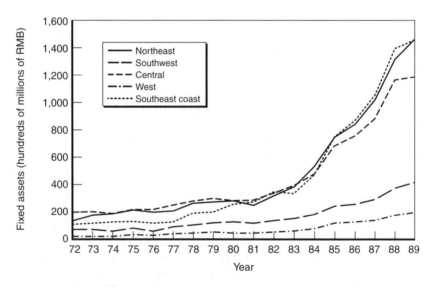

Figure 8.11. Value of Increase in Fixed Assets in the PRC: 1972–1989

85   Tien-tung, Hsueh Li Qiang, and Liu Shucheng (1993).

ager hostage as 20,000 laborers stormed city hall. Beijing recognizes that the strikes and threats by Russian workers, left unpaid for months, would pale in significance to a movement by China's workers. Knowing that it must balance the interests of the peasant mass, urban residents, and industrial workers, China's leadership looks for palatable policy options. In the effort to promote political liberalization in China, assistance in the modernization of the interior provinces may be one lever available to the United States. Even more helpful would be assistance in the retraining of China's soon-to-be unemployed. As the SOE reforms translate into the closing of factories, China will be forced to find jobs for hundreds of millions of out-of-work laborers.

Of course, the U.S. ability to effect such change depends on the larger context of the U.S.-PRC relationship. Key issues such as trade, human rights, arms proliferation, and migration all find China and the United States at the center of the debate.

Pye believes that although the relationship between the United States and China has "just too many fundamental obstacles in political cultures, history and ideologies for the political relationship to be a warm one," it can be a mutually beneficial one if the United States formally and publicly announces its hopes for China's future and rejects the traditional diplomatic channels of closed door meetings.[86]

Whether the relationship becomes warm and fuzzy or not, it is already complex and significant. Figure 8.12 shows the increasingly important trade ties between the two countries—ties that neither is willing to fray, let alone sever.[87]

Institution building and constructive dialogue, coupled with a more coherent and transparent China policy by the United States, may go a long way in strengthening the U.S.-China relationship, but the best opportunities for the Chinese people to experience democracy lie in continued economic liberalization. Expanded markets and the broadening of opportunity will restructure the societal contract and promote a greater balance of power between the public and private domains.

Authoritarianism can be eroded by resisting its integration into the regime, guarding zones of autonomy against it, disputing its legitimacy, and raising the costs of authoritarian rule.[88] A well-functioning private sector achieves all of those things. A viable market creates a competing

86   Pye (1996).
87   Lardy (1994, p. 30).
88   Stephan (1993).

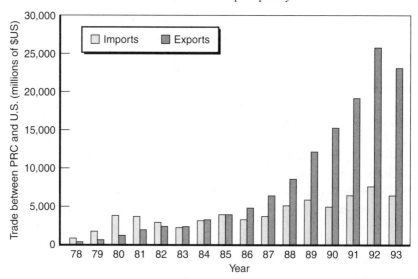

Figure 8.12. Increase in Trade Between the PRC and the United States: 1978–1993

power base that erodes the control of the central government. It also necessitates the need for a formal rule of law to protect property rights and settle business disputes. Arbitrary injunctions and the lawlessness of authoritarian regimes cannot be permitted if the private sector is to run efficiently. The costs of authoritarian rule are high if the foreign investment community remains skeptical about the safety of its investments. Ultimately, private voices cannot be silenced in a market economy.

Dai Qing, a leading dissident journalist, wrote in the *Asian Wall Street Journal* that "the [Chinese] media are more lively than they have been for several years. It is the result of economic reform, not of political reform. Now the party says as long as you don't curse us, and as long as you don't demand that we step down, you can say anything you want."[89] As each year passes and the market matures, more channels of communication, association, and, ultimately, dissent are created. In the December 1995 issue of the *Far Eastern Economic Review*, a survey of Chinese citizens found that "while fewer Chinese care to protest openly, more are using newly opened channels to voice their opinions,"

89   Sampson (1993, p. 9).

including increased press freedoms and uncensored radio call-in shows.[90] Still categorizing China as "not free" and ranking it with the lowest score on both the civil rights and political liberties index, Freedom House does report that "in the past few years social and cultural restrictions have been eased, and sexual morality is no longer rigidly enforced. More than 1,600 newspapers and 6,400 magazines are published. . . . Freedoms of press, political expression and association are nonexistent. However the spread of satellite dishes and short-wave radios has made it harder for the government to control access to information."[91]

As China solidifies its new leadership under Jiang Zemin, political liberalization rests on a cusp—ready to become viable after years of dormancy or waiting to backslide to the dark years of the hardline regimes. Much will depend on whether the economy continues its reform, opportunities extend to the provinces, the door to foreign investment remains open, and the power between the government and citizens transitions to a more equitable distribution. Although Jiang Zemin has solidified power, he may still find himself fighting to retain both his own and the CCP's legitimacy if the economy collapses. Jiang recognizes that he must push for further reforms, despite the potential for short-term unrest. In his speech before the Fifteenth National Congress in September 1997, Jiang announced:

> We are fully aware that there are still quite a few problems and difficulties on the road ahead, and that there are also shortcomings and defects in our work. The following are the main ones: The quality and efficiency of the national economy as a whole remains fairly low, the irrational economic structure still poses a rather outstanding problem . . . corruption, extravagance and waste and other undesirable phenomena are still spreading and growing. . . . Things have yet to be straightened out in the matter of income and distribution, uneven regional development is obvious, and part of the urban and rural residents still live in poor circumstances. Population growth and economic development have caused great strains on resources and the environment.

At first glance it seems like an astute reading of his country's dilemmas, but Jiang went on to announce that in "the press . . . we must adhere to the principle of keeping the Party spirit, persist in seeking truth from facts and maintain a correct orientation for public opinion. We

90 Gilley (1995, p. 35).
91 Finn (1994, p. 202).

should strengthen supervision over the press and publishing."[92] Fortunately, it is highly unlikely that Jiang's intentions for the press will be able to stand if his broader societal and economic reforms are implemented.[93]

A deep-seated fear that may stymie attempts at political reform in the near term is the Chinese dread of national disintegration. To avoid triggering such an implosion, the populace may be willing to tolerate a known commodity in exchange for relative stability. Many believe that promises for political reform could lead to an uprising of the people when reality fails to equal expectations. Rong Jian of the People's University argues that "unless the people's democratic [and, it should be added, economic] demands can be met and realized through normal means, they are bound to be vented through abnormal means, such as demonstrations, protests, strikes, and even violent behavior."[94]

The question for U.S. policymakers is, How can the United States assist the Chinese in meeting and realizing their democratic and economic demands through normal means? A continued push for reform through institution building within the capital markets, incentives for foreign joint ventures, and modernization of the provinces will help extend the economic autonomy of the populace and move the nation toward a restructuring of the societal contract to favor political liberalization.

92 "China: Jiang Zemin Congress Report" (1997).
93 Nathan (1993b) writes that democracy may arise with a "mixture of democratic and authoritarian elements, openness and secrecy, idealism and selfishness, turbulence and stability . . . characterized by moral and symbolic posturing with a stress on personal loyalty, frequent betrayals, extreme rhetoric, emotional intensity, fractionalization of viewpoints and organizations, moralization of political issues, and consequent difficulty in pragmatic compromise." Jiang's speech seems a good example of this reasoning.
94 Rosen and Zou (1990–1991, p. 60).

Part Three

Conclusions and Policy Implications

9

Conclusions and policy implications

PROSPECTS FOR DEMOCRACY IN EAST ASIA

The quantitative analysis of data from seven East and Southeast Asian nations (China, Indonesia, Korea, Malaysia, Singapore, Taiwan, and Thailand) and the detailed country studies of Korea, Taiwan, Indonesia, and China suggest that marketization increases the likelihood for a country to create and sustain democracy. Previous literature in the field of economic and political liberalization has tended to focus on economic development (usually measured by a rising GDP per capita) as the most likely basis for democracy, but theoretically and empirically, a stronger case can be made that marketization, as opposed to prosperity, provides the best path toward political liberalization. Marketization, a movement from a centrally controlled economy toward an open market, creates the foundation for democracy in numerous ways. First, when citizens are introduced to the concepts of choice and competition, they are able to achieve their highest economic utility preference given their budgetary constraint. Choice in the marketplace, and the resulting satisfaction of self-determination, seems often to transfer into a desire for political self-determination. Broadened markets also create very practical reasons for political liberalization. An efficient free market requires the security of property rights; freedom of association; a stable, just, and rational rule of law; and a minimization of the government's role in the daily life of the citizen. The best form of government to achieve these things is a democracy—a form of government where the power is held by the people, public accountability is ensured by frequent elections, and the role of the state is far more circumscribed than in authoritarian regimes.

223

Although there is strong prima facie validity in the above arguments, wise policy must be based on empirical research. This study provides evidence that within East Asia, the creation of free markets lays the best path for a country's movement away from authoritarianism and toward democracy. The econometric model described in Chapter 4 shows that marketization, measured by *mtwo* (currency plus demand and time deposits) as a percentage of GDP—a measure of liberalization within the financial sphere—leads to an increase in political liberalization. A strong word of caution must be included at this point to warn policymakers away from mistaking *mtwo* as the sole program variable needed to obtain marketization. This is distinctly not the case. Although *mtwo* accurately reflects the level of marketization within a country, manipulating this instrument will not necessarily bring about greater financial openness and may, under certain circumstances, distort its reliability as a measure. More research must be undertaken to link this variable with viable policy instruments.

The *prosperity* construct (measured by the log of GDP per capita) was not significant. This finding is consistent with the theory that it is the development of the individual as a result of marketization, not an overall increase in a country's wealth, that forms the desire for self-government and the means for achieving it. The strengthening of the individual via the lessons of the private market is especially important in the People's Republic of China, a country where, for the better part of a century, individualism was linked with moral decay and civil chaos.

The rise of the market, and the attendant birth of the Chinese entrepreneur, is slowly crippling the Chinese Communist Party by replacing the primacy of class and political faction with the primacy of the individual. The econometric model suggests that by increasing marketization by 50 percent, democracy in China would rise by 49 percent, creating a political environment in China akin to that in Indonesia. Still deplorable by Western standards, such an increase in political rights and civil liberties would be a significant improvement from the fierce political repression in the PRC.

The measures of *technology* (investment as a percentage of GDP and the number of telephones per 100 people) were also found to increase democracy. Information and open lines of communication are not only vital for a well-functioning market, they also underpin the high level of political activity needed to create a democratic opposition.[1]

The modern day economic and political histories of Korea, Taiwan, Indonesia, and China provide support for these findings. To address the same question that motivated the econometric study (i.e., Does marketization increase the level of democracy within a country?), a qualitative, comparative country study was undertaken, which enriched the conclusions of the model. The country study confirmed that although the particular road from marketization to democracy may differ, the direction and overall course remain the same. Marketization instills the importance of a separate and distinct private sphere. The resulting diminution of government control lays the foundation for the rise of a democratic opposition.

Korea, the first of the countries examined to move toward political openness, based its economic liberalization program on land reform and the rise of the chaebol. Although it may seem unlikely that the monopolistic conglomerates could in any way create the environment for an individual entrepreneur to flourish, the chaebol were instrumental in preparing the ground for democracy by siphoning power away from an authoritarian government. The shift in power from the state to the private sphere had the effect of de-legitimizing the regime while at the same time opening up the system to new interest groups. Driven less by ideology and more by profit incentives and progress, the chaebol had no cause to silence voices challenging the traditional social and political structure, as long as the voices did not compromise the burgeoning economy. Finding common ground in the desire for a reduced role of government and a more efficient channeling of resources, the large business concerns began to support a democratic opposition. Only after this support was garnered did true change occur. Confident that his

---

1   Robinson (1991) writes that "technology begets the information revolution, which greatly enhances cross-cultural communication and hence knowledge of the world; favors product uniformity across national boundaries; makes access to foreign cultures more efficient; . . . and becomes a driving force for broadly improving material standards of living. While none of these alone is essential for democracy, in combination they are a powerful impetus."

proposals would be backed by the increasingly powerful private sector, Roh Tae Woo, in 1988, restored a free press, ratified a new constitution preserving individual liberty, and removed the military from the political sphere. Democracy had arrived in Korea.

As a result of the financial crisis of 1997, a new stage of Korean development may have begun. The chaebol are being broken up and the pernicious links between government and business are being weakened, if not severed. Such market-opening measures not only will strengthen the economy but will also fortify the Korean system of governance. During the age when the chaebol reigned supreme, ordinary citizens, who could never have made the large political "contributions" routinely given by businesses, were effectively shut out of the political system. With the downsizing of the conglomerates and a severe curtailment of their influence in the political sphere, the Korean system of government will become more democratic.

Unlike Korea, the transformation of Taiwan from an authoritarian regime to a functioning democracy occurred on a much more personal level. The land reform that led to the expansion of the small and medium-sized firm sector simultaneously reduced the influence of the government within the economy. The entrepreneurs, most of whom were Taiwanese, began to gather enough clout in the early 1980s to enter the political sphere, a domain closed to them since the arrival of the KMT in 1949. Like the cracks in Korea's authoritarian system that appeared with the shifting of power from the state to the chaebol, the creation of an entrepreneurial class in Taiwan expanded the circle of ruling elites. In both Korea and Taiwan, political liberalization was seen as a necessity for continued economic expansion and modernization. Excessive government involvement in the intricate workings of the market created inefficiencies. A market less fettered by political decisions would lead to a more vibrant economy, one that could effectively compete in an international environment. As the free market expanded, economic autonomy was granted to vast segments of the Korean and Taiwanese populations. These citizens no longer willingly obeyed the dictates of the regime. Rather, they set about creating special interest groups that would represent their concerns in government.

Distinct from Korea and Taiwan, Indonesia and China should be considered works in progress. These two countries are experiencing the effects of economic reform in the agricultural and financial sectors implemented in the late 1970s and early 1980s but have yet to experience the political liberalization that may follow. However, the signs of this transformation are present. Freedoms never thought possible a decade ago are beginning to become routine in both Indonesia and China. Indonesia is undergoing a radical transformation, with the ouster of President Suharto and the lifting of the ban on the formation of political parties. The financial crisis of 1997 that left the Indonesian economy in ruins may be the catalyst that transforms the country's political system. The IMF has forced the hand of the government to institute economic reforms aimed at increasing transparency and decreasing corruption. The biggest push for political liberalization, however, may come from the rising middle class. Small business owners have begun clamoring for the kind of political change needed to ensure a lasting economic recovery. In this quest, they should be heartened by their Thai counterparts. On September 22, 1997, thousands of Thai small businessmen marched on Bangkok's Silom Road (Thailand's Wall Street) to rally for a series of political reform measures contemplated by the government. The march was organized by the Businessmen for Democracy Club, a group formed with the purpose of promoting democracy in recognition that political liberalization is needed for economic prosperity.[2] As Indonesians continue down the path of democratic learning, it would not be surprising to find a chapter opening in Jakarta.

In China, the economically powerful coastal provinces are blatantly ignoring the dictates from Beijing and formulating their own social, legal, and foreign policies. Rural elections are now permitted in most of the inland provinces, and these rudimentary experiments with democracy are gaining wide support throughout the country. International pressure to formalize China's rule of law to ensure fair business practices is having widespread effects on the entire civil justice system. Greater international scrutiny of China's human rights abuses, made possible through the increasing links between China and the West, is also raising the cost of repression to the regime.

Nevertheless, it would be disingenuous to suggest that China and Indonesia have become even quasi-democratic. Both countries rank among the world's worst human rights violators, and both continue to engage in systematic abuses of civil and political liberties. If, however, marketization is a key determinant in a country's transition toward political liberalization, as this study indicates, what policies are available to the United States to encourage this movement?

2 Tasker (1997).

Over the past decade, U.S. foreign policy toward East Asia has lacked a coherent framework based on realizable goals. In regard to China, the United States has swung between extremes—between reconciling itself to a China that will never become a democracy and could, at best, become a full market economy and a valuable trading partner, to hoping that China will undergo an overnight transformation akin to the lowering of the Iron Curtain in Eastern Europe. Such extremism belies an understanding of the forces at work, politically and economically, in East Asia.

Three lessons should be learned from the modern histories of Korea and Taiwan. The first is that one should never say "never" when speaking about possible political outcomes. Those who conjectured that Korea and Taiwan would forever remain ruled by authoritarian regimes have been proven stunningly incorrect. The second lesson is that it is imperative for the United States to retain a prominent position in shaping the economic and security framework of East Asia. The United States played a formative role in the transformation of South Korea and Taiwan into functioning democracies by assisting in the monumental tasks of land reform, market restructuring, and institution building. The same services should be offered to other East Asian nations. To be in a position to render such services, the United States must consider replacing its "soft engagement" policy with a more active, committed, hands-on involvement. Forthright statements of goals and missions may clear up many sources of confusion within the relationships, but well-intentioned offers to assist in economic transformations increase the likelihood of political reform.

Finally, U.S. policymakers must realize that the perception of time is not a constant throughout the world. An overnight transition in the United States can literally mean overnight, whereas in China, 20 years may describe the same time period. In fashioning effective policy in East Asia, it is essential that the United States extend the typical time horizon for accomplishing goals. It is unlikely that China will transform itself into a democracy at the same breakneck speed as occurred in Eastern Europe, but if the pace of political reforms experienced over the last decade continues for the next 10 years, remarkable progress will be made. On the other hand, who could have predicted that Asia's longest-serving autocrat, President Suharto of Indonesia, would be forced out of office by a band of unruly university students? Nonetheless, the United States should accept a gradual transition and be prepared that the signs reflecting this transformation may be less astonishing than the sight of the Berlin Wall falling. A steady increase in newspaper circulation, a law permitting organization and peaceful protest, or one granting the right to sue the government—these must be heralded as positive movements. Most important, any political, social, or economic change that decreases the role of the government in the everyday affairs of citizens should be viewed as a step toward political liberalization.

As suggested throughout this study, the best way to diminish central authority and broaden the basis of power throughout the citizenry is through the promotion of a private domain. By delineating the sphere of influence of the government over economic activity, politically open societies are likely to result.

As a foreign entity with no right to interfere in the internal workings of another country, the United States still has numerous foreign policy tools available for fostering democracy abroad. Three main venues for the implementation of democratic policies are the U.S. government, the private sector, and multilateral/multinational organizations. By promoting freer trade, financial transparency, institution building, and education, each venue provides the opportunity to increase the breadth and depth of the private domain in East Asia. Before discussing the practical aspects of implementing policies to bring about the creation and expansion of marketization and, hopefully, political liberalization, the thorny issue of "Asian democracy" must be addressed.

"ASIAN DEMOCRACY"

For too long, U.S. policies for East Asia have lacked a coherent framework and have been viewed as incredibly condescending. Beijing's *International Trade Journal* describes the U.S.-China relationship this way:

> Because of reasons known to all (such as differences in levels of economic development, social systems, ideology, culture, and value concepts, as well as adverse balances of trade resulting from differences in statistical principles), trade frictions between the two countries have been constant, and quarrels frequent. Since 1989, acting on the basis of its own laws and without regard for China's circumstances, the United States has resorted to sanctions and retaliation at every turn to handle various issues such as market access, open services trade, "dumping," labor reform products, protection of intellectual property rights, and it has adopted a

haughty attitude. For the thin skinned Chinese, this is unacceptable. What is more, the United States uses, or manufactures, trade friction to attain its political goals, thereby politicizing trade issues . . . . China's transition from a planned to a market economy requires a process of practice and feeling the way.[3]

To accomplish its goals, the United States must back away from the indiscriminate use of the bludgeon as a policy instrument and rely on incentives, inducements, and mutually beneficial cooperative agreements. There is no reason to believe that the countries of East Asia will respond positively to bullying by the United States. However, there is even less reason to believe that they will respect or listen to a mighty nation that comes, hat in hand, apologizing for its success and couching its true goals in the language of "soft engagement." Pollack proposes that "a clearly articulated U.S. policy that is presented fully and fairly to China's leaders is far more likely to elicit a considered response from them than one that obscures American policy preferences."[4]

U.S. foreign policy must shed its insecurities and recognize that the majority of the world strives to implement the engines of political and economic machines that were invented in the United States and have created this mighty nation. Good-willed offerings of assistance to help promote long-term economic viability will do more to transform the countries of East Asia than will confrontation, sanctions, or threats, all of which may provoke nationalist sentiments and result in a closing of borders to trade and democratic ideals.

In any discussion over how to best promote democracy abroad, the question of whether by doing so America is engaging in philosophical hegemony arises. Alagappa suggests that the governing elite of East Asia "strongly contest the projection of democracy . . . as universally valid norms."[5] In particular, the liberal elements of democracy (protection of the individual) are viewed as peculiar to Anglo-Saxon culture. Alagappa writes that East Asian leaders believe that "Asian" democracy, when it arrives, will be based on the primacy of the community over the individual and a stable dominant party over a competitive political environment. Huntington agrees that the "interaction of

3   "Economic Relations with U.S., Japan Reviewed" (1995).
4   Pollack (1996b, pp. 124–125).
5   Alagappa (1994).

economic progress and Asian culture appears to have generated a distinctly East Asian variety of democratic institutions"—namely, where there is "competition for power but not alternation in power, and participation in elections for all, but participation in office only for those in the 'mainstream' party."[6] Plattner builds on Huntington's theories by suggesting that East Asia may be developing a new ideology, that the Asian variant of democracy may not be a stepping stone to a more Western version.[7]

East Asian democracies may indeed have differentiating characteristics, but liberty, self-determination, political pluralism, and individualism must remain as cornerstones. The idea that East Asians will not, or cannot, develop a system in which individuals are free to pursue their own interests is ludicrous. It is the very "non-Asian" notion of individualism that provides the foundation of a market economy—a lesson that has been rapidly learned in Korea and Taiwan. The Chinese government has stressed that economic development supersedes human rights and democracy and may even entail sacrificing the latter to obtain the former. The scholar Liu Qing argues that although many in China

> view human rights as a product of Western culture, a value system, that the West wants to impose on China which is not suitable to Chinese sentiments . . . human rights and democracy [are] a better social system for safeguarding human dignity and interests and also a way for China to avoid its past road of pain and suffering.[8]

There is no shying away from the fact that democracy is a moral system and the United States should be its strongest promoter to those in the world who live without freedom and without liberty.

Promoting democracy in countries with long histories of authoritarian/totalitarian regimes can be accomplished peacefully and, odd as it may seem, at the behest of the ruling elite. Through the promotion of marketization, and the concomitant strengthening of the individual, countries will make a natural progression toward political liberalization. Each new relationship the United States forges with the peoples of the developing countries of East Asia conveys the advantages of living in a democratic society.

6   Huntington (1993, pp. 17–18).
7   Plattner (1993).
8   Liu (1996).

THE ROLE OF THE U.S. GOVERNMENT

The first venue available to the United States in promoting marketization and political liberalization in East Asia is official government channels. The Department of Commerce and the U.S. Trade Representative can be extremely effective in structuring and overseeing the implementation of bilateral agreements to promote freer trade. Trade liberalization promotes price competition, broadens the choices available to consumers, and spurs entrepreneurs to become more efficient and more creative to keep and expand their markets. The maturation of the individual, an outgrowth of a strong entrepreneurial system, facilitates the creation of a politically open system by providing the populace with the desire and the means for self-government.

Cooperation between governmental agencies and their East Asian counterparts should also be encouraged. Conferences pairing the Securities and Exchange Commission (SEC), Internal Revenue Service (IRS), and Federal Reserve with analogous overseas institutions can be invaluable in helping foreign nations create a market framework. Such assistance is desired by many rapidly developing East Asian nations, since the turbulence of partial reforms or of reforming systems can easily trigger hyperinflation and other incendiary pressures on the economy. Understanding and implementing efficient macroeconomic management, complete with the creation of a powerful central bank, a transparent and rational tax system, and coordinated and comprehensive property rights laws, may help eliminate such pitfalls of an economic restructuring. Consequently, aiding the governments of East Asia in implementing sound fiscal and monetary policies should be viewed as a top priority.[9]

As such, particular assistance should be geared toward freeing prices from government controls, ensuring tight money through an independent central bank, making the domestic currency completely convertible, privatizing state-owned entities in an orderly and well-paced manner, encouraging new businesses through stock and bond markets, and opening borders to international trade.

---

9 Fukuyama (1995) writes, "China needs, at a minimum, political stability born of a basic legitimacy of its political institutions and a competent state structure. . . . An unstable China . . . will not be a propitious environment for wise economic policymaking. Nor will an economic environment in which a strong state is constantly required to step in to guide development be favorable to the growth of Chinese democracy."

To increase the likelihood that such policies will be accepted and effective, particular attention must be paid to the individual histories and economies of the countries in question. In achieving marketization, Taiwan encouraged a balanced shift from the agricultural to the non-agricultural sector. Korea, in contrast, depended on large-scale, urban, and export-oriented growth and was more dependent on foreign capital.

Learning from the lessons of Taiwan and Korea—countries that arrived at marketization and political liberalization on different roads—means understanding that the same policies that will assist China in its transformation will be useless at best, and counterproductive at worst, when applied to Indonesia. For instance, promoting provincial autonomy in China and encouraging local authorities to experiment with market-opening policies would not only assist China in its transition to a freer market but would be accepted by Beijing as a continuation of an on-going policy. A similar strategy of by-passing the ruling Javanese elites in Indonesia would risk the expulsion of U.S. interests. Nearly all private wealth is controlled by Javanese interests, and any move by a foreign entity to create greater inter-island tensions would not be well received. A better strategy would be to gradually increase marketizing forces across the country, expanding the pie so to speak, without directly threatening the well-entrenched power base.

THE ROLE OF THE U.S. PRIVATE DOMAIN

The second venue for the promotion of markets abroad is the U.S. private sphere. Cross-border business-to-business relations, joint ventures, foreign direct investment, and exchange programs sponsored by professional associations are perhaps the strongest way for the United States to support the countries of East Asia in their transition to a market economy. The expertise of the U.S. business community can be instrumental in developing the large, modern, and professionally managed corporations that are necessary for economic liberalization. As opposed to governmental policies, policies originating and developed by the private domain are less likely to be viewed as politically motivated and, consequently, are more likely to be accepted.[10]

10   As Shinn (1996, p. 56) writes, "It is important for governments not to interfere with China's growing market dependence. One of the most emphatic recommendations of conditional engagement is that the slowly developing benefits of China's economic integration should not be put at risk or interfered with in favor of short-term political objectives."

U.S. business interests can claim responsibility for some of the most significant milestones in East Asia's marketization. Foreign direct investors and joint venture partners were the leading advocates of the Chinese adopting the U.S.-based Generally Accepted Accounting Principles. In 1992–1993, the Chinese agreed to implement the Accounting System for Foreign Investment Enterprises, the Accounting System for Joint Stock Companies, and the General Accounting Standard for PRC Enterprises, bringing China closer to the international norm. Although seemingly mundane, improvements in the procedure by which business transactions occur can have wide-ranging effects. Trade hurdles are lowered, cooperation between countries increases, and transparency in business transactions fosters a more efficient allocation of resources and a consequent broadening of market forces.

Increased economic ties between U.S. businesses and their East Asian counterparts have also led to a rapidly developing rule of law. In May 1992, a cooperation agreement between the Beijing Conciliation Centre and the American Arbitration Association Conciliation Centre was ratified. The agreement structures the process through which the two organizations can offer mediation services for commercial and maritime disputes. Under the agreement, each association may assist the other in communicating with organizations or persons in its country; getting factual and legal information; obtaining affidavits, testimony, or access to local expert testimony; and arranging for translation. The mission statement of the agreement is for a betterment of U.S.-Chinese business relations through a strengthening of the arbitration/mediation industry and a better understood civil justice system.

The introduction of U.S. jurisprudence into the Chinese market will have crossover importance for a free Chinese judiciary. This will, no doubt, be aided by the American Bar Association's recent announcement that it sets a high priority on increasing the number of private law offices throughout China. Currently, there are approximately 50,000 lawyers in China, an extremely small number given the population of the country, but a significant increase over a decade ago.[11] The increase in the number of Chinese lawyers, a necessity as China becomes more connected to the global economy, has led to systemic changes throughout China, including the passage of the 1990 Administrative Procedures Law allowing citizens to sue the government for abuses.

11   Young (1995).

Other recent developments include the approval of 16 international law firms by China's Justice Ministry (bringing the total number of foreign firms working in China to 73).[12] Strengthening the rule of law within developing East Asian nations is essential for the creation of a civil society, one that respects individual rights and liberties.

The private domain in the United States can also be instrumental in building the institutions necessary to establish political liberalization abroad. Cultural and educational exchange programs can prepare a citizenry unfamiliar with the fundamental mechanics of democracy. The "Berkeley Mafia" of Indonesia, the economists schooled at Berkeley during the 1960s and 1970s, became the most ardent economic reformers within the government as well as supporters of general liberalization within the regime. Schooling a new generation of business leaders, policymakers, and activists will go far in moving a country toward democracy and strengthening the ties of internationalization. As the developing countries of East Asia become more integrated into the world economy, they will have no choice but to conform to internationally accepted norms or suffer the consequences of international censure. As Shinn remarks, the "tyranny of markets will have the bluntest impact on decisionmakers in Beijing. China's economy is becoming increasingly dependent on world markets for essential inputs: energy, food, technology, and capital. The tyranny of markets means that immoderate international behavior and breaking the rules impose an economic cost on China, either by cutting off the supply of these critical inputs from abroad or by raising their price."[13]

THE ROLE OF MULTINATIONAL/MULTILATERAL ORGANIZATIONS

Finally, multilateral/multinational organizations such as the World Bank, the IMF, the Asian Development Bank, and APEC allow the United States to maintain its involvement in the economies of East Asia without unilateral arm twisting. Hosting the 1993 APEC summit in Seattle garnered the United States much needed visibility for promoting its policies of open trade and human rights. By taking an active and unapologetic stance in publicizing and promoting not only its goals but its means for achieving them, the United States can work with the countries of East Asia to create a more efficient and open society.

12   Faison (1996).
13   Shinn (1996, p. 33).

The 1997 Asian financial crisis provides the IMF with an unprecedented opportunity to assist in the political and economic restructuring of East Asia. Armed with billions of dollars in loans and assistance, the IMF has convinced South Korea, Thailand, and Indonesia to open their markets and embark on a major economic restructuring. If seen to completion, these measures may serve as the needed catalyst to strengthen democracy in South Korea and lay the foundation for political liberalization in Indonesia.

CONCLUDING REMARKS

The three venues of governmental, private, and multilateral/ multinational organizations can be used as vehicles for introducing market concepts to the developing countries of East Asia. Cooperation in achieving the goal of economic modernization, a goal shared by both the United States and East Asia, will go much further in bringing these nations closer to political liberalization than will a heavy-handed use of sanctions, humiliations, and threats. If these economies are transformed into free and open markets, central governmental authority over the daily lives of citizens will decrease, individualism will flourish, and the desires and means for political liberalization will increase.

Appendix A

Two-stage least squares

Since the research design of ths study entailed collecting observations for several individual units (the countries of China, Indonesia, South Korea, Malaysia, Singapore, Taiwan, and Thailand) over the time period 1976–1992, it was necessary to employ some method of combining these data. When pooling cross-sectional and time-series data, there are p distinct decision units indexed by i = 1, . . . p and m successive time periods indexed by t = 1, . . . m, giving a total of n = pm sample points. A variety of models can be fitted to pooled data, but certain assumptions must be made about the intercept, the slope coefficients, and the disturbance term. Assuming that the intercept term varies over cross-sectional units, dummy variables can be used to measure shifts in the regression line arising from unobserved variables that are contained within countries over time (a covariance model). The present model includes six dummy variables (N – 1). One variable (China) is omitted, since its inclusion would result in perfect collinearity.

To define the system of equations, there must be a separate equation for each endogenous variable *(democracy, marketization, and prosperity)*. These structural equations are presented below, followed by the reduced-form equation of each. The reduced form explains the endogenous variable as a function of only exogenous (predetermined) variables. The goal in estimating the following equations is to understand the determinants of democracy and the underlying connections between marketization and democracy.

Democracy = f (marketization, prosperity, internationalization, technology, dummy variables, time) + μ1

237

$$[Y_1 = f(Y_2, Y_3, Z_1, Z_2 \ldots Z_6 \ldots Z_{11}, Z_{12} + \mu_1]$$

Marketization = f (democracy, technology, stocks, dummy variables, time) + μ_2

$$[Y_2 = f(Y_1 \ldots Z_2, Z_3 \ldots Z_6 \ldots Z_{11}, Z_{12}) + \mu_2]$$

Prosperity = f (marketization, internationalization, technology, education, urbanization, dummy variables, time) + μ_3

$$[Y_3 = f(Y_2 \ldots Z_1, Z_2 \ldots Z_4, Z_5, Z_6 \ldots Z_{11}, Z_{12}) + \mu_2]$$

Consequently, the reduced-form equations are:

$$Y_1 = f(Z_1, Z_2, Z_3, Z_4, Z_5 \ldots Z_6 \ldots Z_{11}, Z_{12}) \qquad (1)$$

Y1 will be measured by the *democracy* index.

$$Y_2 = f(Z_1, Z_2, Z_3, Z_4, Z_5, Z_6 \ldots Z_{11}, Z_{12}) \qquad (2)$$

Y2 will be measured by *mtwo*/GDP.

$$Y_3 = f(Z_1, Z_2, Z_3, Z_4, Z_5, Z_6 \ldots Z_{11}, Z_{12}) \qquad (3)$$

Y3 will be measured by log GDP per capita.

To obtain values of the structural parameters from the reduced forms, the equation must be identified because, as shown above, different sets of structural-parameter values can give rise to the same set of reduced-form parameters. To check for identification, the equations must meet two conditions: order and rank.

For the order condition to be satisfied, the number of predetermined variables excluded from the specific structural equation must be greater than or equal to the number of included endogenous variables minus 1. The identification process allows for extraneous information to be used to identify the equation in question.

Equation (1): Y1 has three endogenous variables (Y1, Y2, Y3) and three excluded predetermined variables (Z_3, Z_4, Z_5). Since 3 > 3 – 1, Y1 *is overidentified.*

Equation (2): Y2 has two endogenous variables (Y1, Y2) and three excluded predetermined variables (Z_1, Z_4, Z_5). Since 3 > 2 – 1, Y2 is overidentified.

Equation (3): Y3 has two endogenous variables (Y2, Y3) and one excluded predetermined variable (Z_3). Since 1 = 2 – 1, Y3 is exactly identified.

In determining whether the equations are identified, however, the order condition is necessary but not sufficient. It is necessary to evaluate each equation according to the rank of its matrix. To evaluate by rank, a matrix of all variables in the system is constructed. Each specific equation is then evaluated by its excluded variables in terms of the other equations in the system. To exclude a specific equation from the matrix, the submatrix must contain an amount of nonzero rows and columns greater than or equal to the number of total endogenous variables in the system minus 1. If this threshold is reached, the equation is identified.

The matrix of equations:

					Variable					
Eq.	Y_1	Y_2	Y_3	Z_1	Z_2	Z_3	Z_4	Z_5	$Z_6 \ldots Z_{11}$	Z_{12}
(1)	X	X	X	X	X	0	0	0	X ... X	X
(2)	X	X	0	0	X	X	0	0	X ... X	X
(3)	0	X	X	X	X	0	X	X	X ... X	X

Equation (1)'s submatrix contains two nonzero rows and three nonzero columns. Compared to $3 - 1 = 2$ endogenous variables in the system, Equation (1) is identified. Equation (2)'s submatrix contains two nonzero rows and four nonzero columns. Compared to $3 - 1 = 2$ endogenous variables in the system, Equation (2) is identified. Equation (3)'s submatrix contains 2 nonzero rows and 2 nonzero columns. Compared to $3 - 1 = 2$ endogenous variables in the system, Equation (3) is identified. To recover the structural parameters of the *democracy* equation, the predicted values of *marketization* and *prosperity* are calculated. This is accomplished by regressing first *marketization*, then *prosperity*, on all predetermined variables. The predicted values of $\ddot{Y}_2$ and $\ddot{Y}_3$ are used as the regressors in the *democracy* equation. $\ddot{Y}_2$ and $\ddot{Y}_3$ are linearly related to the predetermined model variables and assumed to be uncorrelated with the error term. This process, known as 2SLS, yields a consistent estimator for the structural parameters. The *democracy* equation becomes:

$$Democracy = \text{ß0} + \text{ß1}(mtwohat) + \text{ß2}(lgdcaphat) + \text{ß3}(fdigdp) +$$
$$\text{ß4}(open) + \text{ß5}(trate) + \text{ß6}(tele) + \text{ß7}(invest)$$
$$+ \text{ß8-ß13}(country\ dummies) + \text{ß14}(time) + \mu$$

Appendix B

Codebook

I. DEMOCRACY

1. *demscale*

Definition:	Democracy scale
Unit of measurement:	0 – 1; 0 is the lowest level
Source:	Freedom House[1]
Notes:	[14 – (political rights + civil liberties)]/ 2[2]

The *democracy* scale comprises two parts: political rights and civil liberties.

1a

Definition:	Political rights
Unit of measurement:	1 – 7; 7 is the lowest level
Source:	Freedom House[3]
Notes:	Checklist for political rights:
	a. Chief authority recently elected through meaningful process

1   Finn *(1994)*.
2   "Summing the two indices, as Gastil does in his more recent work, and which seems to be supported . . . gives a measure that takes the value 2 for the most democratic and 14 for the least democratic systems. This is linearly transformed to make the [Freedom Scale], ranging from 0 for no freedoms to 1.0 for fully democratic systems." (See Helliwell, 1992a, p. 5.)
3   Finn (1994).

    b. Legislature recently elected through
       meaningful process
       Alternatives for (a) and (b):
       1. no choice; possibility of rejection
       2. no choice; some possibility of rejection
       3. government or single-party-selected
         candidates
       4. choice only among government-selected
         candidates
       5. relatively open choices only in local
         elections
       6. open choice; restricted range
       7. open choice; all elections
    c. Fair election laws, campaigning
       opportunity, polling and tabulation
    d. Fair reflection of voter preference in
       distribution of power
    e. Multiple political parties
       1. only dominant party allowed effective
         opportunity
       2. open to rise and fall of competing parties
    f. Recent shifts in power through elections
    g. Significant opposition vote
    h. Free of military or foreign control
    i. Major group(s) denied reasonable self-
       determination
    j. Decentralized political power
    k. Informal consensus; de facto opposition
       power

1b

Definition:	Civil liberties
Unit of measurement:	1 – 7; 7 is the lowest level
Source:	Freedom House[4]
Notes:	Checklist for civil liberties:

    a. Media/literature free of political censorship
       1. Independent press
       2. Independent broadcasting

---

4   Finn (1994).

  b. Open public discussion
  c. Freedom of assembly and demonstration
  d. Freedom of political or quasi-political
   organization
  e. Nondiscriminatory rule of law in politically
   relevant cases
   1. independent judiciary
   2. security forces respect individuals
  f. Free from unjustified political terror or
   imprisonment
   1. free from imprisonment or exile for
    reasons of conscience
   2. free from torture
   3. free from terror by groups not opposed
    to the system
   4. free from government organized terror
  g. Free trade unions, peasant organizations, or
   equivalents
  h. Free businesses or cooperatives
  i. Free professional or other organizations
  j. Free religious organizations
  k. Personal social rights including: property;
   internal and external travel; choice of
   residence; marriage and family
  l. Socioeconomic rights including: freedom
   from dependency on landlords, bosses,
   union leaders, or bureaucrats
  m. Free from gross socioeconomic inequality
  n. Free from gross government indifference or
   corruption

II. MARKETIZATION

2. *mtwo*

Definition:	M2 as a percentage of GDP
Unit of measurement:	Percentage
Source:	IMF[5]

---

5 International Monetary Fund, *International Financial Statistics*, various
 years.

Notes: Measures whether the financial system is "repressed"; financial deepening is represented by a growing or high M2/GDP.[6] The size of financial intermediaries is positively correlated to the provision of financial services.

3. *stock*

Definition: Stock market capitalization

Unit of measurement: $millions U.S.

Source: Merrill Lynch & Co., Inc.; IFC[7]

III. PROSPERITY

4. *lgdpcap*

Definition: Log of real per capita GDP; current $ U.S.

Unit of measurement: Log of $ U.S.

Source: Penn World Table [CGDP][8]

5. *edu*

Definition: Gross educational enrollment of all ages as a percentage of children in the appropriate age group

Unit of measurement: Percentage

Source: World Bank; CIESIN[9]

6. *urban*

Definition: Percentage of population residing in major cities

Unit of measurement: Percentage

Source: World Bank; Taiwan Yearbook[10]

---

6 McKinnon (1993).

7 International Finance Corporation, Datastream International; Merrill Lynch & Co., Inc. (1995).

8 Summers and Heston (1991).

9 World Bank, *Social Indicators of Development,* various years; Consortium for International Earth Sciences Information Network, n.d.

10 World Bank, *World Tables,* various years; *Statistical Yearbook of the Republic of China* (1993).

IV. TECHNOLOGY

7. *invest*
Definition: Real investment as a percentage of GDP;
                       current $ U.S.
Unit of measurement: Percentage
Source: Penn World Tables[11]

8. *tele*
Definition: Telephones per 100 inhabitants
Unit of measurement: Percentage
Source: UN; Taiwan statistics; Korea statistics;
                       China statistics[12]

V. INTERNATIONALIZATION

9. *fdigdp*
Definition: Foreign direct investment as a percentage
                       of GDP ($ U.S.)
Unit of measurement: Percentage
Source: IMF, Taiwan financial statistics[13]

10. *open*
Definition: (Imports + exports)/GDP ($ U.S.)
Unit of measurement: Percentage
Source: IMF, Taiwan National Economic Trends[14]

11. *trate*
Definition: Tariff rates: international tariffs/ (imports +
                       exports), $ U.S.
Unit of measurement: Percentage
Source: IMF, Taiwan financial statistics[15]

11   World Bank, *World Tables,* various years; *Statistical Yearbook of the Republic of China* (1993).
12   United Nations, *Statistical Yearbook,* various years; *Essential Statistics of Taiwan* (1993); Economic Planning Board, various years; *Statistical Yearbook of China,* various years.
13   International Monetary Fund, *Government Statistics,* various years; *Financial Statistics, Taiwan District,* various years.
14   International Monetary Fund, *International Financial Statistics,* various years; *Quarterly National Economic Trends, Taiwan Area* (1994).
15   International Monetary Fund, *Government Statistics,* various years; *Financial Statistics, Taiwan District,* various years.

Appendix C

━━

Serial correlation

Serial correlation, a common occurrence in time-series data, occurs when a shock in one period continues to affect the next period, resulting in the errors correlated across different time periods. In such a case, the assumed error structure would be $U_t = \beta u_{t-1} + e_t$. With serial correlation, OLS has unbiased and consistent estimators; however, the statistical inferences may be unreliable. To test for the presence of serial correlation, each structural equation was estimated and the errors predicted. Because of the nature of the dataset (country blocks), a separate Durbin Watson (DW) statistic was calculated for each block. For each of the seven countries, the null hypothesis of no serial correlation was rejected. The DW statistics tended toward zero, reflecting the presence of positive serial correlation.

To correct for the serial correlation, a correction coefficient *(rhohat)* was constructed from the DW statistic. Again, a separate coefficient was constructed for each of the country blocks. Using the correction coefficient, the raw data were transformed ($Y_t^* = Y_t - rhohat\ Y_{t-1}$) and included in the structural equation regressions. It should be noted that the small sample size of the country blocks used in the correction technique may affect the ability of *rhohat* to correct the serial correlation.

Bibliography

"A Little Booing from the Audience," *The Economist*, March 25, 1996.

"Acceleration of Foreign Exchange Reforms Studied," *The Korea Times*, June 28, 1995, p. 9, reprinted in *FBIS*, June 30, 1995.

"Address by Kim Tae-chun," *FBIS-EAS-97-513*, Seoul KBS-1 Television Network, December 19, 1997.

Adelman, I., and C. T. Morris, *Society, Politics, and Economic Development*, The Johns Hopkins University Press, Baltimore, Maryland, 1967.

Adelman, Irma, and Cynthia Taft Morris, *Economic Growth and Social Equity in Developing Countries*, Stanford University Press, Stanford, California, 1973.

Ahn, Byung-Joon, "Korea's International Environment," in Thomas W. Robinson (ed.), *Democracy and Development in East Asia*, AEI Press, Washington, D.C., 1991.

Alagappa, Muthiah, *Democratic Transition in Asia: The Role of the International Community*, East-West Center Special Reports, No. 3, October 1994.

Almanac of China's Economy, Beijing, 1988.

Almond, Gabriel A., and James S. Coleman, *The Politics of Developing Areas*, Princeton University Press, Princeton, New Jersey, 1960.

Alwin, D. F., and R. M. Hauser, "The Decomposition of Effects in Path Analysis," *American Sociological Review*, February 1975.

Amsden, Alice, *Asia's Next Giant*, Oxford University Press, New York, 1989.

Anderson, Benedict, from a speech entitled "Elections and Democratization in Southeast Asia: Thailand, the Philippines and Indonesia" reprinted in Adam Schwarz, *A Nation in Waiting*, Westview Press, Boulder, Colorado, 1994.

Arat, Zehra F, "Democracy and Economic Development—Modernization Theory Revisited," *Comparative Politics*, Vol. 21, 1988.

"Army Chief: No Need to Change Election System," reprinted in *FBIS-EAS-95-123*, June 27, 1995, p. 56, from *Jakarta Republika*, June 25, 1995.

Arrow, Kenneth, *Social Choice and Individual Values*, Yale University Press, New Haven, Connecticut, 1963.

Australian National Korean Studies Center, *Korea to the Year 2000: Implications for Australia*, Department of Foreign Affairs and Trade, Australia, 1992.

Auw, David C. L., "Political Evolution in Post-Martial Law Taiwan: Issues, Problems, and Prospects," *Issues and Studies*, Vol. 30, No. 6, June 1994.

Bachman, David, "China in 1993: Dissolution, Frenzy, and/or Breakthrough?" *Asian Survey*, Vol. XXXIV, No. 1, January 1994.

Baker, Richard W., *Indonesia—Moving to the End Game*, East-West Center, August 1996.

Barrett, Richard E., "Autonomy and Diversity in the American State on Taiwan," in Edwin Winckler and Susan Greenhalgh (eds.), *Contending Approaches to the Political Economy of Taiwan*, M. E. Sharpe, Inc., Armonk, New York, 1988.

Barro, R. J., "Economic Growth in a Cross Section of Countries," *Quarterly Journal of Economics*, Vol. 106, 1991, pp. 407–444.

Barro, Robert, *Determinants of Economic Growth*, MIT Press, Cambridge, Massachusetts, 1997.

Barro, Robert, "Pushing Democracy Is No Key to Prosperity," *The Wall Street Journal*, December 14, 1993.

Bates, R. H, "The Economics of Transitions to Democracy," *Political Science and Politics*, Vol. 24, 1991.

Bauer, Peter, "Transition in the East: Democracy and Market," *Cato Policy Report*, March/April 1992.

Baum, Julian, "Adapt or Perish," *Far Eastern Economic Review*, August 19, 1993.

Becker, Gary S., "A Theory of Competition Among Pressure Groups for Political Influence," *Quarterly Journal of Economics*, Vol. 98, No. 3, August 1983, pp. 371–400.

Bedeski, Robert E., *The Transformation of South Korea*, Routledge Press, New York, 1994.

Beijing Review, Beijing, November 9–15, 1987.

Bell, Michael W., Hoe Ee Khor, and Kalpana Kochhar, *China at the Threshold of a Market Economy*, International Monetary Fund, Washington, D.C., September 1993.

Benjamin, Roger W., "Korean Political Participation as Collective Action," in Chong Lim Kim (ed.), *Political Participation in Korea: Democracy, Mobilization and Stability*, CLIO Press, Oxford, 1980.

Bennett, John T., "Economic Developments in the Republic of Korea," in Thomas W. Robinson (ed.), *Democracy and Development in East Asia*, AEI Press, Washington, D.C., 1991.

Berleson, Bernard R., Paul F. Lazarsfeld, and William N. McPhee, "Democratic Practice and Democratic Theory" (1954), in Samuel Hendel (ed.), *Basic Issues of American Democracy*, Prentice Hall, New Jersey, 1976.

Bhagwati, Jagdish, *The Economics of Underdeveloped Countries*, McGraw-Hill, New York, 1966.

Bollen, Kenneth A., "Political Democracy: Conceptual and Measurement Traps," *Studies in Comparative International Development*, Spring 1990.

Bollen, Kenneth, "Political Democracy and the Timing of Development," *American Sociological Review*, 1979, p. 44.

Bos, Theodore, and Thomas A. Fetherston, "Asian Capital Markets Gaining Recognition and Maturity," in *Rising Asian Capital Markets: Empirical Studies, Research in International Business and Finance*, Vol. 10, JAI Press, London, 1993.

Bowles, Samuel, and Herbert Gintis, *Democracy & Capitalism*, Basic Books, Inc., New York, 1986.

Brick, Andrew B., "China's Revolution Without Borders," *Asian Wall Street Journal*, March 16, 1992.

Bush, George, U.S. State Department Dispatch, May 29, 1991.

Bustelo, P., "Economic Development and Political Transition in Taiwan and Spain—A Comparative Analysis," *Issues and Studies*, Vol. 28, 1992.

Chan, Steve, *East Asian Dynamism*, Westview Press, Oxford, 1990.

Chase, Robert, Emily B. Hill, and Paul Kennedy, "Pivotal States and U.S. Strategy," *Foreign Affairs*, Vol. 75, No.1, January/February 1996.

Chen, Hurng-yu, "China's Political Division and Chinese Communities in Southeast Asia," *Issues and Studies*, Vol. 27, No. 4, April 1991.

Cheng, Chu-yuan, "The ROC's Role in the World Economy," *Issues and Studies*, November 1992.

Cheng, Lucie, and Ping-Chun Hsiung, "Women, Export-Oriented Growth, and the State," in Joel D. Aberbach, David Dollar, and Kenneth L. Sokoloff (eds.), *The Role of the State in Taiwan's Development*, M. E. Sharpe, Inc., Armonk, New York, 1994.

Cheng, Tun-jen, and Stephan Haggard, *Political Change in Taiwan*, Lynne Rienner Publishers, Boulder, Colorado, 1991.

Chiang, Antonio, *Taiwan Communiqué*, International Committee for Human Rights in Taiwan, No. 64, January 1995.

Chien, Frederick F., "A View from Taipei," *Foreign Affairs*, Vol. 70, No. 5, Winter 1991–1992.

China Daily, January 6, 1992, Foreign Broadcast Information Service (FBIS).

China Daily, September 13, 1991, Foreign Broadcast Information Service (FBIS).

China: Foreign Trade Reform, A World Bank Country Study, Washington , D.C., 1994.

"China: Jiang Zemin Congress Report," *Beijing Xinhua*, September 21, 1997, Foreign Broadcast Information Service (FBIS), FBIS-CHI-97-266.

China News Analysis, No. 1524, December 15, 1994.

"China's Arbitrary State," *The Economist*, March 23, 1996.

Choi, Ho Chin, *The Economic History of Korea*, Freedom Library, Seoul, 1971.

Chu Yun-han, "Constitutional Reform and Democracy," in Jason C. Hu (ed.), *Quiet Revolutions*, Kwang Hwa Publishing Co., Taipei, 1994.

Claeesens, Stijn, Susmita Dasgupta, and Jack Glen, "Return Behavior in Emerging Stock Markets," *The World Bank Economic Review*, Vol. 9, No. 1, January 25, 1996.

Clark, Cal, *Taiwan's Development: Implications for Contending Political Economy Paradigms*, Greenwood Press, 1989.

Clifford, Mark, "Filing for Divorce," *Far Eastern Economic Review*, April 21, 1988.

Cohen, Carl, *Democracy*, University of Georgia Press, Georgia, 1971.

Cohen, Margot, "To the Barricades," *Far Eastern Economic Review*, May 14, 1998.

Cole, David C., and Betty F. Slade, *Building a Modern Financial System*, Cambridge University Press, Cambridge, 1996.

Collier, D., "Timing of Economic Growth and Regime Characteristics in Latin America," *Comparative Politics*, Vol. 7, 1975.

Consortium for International Earth Sciences Information Network, n.d.

Coppedge, Michael, and Wolfgang H. Reinicke, "Measuring Polyarchy," in Alex Inkeles (ed.), *On Measuring Democracy*, Transaction Publishers, New Jersey, 1991.

Cotton, James, "The Military Factor in South Korean Politics," in Viberto Selochan (ed.), *The Military, the State, and Development in Asia and the Pacific*, Westview Press, Boulder, Colorado, 1991.

Crouch, Harold, *The Army and Politics in Indonesia*, Cornell University Press, Ithaca, New York, 1988.

Cumings, Bruce, "The Origins and Development of the Northeast Asian Political Economy: Industrial Sectors, Product Cycles, and Political Consequences," in Frederic C. Deyo (ed.), *The Political Economy of the New Asian Industrialism*, Cornell University Press, Ithaca, New York, 1987.

Cuomo, Mario, and Harold Holzer (eds.), *Lincoln on Democracy*, Harper Collins Publishers, New York, 1990.

Cutright, Philips, "National Political Development: Its Measurement and Social Correlates," in Nelson W. Polsby, Robert A. Dentler, and Paul A. Smith (eds.), *Politics and Social Life*, Houghton Mifflin Company, Boston, Massachusetts, 1963.

Dahl, Robert A., *Polyarchy; Participation and Opposition*, Yale University Press, New Haven, Connecticut, 1971.

Davies, Powell A., *Man's Vast Future: A Definition of Democracy*, Farrar, Straus and Young, New York, 1951.

Denison, Edward F., *Trends in American Economic Growth*, The Brookings Institution, Washington, D.C., n.d.

Deutsch, Karl W., "Social Mobilization and Political Development," *American Political Science Review*, Vol. 55, 1961.

Diamond, Larry, in Larry Diamond, Juan J. Linz, and Seymour Martin Lipset (eds.), *Democracy in Developing Countries*, Vol. 3, Lynne Rienner Publishers, Boulder, Colorado, 1988.

Dick, G. W., "Authoritarian versus Nonauthoritarian Approaches to Economic Development," *Journal of Political Economy*, 1974.

Directorate-General of Budget, Accounting, and Statistics, *The Report on 1985 Agricultural and Fishery Census*, Taiwan, 1987.

Eberstadt, Nicholas, "Some Comments on Democracy and Development in East Asia," in Thomas W. Robinson (ed.), *Democracy and Development in East Asia*, AEI Press, Washington, D.C., 1991.

Economic Planning Board, *Major Statistics of the Korean Economy*, Seoul, various years.

"Economic Relations with U.S., Japan Reviewed," *Beijing Guoji Maoyiwenti (International Trade Journal)*, No. 5, May 19, pp. 2–6, Foreign Broadcast Information Service (FBIS), CHI95-147, August 1995.

Engardio, Pete, and George Wehrfritz, "Suddenly, All Bets Are Off in Taiwan," *Business Week*, August 23, 1993.

Espinal, R., "Development, Neoliberalism and Electoral Politics in Latin America," *Development and Change*, Vol. 23, 1992.

Essential Statistics of Taiwan, Taipei, 1993.

Faison, Seth, "16 Foreign Law Firms Cleared to Open Offices in China," *The New York Times*, June 27, 1996.

Far Eastern Economic Review, June 8, 1989, p. 85.

Far Eastern Economic Review, December 31, 1987.

Fei, John C. H., "The Taiwan Economy in the Seventies," in Shao-chuan Leng (ed.), *Chiang Ching-Kuo's Leadership in the Development of the Republic of China on Taiwan*, The Miller Center, University of Virginia, University Press of America, New York, 1993.

Feierabend, Ivo K., and Rosalind L. Feierabend, "Coerciveness and Change: Cross-National Trends," *American Behavioral Scientist*, Vol. 15, 1972, pp. 911–928.

Financial Statistics, Taiwan District, ROC, various years.

Finkel, S. E., E. N. Muller, and M. A. Seligson, "Economic Crisis, Incumbent Performance and Regime Support—A Comparison of Longitudinal Data from West Germany and Costa Rica," *British Journal of Political Science*, Vol. 19, 1989.

Finn, James (ed.), *Freedom in the World*, Freedom House, New York, 1994.

Fleming, P. T. Jardine, "Indonesia," *World Equity Markets*, Euromoney, Nusantara, Jakarta, London, 1993.

French, J.R.P., and B. Raven, "The Bases of Social Power," in D. Cartwright and A. Zander (eds.), *Group Dynamics*, Harper and Row, New York, 1968.

Friedman, Edward, *National Identity and Democratic Prospects in Socialist China*, M. E. Sharpe, Armonk, New York, 1995.

Friedman, Milton, *Capitalism and Freedom*, University of Chicago Press, Chicago, Illinois, 1962.

Friedman, Milton, "Which Way for Capitalism?" in Robert W. Poole, Jr., and Virginia I. Postrel (eds.), *Free Minds & Free Markets*, Pacific Research Institute for Public Policy, San Francisco, California, 1993.

Friedman, Thomas L., "The New China Consensus," *The New York Times*, May 26, 1996.

The Fuji Bank Ltd., "The Stock Market of Shenzhen," in Institute of Global Financial Studies, *The Stock Markets in Asia*, June 1994.

Fukasaku, Kiichiro, and David Wall, *China's Long March to an Open Economy*, *Development Centre Studies*, OECD, Paris, 1994.

Fukuyama, Francis, "Social Capital and the Global Economy," *Foreign Affairs*, Vol. 74, No.5, September/October 1995, pp. 89–103.

"Full text of letter to people by the Ministry of Finance and Economy," *Seoul Sinmun*, November 24, 1997, Foreign Broadcast Information Service, FBIS-EAS-97-334.

Gaouette, Nicole, "Indonesia Faces Unsettling Prospect of Real Democracy," *The Christian Science Monitor,* June 1, 1998.

Gasiorowski, M. J., "Economic Dependence and Political Democracy—A Cross National Study," *Comparative Political Studies*, Vol. 20, 1988.

Gastil, R. D., "The Comparative Survey of Freedom: Experiences and Suggestions," *Studies in Comparative International Development*, Vol. 25, 1990, pp. 25–50.

Gelb, Alan, Gary Jefferson, and Inderjit Singh, "Can Communist Economies Transform Incrementally?" Policy Research Department, The World Bank, Washington, D. C., WPS 1189, October 1993.

Geller, D. S., "Economic Modernization and Political Instability in Latin America—A Causal Analysis of Bureaucratic Authoritarianism," *Western Political Quarterly*, Vol. 35, 1982.

Ghose, Ajit Kumar, "The New Development Strategy and Rural Reforms in Post-Mao China," in Keith Griffin (ed.), *Institutional Reform and Economic Development in the Chinese Countryside*, M. E. Sharpe, Inc., Armonk, New York, 1984.

Gilley, Bruce, "Whatever You Say," *Far Eastern Economic Review*, December 7, 1995.

Gillis, Malcolm, "Episodes in Indonesian Economic Growth," in Arnold C. Harberger (ed.), *World Economic Growth*, San Francisco, California, 1984.

Gold, Thomas B., "Autonomy Versus Authoritarianism," in George Hicks (ed.), *Broken Mirror*, St. James Press, Chicago, Illinois, 1990.

Gold, Thomas B., *State and Society in the Taiwan Miracle*, M. E. Sharpe, Inc., Armonk, New York, 1986.

Goldman, Merle, *Sowing the Seeds of Democracy in China*, Harvard University Press, Cambridge, Massachusetts, 1994.

Goldstein, Carl, Lincoln Kaye, and Anthony Blass, "Get Off Our Backs," *Far Eastern Economic Review*, July 15, 1993.

Goldstein, Steven M., *Continuing the "Miracle": Taiwan Faces the Twenty-First Century*, Foreign Policy Association, Summer 1997.

Goldstein, Steven M., "Reforming Socialist Systems: Some Lessons of the Chinese Experience," *Studies in Comparative Communism*, Summer 1988.

Gonick, L. S., and R. M. Rosh, "The Structural Constraints of the World Economy on National Political Development," *Comparative Political Studies*, Vol. 21, 1988.

Gordon, Richard, and Carma Hinton, *The Gate of Heavenly Peace*, documentary interview with Wan Dan, 1995.

"The Guinier Battle: Where Ideas That Hurt Guinier Thrive," *The New York Times*, Section B, May 14, 1993.

Hamrin, Carol Lee, *China and the Challenge of the Future*, Westview Press, Boulder, Colorado, 1990.

Harding, Harry, *China's Second Revolution*, The Brookings Institution, Washington, D.C., 1987.

Harding, Harry, "Political Development in Post-Mao China," in A. Doak Barnett and Ralph N. Clough (eds.), *Modernizing China: Post-Mao Reform and Development*, Westvew Press, Boulder, Colorado, 1986.

Haseman, John B., "Catalyst for Change in Indonesia," *Asian Survey*, Vol. XXXV, No. 8, August 1995.

Helliwell, John F., "Empirical Linkages between Democracy and Economic Growth," *National Bureau of Economic Research*, Cambridge, Massachusetts, 1992a.

Helliwell, John, *National Bureau of Economic Research Working Paper*, No. 4066, May 1992b.

Hill, Hal, *The Indonesian Economy Since 1966*, Cambridge University Press, Cambridge, 1996.

Ho, Samuel P. S., *Economic Development of Taiwan, 1860–1970*, Yale University Press, New Haven, Connecticut, 1978.

Holt, Robert T., and John E. Turner, *The Political Basis of Economic Development*, Van Nostrand, Princeton, New Jersey, 1966, in Robert M. Marsh, "Does Democracy Hinder Economic Development in the Latecomer Developing Nations?" *Comparative Social Research*, Vol. 2, 1979.

"How and Why to Survive Chinese Tax Torture," *The Economist*, December 12, 1995.

Howell, Jude, "The Impact of the Open Door Policy on the Chinese State," in Gordon White (ed.), *The Chinese State in the Era of Economic Reform*, M. E. Sharpe, Inc., Armonk, New York, 1991.

Hsieh, Winston, "Migrant Peasant Workers in China: The PRC's Rural Crisis in an Historical Perspective," in George T. Yu (ed.), *China in Transition*, University Press of America, New York, 1993.

Hsin-Huang, Michael Hsiao, "Political Liberalization and the Farmers' Movement in Taiwan," in Edward Friedman (ed.), *The Politics of Democratization*, Westview Press, Oxford, 1994.

Hu, Jason C.,"Freedom of Expression and Development of the Media," in Jason C. Hu (ed), *Quiet Revolutions,* Kwang Hwa Publishing Co., Taipei, 1994.

Hu, Jason C. (ed), *Quiet Revolutions,* Kwang Hwa Publishing Co., Taipei, 1994.

Huang, Teh-fu, "Electoral Competition and Democratic Transition in the Republic of China," *Issues and Studies*, October 1991.

Huang, Yasheng, *Inflation and Investment Controls in China*, Cambridge University Press, Cambridge, 1996.

Huber, Evelyne, Dietrich Rueschmeyer, and John D. Stephens, "The Impact of Economic Development on Democracy," *Journal of Economic Perspective*, Vol. 7, No. 3, Summer 1993.

Huntington, Samuel, "Democracy's Third Wave," in Larry Diamond and Marc F. Plattner (eds.), *The Global Resurgence of Democracy*, The Johns Hopkins University Press, Baltimore, Maryland, 1993.

Huntington, Samuel, *Political Order in Changing Societies*, Yale University Press, New Haven, Connecticut, 1968.

Huntington, S. P., and J. I. Dominguez, "Political Development," in F. I. Greenstein and N. W. Polsby (eds), *Handbook of Political Science*, Addison-Wesley, Massachusetts, 1975.

Il Sakong, *Korea in the World Economy*, Institute for International Economics, Washington, D.C., 1993.

"Indonesia: Camdessus Views Indonesia's Economic Reform," Jakarta TVRI Television Network, Foreign Broadcast Information Service, FBIS-EAS-98-015.

Indonesia Financial Statistics, Bank of Indonesia, various years.

"Indonesia: Minister Unveils Revised State Budget," Jakarta TVRI Television Network, Foreign Broadcast Information Service, FBIS-EAS-98-023.

Inkeles, Alex, and David Smith, *Becoming Modern: Individual Change in Six Developing Countries,* Harvard University Press, Cambridge, Massachusetts, 1974.

International Finance Corporation, Datastream International.

International Monetary Fund, *Government Statistics,* Washington, D.C., various years.

International Monetary Fund, *International Financial Statistics,* Washington, D.C., various years.

Investing in China, Ernst & Young, New York, 1994.

Investment Commission, Ministry of Economic Affairs, Republic of China, various years.

Jackman, R. W., "Relation of Economic Development to Democratic Performance," *American Journal of Political Science,* Vol. 17, 1973.

Jefferson, Gary H., and Wenyi Xu, "The Impact of Reform on Socialist Enterprises in Transition: Structure, Conduct and Performance in Chinese Industry," *Journal of Comparative Economics,* Vol. 15, 1992.

Jefferson, Thomas, *On Democracy,* selected and organized with an introduction by Saul K. Padover, D. Appleton-Century Company, 1959.

Jenkins, David, *Soeharto and His Generals,* Cornell Modern Indonesia Project, Monograph No. 64, Ithaca, New York, 1984.

Jia, Wei, *Chinese Foreign Investment Laws and Policies,* Quorum Books, Westport, Connecticut, 1994.

Johnson, Bryan T., and Thomas P. Sheehy, *The Index of Economic Freedom,* The Heritage Foundation, Washington, D.C., 1995.

Johnson, Chalmers, "Inflation," in George Hicks (ed.), *The Broken Mirror,* St. James Press, London, 1990.

Jones, Leroy, *Public Enterprise and Economic Development: The Korean Case,* Korea Development Institute, Seoul, 1975.

Kainz, Howard P., *Democracy: East and West,* Macmillan Publishing Company, Hong Kong, 1984.

"Keeping the Wheels Turning," *Review Indonesia (Economic and Business)*, No. 82, November 6, 1993.

Kelliher, Daniel, *Peasant Politics in China: The Era of Rural Reform: 1979–1989*, Yale University Press, New Haven, Connecticut, 1992.

Kelliher, Daniel, "Privatisation and Politics in Rural China," in Gordon White (ed.), *The Chinese State in the Era of Economic Reform*, M. E. Sharpe, Inc., Armonk, New York, 1991.

Khadka, N., "Democracy and Development in Nepal—Prospects and Challenges," *Pacific Affairs*, Vol. 66, 1993.

Khan, Azizur Rahman, "The Responsibility System and Institutional Change," in Keith Griffin (ed.), *Institutional Reform and Economic Development in the Chinese Countryside*, M. E. Sharpe, Inc., Armonk, New York, 1984.

Kim Kwang-suk and Park Joon-kyung, *Sources of Economic Growth in Korea: 1963–1982*, Korea Development Institute, Seoul, 1985.

King, Dwight, "Indonesia's Foreign Policy," in David Wurfel and Bruce Burton (eds.), *The Political Economy of Foreign Policy in Southeast Asia*, St. Martin's Press, New York, 1991.

King, Robert G., and Ross Levine, "Finance and Growth: Schumpeter Might be Right," *Quarterly Journal of Economics*, August 1993.

Kleinberg, Robert, *China's "Opening" to the Outside World*, Westview Press, Boulder, Colorado, 1990.

Klitgaard, Robert, "Better States, Better Markets," Invited paper presented at the South African Economics Society Biennial Conference, Pretoria, October 11–12, 1993.

Klitgaard, Robert, in Larry Diamond, Juan J. Linz, and Seymour Martin Lipset (eds.), *Democracy in Developing Countries*, Vol. 3, Lynne Rienner Publishers, Boulder, Colorado, 1988.

Kohli, Atul, "Democracy and Development," *Development Strategies Reconsidered*, Overseas Development Council, Washington, D.C., 1986.

Korea Labor Institute, *Quarterly Labor Review*, Seoul, 1992.

The Korea Times, May 4, 1988.

Korea to the Year 2000, Korea Development Institute, Seoul, 1986.

Korean Industrial Research Institute, Seoul, various years.

Korzeniewicz, R. P., and K. Awbrey, "Democratic Transitions and the Semiperiphery of the World-Economy," *Sociological Forum*, Vol. 7, 1992.

Kuznets, Simon, *Economic Growth of Nations: Total Output and Production Structure*, Harvard University Press, Cambridge, 1971.

Kuznets, Simon, "Quantitative Aspects of the Economic Growth of Nations," *Economic Development and Cultural Change*, October 1956.

Landay, Jonathan S., "U.S., China Struggle to Uncover Reach of North Korea Famine," *The Christian Science Monitor*, May 15, 1997.

Lardy, Nicholas R., *China in the World Economy*, Institute for International Economics, Washington, D.C., 1994.

Lasater, Martin L., "Taiwan's International Environment," in Thomas Robinson (ed.), *Democracy and Development in East Asia*, The AEI Press, Washington, D.C., 1991.

Lau, Lawrence J. (ed.), *Models of Development*, ICS Press, San Francisco, California, 1986.

Leifer, Michael, *Indonesia's Foreign Policy*, George Allen and Unwin, London, 1983.

Lerner, Daniel, *The Passing of Traditional Society*, The Free Press, Glencoe, Illinois, 1958.

Li, Kwoh-ting, *Economic Transformation of Taiwan, ROC*, Shepheard-Walwyn Ltd., London, 1988.

Lilley, James, "Freedom Through Trade," *Foreign Policy*, No. 94, Spring 1994.

Lin, Zhimin, "Walking on Two Legs: The Domestic Context of China's Policy Toward the Asian-Pacific Region in the 1990s," in George T. Yu (ed.), *China in Transition*, University Press of America, New York, 1993.

Lindblom, Charles, *Politics and Markets*, Basic Books, Inc., New York, 1977.

Ling, Zhu, "The Chinese Role of the State in Chinese Agriculture," in Gordon White (ed.), *The Chinese State in the Era of Economic Reform*, M. E. Sharpe, Inc., Armonk, New York, 1991.

Linz, Juan J., "Totalitarian and Authoritarian Regimes," in Fred I. Greenstein and Nelson W. Polsby (eds.), *Macropolitical Theory*, Addison-Wesley, Reading, Massachusetts, 1975.

Lipset, Seymour M., "Capitalism, Socialism and Democracy," *Commentary*, Vol. 65, 1978.

Lipset, Seymour M., "Democracy at the Polls—An Expository Review," *Electoral Studies*, Vol. 1, 1982.

Lipset, Seymour M., "Some Social Requisites of Democracy: Economic Development and Political Legitimacy," *American Political Science Review*, Vol. 53, March 1959.

Lipset, Seymour Martin, *The First New Nation*, Basic Books, Inc., New York, 1963.

Liu Qing, "Human Rights, Democracy and China," *Journal of International Affairs*, Vol. 49, No. 2, Winter 1996.

The Long Term Credit Bank of Japan, "Securities Market in Korea," in Institute of Global Financial Studies, *The Stock Markets in Asia*, Tokyo, 1994.

Lu Ya-Li, "Political Developments in the Republic of China," in Thomas Robinson (ed.), *Democracy and Development in East Asia*, The AEI Press, Washington, D.C., 1991.

Madison, James, *The Federalist Papers*, Mentor Book Edition, New American Library, New York, 1961.

Marsh, R. M., "Authoritarian and Democratic Transitions in National Political Systems," *International Journal of Comparative Sociology*, Vol. 32, 1991.

Marsh, Robert M., "Does Democracy Hinder Economic Development in the Latecomer Developing Nations?" *Comparative Social Research*, Vol. 2, 1979.

McBeth, John, "Ground Zero," *Far Eastern Economic Review*, January 22, 1998a.

McBeth, John, "Heavy Hand," *Far Eastern Economic Review*, June 29, 1995a.

McBeth, John, "The Line of Fire," *Far Eastern Economic Review*, May 21, 1998b.

McBeth, John, "Murky Waters," *Far Eastern Economic Review*, November 30, 1995b.

McBeth, John, "Technical Problems," *Far Eastern Economic Review*, September 4, 1997.

McKinnon, Ronald I., *The Order of Economic Liberalization*, The Johns Hopkins University Press, Baltimore, Maryland, 1993.

McLeod, Ross, "Financial Institutions and Markets in Indonesia," in Michael T. Skully (ed.), *Financial Institutions and Markets in Southeast Asia*, St. Martin's Press, New York, 1984.

Merrill Lynch & Co., Inc., 1995.

Metraux, Daniel, *Taiwan's Political and Economic Growth in the Late Twentieth-Century*, The Edwin Mellen Press, Lewiston, New York, 1991.

Midlarsky, M. I., "The Origins of Democracy in Agrarian Society— Land Inequality and Political Rights," *Journal of Conflict Resolution*, Vol. 36, 1992.

Mini Dragons: South Korea, Maryland Public Television, NHK, Film Australia, and InCA, Ambrose Video Publishing, Inc., New York, 1991.

"Minister Cites Prevalence of Corruption," *Jakarta Kompas*, July 21, 1995, Foreign Broadcast Information Service, FBIS-EAS-95-167, August 29, 1995, p. 60.

"Minister Stresses Importance of Small Businesses," *Suara Pembaruan*, June 26, 1995, Foreign Broadcast Information Service, FBIS-EAS-95-125, June 29, 1995, p. 59.

Moody, Peter R., Jr., *Political Change on Taiwan*, Praeger, New York, 1992.

Moreno, Ramon, *Exchange Rate Policy and Insulation from External Shocks: The Experiences of Taiwan and Korea—1970–1990*, Center for Pacific Basin Monetary and Economic Studies, Federal Reserve Bank, Working Paper PB93-05, 1993.

Morrison, Donald (ed.), *Massacre in Beijing*, Time Inc., New York, 1989.

Moy, Roland F., *A Computer Simulation of Democratic Political Development*, Sage Publications, Beverly Hills, California, 1970.

Muller, E. N., "Democracy, Economic Development and Income Inequality," *American Sociological Review*, Vol. 53, 1988.

Muller, E. N., "Dependent Economic Development, Aid Dependence on the United States and Democratic Breakdown in the Third World," *International Studies Quarterly*, Vol. 29, 1985.

Myers, Ramon H., "Building the First Chinese Democracy: The Crises and Leadership of President Lee Teng-hui," in Jason C. Hu (ed), *Quiet Revolutions*, Kwang Hwa Publishing Co., Taipei, 1994.

Nam, Chang-Hee, "South Korea's Big Business Clientelism in Democratic Reform," *Korea Observer*, Vol. XXV, No. 2, Summer 1994.

Nandy, A., "Economic and Psychoeconomic Contexts of Political Commitment and Dissent," *Economic Development and Cultural Change*, Vol. 23, 1975.

Nathan, Andrew, "Chinese Democracy: The Lessons of Failure," *Journal of Contemporary China*, No. 4, Fall 1993a.

Nathan, Andrew J., "Is China Ready for Democracy," in Larry Diamond and Marc F. Plattner (eds.), *The Global Resurgence of Democracy*, The Johns Hopkins University Press, Baltimore, Maryland, 1993b.

Nathan, Andrew J., and Helena V.S. Ho, "Chiang Ching-Kuo's Decision for Political Reform," in Shao-chuan Leng (ed.), *Chiang Ching-Kuo's Leadership in the Development of the Republic of China on Taiwan*, The Miller Center, University of Virginia, University Press of America, New York, 1993.

Naughton, Barry, "China's Reforms: Structural and Welfare Aspects," *AEA Papers and Proceedings*, May 1994.

Naughton, Barry, *Growing Out of the Plan*, Cambridge University Press, Cambridge, 1996.

Naughton, Barry, "Implications of the State Monopoly over Industries and Its Relaxation," *Modern China*, Vol. 18, No. 1, 1992.

Neher, Clark, "Democratization in Thailand," *Asian Affairs*, Vol. 21, No. 4, Winter 1995.

Neher, Clark D., and Ross Marlay, *Democracy and Development in Southeast Asia*, Westview Press, Boulder, Colorado, 1995.

Neubauer, Deane E., "Some Conditions of Democracy," *American Political Science Review*, 1967.

The Nikko Securities Co., Ltd., "Securities Market in Malaysia," in Institute of Global Financial Studies, *The Stock Markets in Asia*, Tokyo, 1994.

"Not So Militant," *The Economist*, June 10, 1995, p. 35.

Notosusanto, Nugroho, *The National Struggle and the Armed Forces of Indonesia*, Department of Defence and Security, Jakarta.

"Observers Comment on National Economic Situation," *Jakarta Republik*, August 8, 1995, Foreign Broadcast Information Service, FBIS-EAS-95-152, August 8, 1995, p. 79.

O'Donnell, Guillermo A., *Modernization and Bureaucratic Authoritarianism: Studies in South American Politics*, Institute of International Studies, University of California, Berkeley, 1973.

"Official on Need for Political Liberalization," *Bisnis Indonesia*, May 8, 1995, Foreign Broadcast Information Service, FBIS-EAS-95-133, July 12, 1995, p. 86.

Oh, John Chung Hwan, "The Future of Democracy and Economic Growth in Korea," *Korea Observer*, Vol. XXV, No. 1, Spring 1994.

Overholt, William H., *The Rise of China*, W. W. Norton and Company, New York, 1993.

Padover, Saul, *On Democracy*, Penguin Books, New York, 1946.

Pae, Sung Moon, *Korea Leading Developing Nations*, University Press of America, Lanham, Maryland, 1992.

Paine, Thomas, *The Rights of Man*, J. M. Dent, London, 1993.

Pei, Minxin, *From Reform to Revolution*, Harvard University Press, Cambridge, Massachusetts, 1994.

People's Bank of China, *Survey of the Distribution of Money in Circulation*, China Finance Press, Beijing, 1988.

Persson, Torsten, and Guido Tabellini, "Politico-Economic Equilibrium Growth: Theory and Evidence," 1990, Draft.

Pindyk, Robert S., and Daniel L. Rubinfeld, *Microeconomics*, 2d ed., Macmillan Publishing Company, New York, 1989.

Pitroda, Sam, "Development, Democracy, and the Village Telephone," *Harvard Business Review*, November-December, 1993.

Plattner, Marc, "The Democratic Moment," in Larry Diamond and Marc F. Plattner (eds.), *The Global Resurgence of Democracy*, The Johns Hopkins University Press, Baltimore, Maryland, 1993.

Plunk, Daryl M., "Political Developments in the Republic of Korea," in Thomas W. Robinson (ed.), *Democracy and Development in East Asia*, AEI Press, Washington, D.C., 1991.

Pollack, Jonathan D., "Technology, Innovation, and Institutional Identity in Modern China," in Kenneth G. Lieberthal (ed.), *Constructing China: The Interaction of Economics and Culture*, Center for Chinese Studies, Ann Arbor, Michigan, 1996a.

Pollack, Jonathan, "Designing a New American Security Strategy for Asia," in James Shinn (ed.), *Weaving the Net*, Council on Foreign Relations, New York, 1996b.

Pourgerami, A., "Authoritarian Versus Nonauthoritarian Approaches to Economic Development—Update and Additional Evidence," *Public Choice*, Vol. 74, 1992.

Pourgerami, A., "The Political Economy of Development—A Cross-National Causality Test of Development, Democracy, Growth Hypothesis," *Public Choice*, Vol. 58, 1988.

Prybyla, Jan S., "Economic Development in the Republic of China," in Thomas Robinson (ed.), *Democracy and Development in East Asia*, The AEI Press, Washington, D.C., 1991.

Przeworski, Adam, and Fernando Limongi, "Political Regimes and Economic Growth," *Journal of Economic Perspectives*, Vol. 7, No. 3, Summer 1993.

Pye, Lucian W., *Asian Power and Politics*, Harvard University Press, Cambridge, Massachusetts, 1985.

Pye, Lucian W., "China's Quest for Respect," *The New York Times*, Op-ed, February 19, 1996, p. A13.

Pye, Lucian, *Aspects of Political Development*, Little Brown, Boston, Massachusetts, 1966.

Quarterly National Economic Trends, Taiwan Area, The Republic of China, 1994.

Ranis, Gustav, "Industrial Development," in Walter Galenson (ed.), *Economic Growth and Structural Change in Taiwan*, Cornell University Press, Ithaca, New York, 1979.

Ravich, Samantha F., *Marketization and Prosperity: Pathways to East Asian Democracy*, RAND Graduate School dissertation, RGSD-132, 1996.

Rawski, Thomas G., "Chinese Industrial Reform: Accomplishments, Prospects, and Implications," *AEA Papers and Proceedings*, May 1994.

Rawski, Thomas G., "Implications of China's Reform Experience," draft, February 1995.

"Reaching an Impasse," *The Economist*, August 6, 1994.

"Red Scare," *The Economist*, November 25, 1995, p. 35.

Remmer, K. L., "The Process of Democratization in Latin-America," *Studies in Comparative International Development*, Vol. 27, 1992.

Rhee, Yung Whee, Bruce Ross-Larson, and Garry Pursell, *Korea's Competitive Edge*, A World Bank Research Publication, The Johns Hopkins University Press, Baltimore, Maryland, 1984.

Rigger, Shelley, "Trends in Taiwan: A Political Perspective," *Issues and Studies*, Vol. 30, No. 11, November 1994.

Robinson, Thomas W., "Democracy and Development in East Asia—Toward the Year 2000," in Thomas Robinson (ed.), *Democracy and Development in East Asia*, The AEI Press, Washington, D.C., 1991.

Robison, Richard, "Indonesia: Tensions in State and Regime," in Richard Robison, Kevin Hewison, and Richard Higgott (eds.), *Southeast Asia in the 1990s—The Politics of Economic Crisis*, 1994.

Roosevelt, Eleanor, *The Moral Basis of Democracy*, Howell Soskin, New York, 1940.

Rosen, S., "Human Capital: A Survey of Empirical Research," in A. B. Atkinson (ed.), *Wealth, Income and Inequality*, Oxford University Press, London, 1980.

Rosen, Stanley, and Gary Zou, "The Chinese Debate on the New Authoritarianism," *Chinese Sociology and Anthropology*, Winter 1990–1991.

Rostow, W. W., *Politics and the Stages of Growth*, Cambridge University Press, Cambridge, 1971.

Rostow, W. W., *Theorists of Economic Growth from David Hume to the Present*, Oxford University Press, New York, 1990.

Rueschemeyer, D., "Different Methods, Contradictory Results— Research on Development and Democracy," *International Journal of Comparative Sociology*, Vol. 23, 1991.

Sampson, Catherine, "China's Media Go to Market," *Asian Wall Street Journal*, February 26–27, 1993.

Scalapino, Robert, "Reflections on Leadership, China, and Chiang Ching-Kuo," in Shao-chuan Leng (ed.), *Chiang Ching-Kuo's Leadership in the Development of the Republic of China on Taiwan*, The Miller Center, University of Virginia, University Press of America, New York, 1993.

Schive, Chi, *Taiwan's Economic Role in East Asia*, Center for Strategic and International Studies, Washington, D.C., 1995.

Schmitter, Philippe C., and Terry Lynn Karl, "What Democracy Is . . . and Is Not," in Larry Diamond and Marc F. Plattner (eds.), *The Global Resurgence of Democracy*, The Johns Hopkins University Press, Baltimore, Maryland, 1993.

Schran, Peter, "The Urbanization and Occupational Diversification of China's Countryside," in George T. Yu (ed.), *China in Transition*, University Press of America, Lanham, Maryland, 1993.

Schumpeter, Joseph A., *Capitalism, Socialism and Democracy*, Harper and Row, New York, 1942.

Schwarz, Adam, *A Nation in Waiting*, Westview Press, Boulder, Colorado, 1994.

Segal, Gerald, "China's Changing Shape," *Foreign Affairs*, May/June 1994.

Sharma, Shalendra, "Markets and States in Development: India's Reformers and the East Asian Experience," *Asian Survey*, Vol. 33, No. 9, September 1993.

Shen, Jia-Dong, and Ya-Hwei Yang, "Taiwan's Financial System and the Allocation of Investment Funds," in Joel D. Aberbach, David Dollar, and Kenneth L. Sokoloff (eds.), *The Role of the State in Taiwan's Development*, M. E. Sharpe, Inc., Armonk, New York, 1994.

Shih, Casper, "Productivity—A Strategy for the Century of the Pacific," in Jason C. Hu (ed), *Quiet Revolutions*, Kwang Hwa Publishing Co., Taipei, 1994.

Shinn, James (ed.), *Weaving the Net*, Council on Foreign Relations, New York, 1996.

Sigur, Gaston, J., "South Korea and the Triumph of Democracy," in Christopher J. Sigur (ed.), *Korea's New Challenges and Kim Young Sam*, Carnegie Council on Ethics and International Affairs, New York, 1993.

Singh, Bilveer, *Dwifungsi ABRI*, Singapore Institute of International Studies, Singapore, 1995.

Sirowy, L., and A. Inkeles, "The Effects of Democracy on Economic Growth and Inequality—A Review," *Studies in Comparative International Development*, Vol. 25, 1990.

Soesastro, M. Hadi, "The Political Economy of Deregulation in Indonesia," *Asian Survey*, Vol. 29, No. 9, September 1989.

Solow, Robert, "Contribution to the Theory of Economic Growth," *Quarterly Journal of Economics*, Vol. 70, February 1956.

Soong, James C. Y., "Political Development in the Republic of Taiwan, 1985-1992: An Insider's View," *World Affairs*, Fall 1992.

South China Morning Post, September 15, 1989, p. 1, Foreign Broadcast Information Service (FBIS), September 15, 1989.

South Korea, A Country Study, Andrea Matles Savada and William Shaw (eds.), Federal Research Division, Library of Congress, Washington, D.C., 1992.

State Statistical Bureau, *State Yearbook of China*, 1981.

Statistical Yearbook of China, Beijing, various years.

Statistical Yearbook of the Republic of China, Taipei, 1993.

Steinberg, David I., *The Republic of Korea*, Westview Press, Boulder, Colorado, 1989.

Stephan, Alfred, "On the Tasks of a Democratic Opposition," in Larry Diamond and Marc F. Plattner (eds.), *The Global Resurgence of Democracy*, The Johns Hopkins University Press, Baltimore, Maryland, 1993.

"Stock Exchange Opened to Small Companies," *Jakarta GATRA,* April 1, 1995, Foreign Broadcast Information Service, FBIS-EAS-95-101, May 25, 1995, p. 69.

"Suharto on Open Economy, Free Trade System," *Jakarta Antara,* November 7, 1995, Foreign Broadcast Information Service, FBIS-EAS-95-217, November 9, 1995, p. 59.

Sukarno, *Sukarno: An Autobiography*, Bobbs-Merrill Co., Indianapolis, 1965.

Summers, R., and A. Heston, "The Penn World Table (Mark 5): An Expanded Set of International Comparisons, 1950–1988," *Quarterly Journal of Economics*, 1991, Vol. 106, pp. 327–368.

Sun Yat-sen, *The International Development of China*, Da Capo Press, New York, 1975 (c. 1922).

Taiwan Communiqué, International Committee for Human Rights in Taiwan, No. 64, January 1995.

Taiwan Statistical Data Book, Taipei, various years.

Taiwan Statistical Yearbook, Council for Economic Planning and Development, Taipei, various years.

Tasker, Rodney, "Mad as Hell," *Far Eastern Economic Review*, October 9, 1997.

Tempest, Rone, "Villages Taste Democracy's Forbidden Fruit in China," *Los Angeles Times*, May 19, 1996.

Terry, Gayle Pollard, "Perspective on Civil Rights," *Los Angeles Times*, July 27, 1993.

Thorbecke, Erik, and Theodore van der Pluijm, *Rural Indonesia: Socio-Economic Development in a Changing Environment*, International Fund for Agricultural Development, New York University Press, New York, 1993.

Tien-tung, Hsueh Li Qiang, and Liu Shucheng (eds.), *China's Provincial Statistics, 1949-1989,* Westview Press, Boulder, Colorado, 1993.

Ting Tin-yu, "Sociocultural Developments in the Republic of China," in Thomas Robinson (ed.), *Democracy and Development in East Asia*, The AEI Press, Washington, D.C., 1991.

Tocqueville, Alexis de, *Democracy in America*, Knopf, New York, 1960.

Tocqueville, Alexis de, *The Old Regime and the French Revolution*, Anchor Books, New York, 1955.

"The Truth About the Case of Shijie Jingji Daobao," *Xinhua*, August 18, 1989, Foreign Broadcast Information Service (FBIS), August 21, 1989.

United Nations, *Monthly Bulletin of Statistics*, New York, various years.

United Nations, *Statistical Yearbook*, New York, various years.

U.S. Department of Commerce, "Marketing in Taiwan," *Overseas Business Reports*, September 1988.

U.S. Department of Defense, *The Security Situation in the Taiwan Strait*, Report to Congress Pursuant to the FY99 Appropriations Bill, February 1, 1999.

U.S. Department of State, *Indonesia Human Rights Practices, 1994*, Washington, D.C., February 1995.

Vatikiotis, Michael R.J., *Indonesian Politics Under Suharto*, Routledge Press, New York, 1992.

Venieris, Y. P., and D. K. Gupta, "Sociopolitical and Economic Dimensions of Development—A Cross Sectional Model," *Economic Development and Cultural Change*, Vol. 31, 1983.

Wachman, Alan M., *Taiwan: National Identity and Democratization*, M. E. Sharpe, Armonk, New York, 1994.

Wade, Robert, *Governing the Market*, Princeton University Press, Princeton, New Jersey, 1990.

Wang Guofa, "Democracy Should Not Go Beyond Social Development," *Liaowang*, August 7, 1989, p. 17, Foreign Broadcast Information Service (FBIS), August 21, 1989, pp. 32–33.

Wang Hui, *The Gradual Revolution*, Transaction Publishers, New Brunswick, New Jersey, 1994.

Wardhana, Ali, "Structural Adjustment in Indonesia: Export and the 'High-Cost Economy'," address at the 24th Conference of South-East Asian Central Bank Governors, Bangkok, January 24, 1989.

Warta Ekonomi Magazine, 1996 (reprinted in *The Christian Science Monitor*, January 21, 1998).

Weede, E., "The Impact of Democracy on Economic Growth," *Kyklos*, Vol. 36, 1983.

Wei Jingsheng, "Democracy or a New Dictatorship," 1979, translated and reproduced in Amnesty International, *China: Violations of Human Rights*, London, 1984.

Weimer, David L., "The Political Economy of Property Rights," in David Weimer (ed), *The Political Economy of Property Rights*, New York, Cambridge University Press, New York, 1997.

Winckler, Edwin A., "Elite Political Struggle," in Edwin Winckler and Susan Greenhalgh (eds.), *Contending Approaches to the Political Economy of Taiwan*, M. E. Sharpe, Armonk, New York, 1988.

Winckler, Edwin, "CCK and Society: Institutional Leadership and Social Development on Taiwan," in Shao-chuan Leng (ed.), *Chiang Ching-Kuo's Leadership in the Development of the Republic of China on Taiwan*, The Miller Center, University of Virginia, University Press of America, New York, 1993.

Wolf, Charles, Jr., *Foreign Aid: Theory and Practice in Southern Asia*, Princeton University Press, Princeton, New Jersey, 1960.

Wolf, Charles, Jr., *Markets or Governments*, The MIT Press, Cambridge, Massachusetts, 1988.

Wong, Christine P. W., "Central Planning and Local Participation under Mao: The Development of Country-Run Fertiliser Plants," in Gordon White (ed.), *The Chinese State in the Era of Economic Reform*, M. E. Sharpe, Inc., Armonk, New York, 1991.

Wong, Jesse, "Ma Fights for Rule of Law in Freewheeling Taiwan," *Asian Wall Street Journal*, April 14–15, 1995.

Woo, Wong Thye, and Liang-Yn Liu, "Taiwan's Persistent Trade Surpluses: The Role of the Underdeveloped Financial Markets," in Joel D. Aberbach, David Dollar, and Kenneth L. Sokoloff (eds.), *The Role of the State in Taiwan's Development*, M. E. Sharpe, Inc., Armonk, New York, 1994.

World Bank, *Indonesia: Strategy for a Sustained Reduction in Poverty*, Washington, D.C., 1990.

World Bank, *Social Indicators of Development*, Washington, D.C., various years.

World Bank, *World Bank Development Report 1980*, Oxford University Press, London, 1980.

World Bank, *World Bank Development Report 1986*, Oxford University Press, London, 1986.

World Bank, *World Tables*, Washington, D.C., various years.

Wu, Jaushieh Joseph, "The 1994 Elections in Taiwan: Continuity, Change, and the Prospect of Democracy," *Issues and Studies*, Vol. 31, No. 3, March 1995.

Yamaichi Securities Co., Ltd., "Shanghai Securities Market," in Institute of Global Financial Studies, *The Stock Markets in Asia*, June 1994.

Yatsko, Pamela, "No Soft Landing," *Far Eastern Economic Review*, November 13, 1997.

Yeager, Leland B., and David G. Tuerck, *Trade Policy and the Price System*, International Textbook Co., Scranton, Pennsylvania, 1966.

Yearbook of Financial Statistics of the ROC, 1988.

Yi, Gang, "A Study of Money Flows in China," in George T. Yu (ed.), *China in Transition*, University Press of America, Lanham, Maryland, 1992.

Young, Stephen M., "Post-Tiananmen Chinese Politics and the Prospects for Democratization," *Asian Survey*, July 1995.

Yu, Tzong-shian, "The Relationship Between the Government and the Private Sector in the Process of Economic Development in Taiwan, ROC," *Industry of Free China*, October 1985.

"Yuan on Controlled Single-Track," *China Advisors*, July 1994.

Zheng, Yongnian, "Development and Democracy: Are They Compatible in China," *Political Science Quarterly*, Vol. 109, No. 2, 1994.

Zhongguo Xinwenshe, January 1, 1987, Foreign Broadcast Information Service (FBIS).

Zuvekas, C., "Concentration of Political Power and Levels of Economic Development in Latin American Countries—Comment," *Journal of Developing Areas*, Vol. 8, 1974.

Index

Modernization theory, 1–2
Most Favored Nation (MFN) status, 19
mtwo
  defined, 2, 32–34
  as a percentage of GDP, 158, 224
Multinational/multilateral organizations.
    See also individual organizations
  role in promoting marketization and
    political liberalization, 235–236
Muslim Intellectuals Association, 165

Networks, global, 19
New elites. *See* Elites
New Korea Democratic Party (NKDP),
    86–87
Noncompetitive markets. *See* Markets
Non-state sector. *See* Private sector
North Korea, 68, 94

Office of Investment Promotion (OIP),
    Korea, 82–84
Oil crisis of 1973
  causing boom in Indonesia, 152–153
  economic effects on Taiwan, 117
OPEC, 138
Open markets. *See* Free markets
Ordinary least squares (OLS) models, 30,
    47
Organization for Economic Development
    and Cooperation (OECD), 91–92, 185
Output. *See* Gross industrial output;
    Industrial output

PAKTO, in Indonesia, 158
Park Chung Hee, Korean President, 71–75,
    86
  assassination of, 79
Participatory government, 13, 21
Peasant income. *See also* Land reform
  increase in from Taiwan's land reform,
    106
People's Bank, 189
People's Communes (PCs) in China, 180
  reforms of, 181–182
People's Republic of China. *See* China,
    People's Republic of
Per capita GDP. *See* GDP
PKI. *See* Indonesia's Communist Party
    (PKI)
Policy considerations, 62, 220–236
  levers for increasing democracy, 1
Political corruption
  reducing level of, 16–17
  in Taiwan, 96, 132
Political demonstrations, 71
Political parties. *See also* Candidacy;
    individual political parties

  in Korea, 74, 86–89
Political power
  cost of obtaining, 29
  means of obtaining, 18
  serendipity in, 49
Polity, theories of, 1, 7–11
Potential, unrealized, 137–176
Poverty, 13–14
Power. *See also* Political power
  consolidation of, 63–94
  establishing a balance of, 17–19, 63–94
PRC. *See* China, People's Republic of
Predicted *versus* actual values, of
    democracy, 49–52, 54
Prerequisites for democracy, 21–29
Private sector
  contributions to gross industrial output
    in China, 212
  contribution to gross social product in
    China, 196
  in Indonesia, 156
  role in promoting marketization and
    political liberalization, 233–235
Privatization, trend toward in the coastal
    and northeast regions of China, 212
Product. *See* Gross social product;
    Provincial product; Total societal
    product
Progress, as an ideology, 66–71
Prosperity, 7, 224, 238, 243. *See also*
    lgdpcap
  increasing, 13–14, 20
Prosperity regression, 55
Provincial product, contribution to total
    societal product in China, 214

Qualitative historical studies, 61–220. *See
    also* individual countries
Quantitative model, 5–58
  empirical evaluation of, 47–56
  summary statistics regarding, 36–47
  theoretical, 31–36

R&D
  expenditures in Korea, 86
  as a percentage of GDP, 20
Real investment, trends in, 42
Real per capita GDP. *See* GDP
Regression model, 47–56
Regressions
  democracy, 48
  marketization, 55
  prosperity, 55
Representative government, 23
Republic of China (ROC). *See* Taiwan
    (Republic of China)